D1327264

MAY 2 3 2016

# THE SEASICK ADMIRAL

# The Seasick Admiral

*Nelson and the Health of the Navy*

KEVIN BROWN

**Seaforth**
PUBLISHING

First published in Great Britain in 2015 by
Seaforth Publishing
Pen & Sword Books Ltd
47 Church Street
Barnsley S70 2AS

British Library Cataloguing in Publication Data
A catalogue record for this book is available from the British Library

ISBN 978 1 84832 217 2

Typeset and designed by M.A.T.S., Leigh-on-Sea, Essex
Printed and bound in Malta by Gutenberg Press Ltd.

359.331
Bro

# Contents

To my own 'Band of Brothers', those friends who have encouraged
me in my research, writing and travels.




'And Sir, the secret of his victories?'
'By his unServicelike, familiar ways, Sir,
He made the whole Fleet love him, damn his eyes!'

Robert Graves, *1805*

# Preface

One of the most evocative and iconic places in British naval history is the orlop deck of *Victory*, scene of the death of Nelson in the hour of his great victory at Trafalgar. In the days when visitors were conducted around *Victory* on tours guided by naval ratings, these fresh-faced young sailors always dwelt with relish on the death of Nelson, the casualties from Trafalgar and the stench and gore of amputations and crude battle surgery in the cockpit painted red to hide the blood. Their accounts were always vivid, sometimes imaginative and sensationalist, perhaps not always accurate, but all the more meaningful for being delivered by Nelson's heirs. The health, medicine and welfare of Nelson's navy always played an important part in their accounts, but what they were perhaps not fully aware of was that their own ruddy good health was a legacy of the importance given to the health of the navy and a reflection down the years of Nelson's own concern for the welfare of his men. Nelson's own medical history indeed reflected wider naval medical practices of the time and his own ill-health translated into a practical concern for the health of his fleet which in turn gave it advantages over some of his enemies.

Nelson himself said that 'I have all the diseases that are, but there is not enough in my frame for them to fasten on'. The story of his health is the story of the illnesses and wounds which beset his contemporaries at sea. Apart from the loss of his right arm and sight in his right eye, Nelson is perhaps most often remembered for suffering from seasickness which did not stop him from pursuing a successful career at sea.

In many ways he was unlucky and as a sickly child ought never to have gone to sea, but the way he overcame these problems to become perhaps the greatest of Britain's maritime heroes tells us something of the nature of the man. However what Nelson's medical history reveals of the wider picture of health and welfare is perhaps even more significant, especially when his own contributions to the health of seaman is taken into consideration.

What I have not done is try to diagnose Nelson's illnesses or medical problems, but have looked at his medical history as it was presented and understood at the time. I am always suspicious of retrospective diagnosis of historical figures as the records upon which these are based are inevitably selective and coloured by the perceptions and prejudices of their age. Those records can never present a full and true picture and can only be understood in context. Any diagnosis after a couple of centuries and based on incomplete information can only ever be tentative; that is not the role of any historian of medicine.

The historical imagination is always helped by visiting the places where things actually happened or seeing an object with a direct link to the past. For Nelson there are so many places and objects, not just the *Victory* or the relics at the National Maritime Museum. Lecturing on the health of Nelson's navy to passengers on a cruise ship, *Independence of the Sea,* as it sailed through the Trafalgar waters will always be memorable, though its timing was nothing but co-incidental, as well as seeing on the same voyage the canon at Tenerife which reputedly fired the shot that resulted in Nelson's amputation in July 1797. I am grateful to Timothy Hall for a tour of Haslar Hospital shortly after it closed. In Gibraltar, Dave Eveson of the Gibraltar History Society showed me around the naval hospital sites and the remains on the Rock that would have been familiar to Nelson's contemporaries. In Menorca, I was honoured to be invited to give a lecture in 2012 by the Amics de l'Illa del Hospital in aid of the restoration of Britain's first naval hospital on Isla del Rey at Mahon and had the opportunity to explore Menorca's naval and medical history, with thanks to General Luis Alexandre Sintre and, most especially, to Lorraine Ure.

As always much of the research for a book like this involves hard slog in archives and libraries. Foremost for the study of British naval history are the resources of the National Maritime Museum at Greenwich, the National Archives at Kew and the Royal Naval

Museum at Portsmouth. Perhaps less known are the collection of Nelson's letters concerning naval medicine held at the Wellcome Library though these are a wonderful resource. I wish to thank the staff at all the institutions I have visited for their role in caring for this great heritage and their helpfulness. After all that archive and library work, it is refreshing to be finishing work on this book in a relaxed environment at sea as a guest lecturer on the history of medicine on the *Pacific Princess*, and once again talking about the health of Nelson's navy through waters he knew.

The topic of health and medicine at sea is a popular one and audiences to my many talks on the subject, especially my Trafalgar Day lectures, have raised many thought-provoking points on naval medicine as indeed have correspondents who have read some of my previous books. I must particularly thank Mick Crumplin for sharing with me his knowledge of military and naval surgery during the French Wars of the Revolutionary and Napoleonic period. John Williamson has shared with me his interest in the history of smallpox and drawn my attention to some sources for the early adoption of variolation and vaccination by the Royal Navy. In addition I wish to thank Lorna Swift, Honorary Librarian of the Garrison Library in Gibraltar, Tudor Allen, Nicholas Webb, Neil Handley of the British Optical Association for allowing reproduction of the portrait of Peter Rainier in his collections, Jane Wickenden, Historic Collections Manager at the Institute of Naval Medicine, and Robert Gardiner and his colleagues at Seaforth Publishing.

Kevin Brown
At sea off Aboukir Bay, Easter Saturday 2015.

# 1

# Going to Sea

Britain's greatest naval hero never should have gone to sea. Horatio Nelson – whose death at the age of forty-seven in the hour of his greatest victory at Trafalgar sealed his lasting, almost legendary, reputation – was a frail child ill-equipped for the ardours of life on the ocean. Although an anonymous poet later considered that the birth of 'that noble Nelson ... most clearly showed he would the world adorn, the warrior of Heaven, hurl'd headlong from the sky',[1] his destiny would have been far from obvious to those who knew him in his youth. He had been so weak at his birth on 29 September 1758 that his christening took place when he was ten days old rather than as scheduled on 15 November. His parents had not expected him to live long.[2] Indeed three of his ten siblings died before they reached the age of two, including an elder brother also named Horatio, born and died in 1751. His forty-two year-old mother Catherine herself died in 1767, being considered by her daughter Susanna to have 'bred herself to death', worn out by childbirth after having borne eleven children in eighteen years of marriage. As a school boy at the Paston School in North Walsham, despite later stories of his daring if always honourable escapades, Horatio was regarded as 'much impaired by an aguish complaint' and succumbed to an epidemic of measles in 1770 which saw him isolated in a 'stable chamber' and 'space over the muck bin' with fellow sufferers.[3] A sickly child, prey to the marsh fevers of his Norfolk home, he was not exactly cut out for the hardships of naval life to which he was despatched at the age of twelve in March 1771.

Nelson's uncle, Captain Maurice Suckling, had very serious doubts about his nephew's suitability for a naval career, asking 'what has poor

Horatio done, who is so weak, that he above all the rest should be sent to rough it out at sea? But let him come, and the first time we go into action a cannon ball may knock off his head and provide for him at once.'[4] Suckling had gone to sea at the age of thirteen sponsored by his family connections with the Walpole family of Holkham Hall and had promised to use his influence to advance one of his nephews. When called out of retirement to take command of the *Raisonable* in 1770, he had been ready to take one of his nephews to sea, but had not expected it to be Horatio who had asked his father to request a place for him.

Patronage was important for any young midshipman not only in obtaining for him a position but also in offering him advice and watching over his welfare. Cuthbert Collingwood promised the MP Walter Spencer-Stanhope that 'I shall be very glad to see your son William, and will take good care of him, and give him the best introduction to the service that I can.' Although the boy proved to have merely the makings of a good officer rather than a great one, Collingwood took pains with him, breakfasting with him every day and regularly reporting on his progress to his father. He had advised against burdening the young man with too much luggage other than the essentials needed for life at sea, but warned that he must bring 'a comfortable bed – that his health requires'.[5] Collingwood was pleased to be able to report to the boy's father that life at sea had improved William both physically and morally: 'his health has improved astonishingly, his body, which was puny and delicate, is become strong, he is grown much in stature, and is as diligent in his learning as can reasonably be expected.'[6]

Nelson too was to find his stamina and physique improved by life at sea. Despite all expectations he thrived on life at sea, first as a captain's servant with his uncle on *Raisonnable* and *Triumph*, then on a year's voyage to the West Indies on the merchantman *Mary Ann*. Toughened by experience at sea, Nelson, by now a midshipman, was robust enough to take part in an expedition to the North Pole in search of the elusive Northeast Passage on the bomb ketch *Carcass* in 1773. The Admiralty had issued special clothing for protection against the cold, variable winds, fog, rain and snow, consisting of six 'fearnought' jackets, two pairs of 'fearnought' trousers, two milled caps, four pairs of milled stockings, a strong pair of boots, a dozen pairs of milled mittens, two cotton shirts and some handkerchiefs. Nelson supplemented this with slops purchased from the purser.[7] It was on this voyage of discovery that Nelson reputedly showed his courage, enterprise and strength by single-handedly pursuing a polar bear.[8] The story would indeed show how much his experiences at sea had made a tough man of the once sickly child had there been any great substance to it. Nelson, not noticeably modest nor reticent about his achievements, never referred to the incident and the log of Master James Allen of the *Carcass* merely records that early in the morning of 4 August 1773 'a bear came close to the ship on the ice, but on the people's going towards him he went away.'[9]

The young midshipman was to suffer from a malady more common among seaman than might be supposed: seasickness. Nelson himself was reticent about admitting to suffering from this, writing in October 1805 to Earl St Vincent that 'I am – don't laugh – dreadfully seasick this day as it blows a Levanter'.[10] It was only in his letters to Emma Hamilton that he referred with any frequency to his susceptibility to it just as it was only to his mistress that he admitted that he had always been prone to colds and coughs. He made no reference to suffering from seasickness in his early years at sea and first admitted that 'I am seasick' in a letter to Lady Hamilton in May 1799,[11] and in August 1801 was 'so dreadfully seasick I cannot hold up my head.'[12] The condition worsened in rough seas when 'I am never well when it blows hard' and could come on suddenly 'in one hour, from the weather like a mill-head, to such a sea as to make me very unwell.'[13] Nelson was to complain to his banker and prize agent Alexander Davison about the sea off Toulon that it was 'such a place for storms of wind I never met with, and I am unfortunately, in bad weather, always seasick.'[14] So severe was this that on occasion 'I am so seasick that I cannot write another line' even to his dear Emma.[15]

Nelson accepted that seasickness was common among men at sea in rough weather. It was in a matter of fact tone that he reported in April 1793 to his wife Fanny that her son Josiah Nisbet, whom he had taken to sea with him aboard the *Agamemnon*, was suffering from *mal de mer*, something that Josiah had not admitted in his own letters to his mother: 'Josiah is with me: yesterday, it blowing a smart gale, he was a little seasick.'[16] He was soon able to reassure her that 'now Josiah has got the better of seasickness, I think he gets stout.'[17] William Hoste, one of Nisbet's fellow midshipmen on *Agamemnon*, was afraid that conditions in the Bay of Biscay in May 1793 would be so rough that they would bring on his seasickness: 'Hitherto, we have had fine weather and pleasant sailing, though scarcely wind enough to give a sickening motion to our vessel. I have not been sick since our last cruise but expect to have a touch of it as we are rolling through the Bay of Biscay.'[18]

Biscay was notorious for its rough seas. Jeffrey Raigersfield, son of the Austrian Chargé d'Affaires and a midshipman on *Mediator*, suffered badly when crossing the Bay:

No sooner were we out of sight of land than I became very sea sick as to be unable to assist myself in the least; indeed when crossing the Bay of Biscay, the waves ran so high and the water out of the soundings caused so bad a smell on board, from the rolling of the ship as it washed from side to side in the between decks, that had anyone thrown me overboard as I lay helpless upon the gangway I should not have made the smallest resistance.[19]

His seasickness offered his fellow midshipmen the opportunity to rob him when he was too weak to be aware of what was going on. He had boarded his ship well-fitted out with a large chest of clothes, a pewter wash hand-basin and supplies of tea and sugar. His chest was soon depleted by petty thieving but, after recovering from a bout of *mal de mer*, went to his sea chest only to find it 'nearly emptied of all superfluities, and excepting three or four shirts and a scanty portion of other necessaries, little remaining of the abundant stock my parents had so carefully put together for a three years' station'. Raigersfield felt helpless but 'I was only laughed at' and 'given to understand that unless I could prove my loss, my complaint would do me harm than good, and I wisely followed this advice which certainly afterwards contributed to my not being made the general fag.'[20]

Even a ship's surgeon was not free from being sea sick. Lionel Gillespie, surgeon on the *Vanguard*, recorded his illness in his medical journal, observing that when 'the ship pitched most intolerably ... most of our people were more or less affected with seasickness.' He himself soon 'became affected with insufferable nausea, spitting dizziness ... and at length vomited two or three times yellow bile'. Chewing ginger seemed to sooth his stomach. He observed that 'my sickness as well as that of several others on board regularly observed the period of a day occurring at noon and going off about the same time'.[21] When the affliction struck him again some eight months later when he was serving on *Racehorse,* he was more analytical in his approach, commenting that 'it is proper to prepare for it by opening the belly previously, by avoiding all cause of indigestion, avoiding the use of fluids, to be abstemious, when at sea to keep in the open air and if possible to work, to pull and haul; or when the stomach has been emptied, to avoid drinking and support a warmth of surface lying abed with much clothing'. He was envious of a boy 'of a thin rather delicate habit with a long neck and consumptive make' he had before him who had never suffered from seasickness, unlike most of his shipmates.[22]

It was an indeed a rite of passage for the young midshipman and also an ordeal for the experienced seaman. Writing to the Earl of Camden – the Secretary of State for War – in 1804 after Camden's sixteen year-old nephew Francis James had abandoned a naval career because he was unsuited to life at sea and suffered badly from seasickness, Nelson expressed his sympathy while stressing that 'it was not ... my fault that your Nephew left the *Victory* but if he did not admire the profession I am sure there can be no comfort', and admitted that ' I am ill every time it blows hard and nothing but my enthusiastic love for my profession keeps me one hour at sea',[23] with the clear implication that Nelson was prepared to suffer for his country though others might be less patriotic. In the last years of his life, his common susceptibility to sea sickness, once little mentioned, had become a badge of endurance, patriotism and heroism.

Seasickness was the least of the problems facing a young midshipman. Nelson, although he himself had gone to sea at the age of twelve, was not entirely in favour of youths entering the navy at too tender an age. When dining on *Foudroyant* with Midshipman George Parsons in 1799, he expressed surprise that 'you entered the service at a very early age to have been in action off St Vincent' and, on being told that Parsons had been eleven, muttered 'much too young.'[24] It was a strange and unfamiliar world to which the new recruit came. William

Dillon 'did not enjoy much sleep that night in the cable tier where I was slung up. The effluvia from the cables was not very agreeable. But knowing there was no bettering my position, I calmly resigned myself to my fate.'[25]

Bullying was common unless the captain's servant or midshipman could count on the protection of older men. The captain was meant to be a 'sea daddy' to the young men under his command. Nelson himself was praised for the attention he showed to his midshipmen, William Hoste enthusing about how 'Captain Nelson is uncommon kind to me' and 'treats me as he said he would'.[26] When Hoste broke his leg during the raid on Alassio in 1795, Nelson 'often comes down to see me and tells me to get everything I want from him'. Indeed, despite hopping about on crutches, fifteen-year-old Hoste believed that 'if I were to go on board of any ship in the British navy, I could not be more happy, nor could I have more care taken of me, since this accident, than has happened on board the *Agamemnon*.' Immediately after the accident he had been taken to the cabin of Lieutenant Maurice William Suckling, who 'has behaved to me like a father' and 'has been with me all the while, except when his duty called him away.' Hoste also relied on the support of his friend and fellow midshipman John Weatherhead, who had 'nearly made himself ill in attending me'.[27] Nelson had also arranged and paid for Hoste to convalesce at Leghorn, but when the boy fractured his other leg on his return to the *Agamemnon*, Nelson commented wryly that 'I have strongly recommended him not to break any more limbs'.[28]

However, the captain was too remote to provide continuous protection for the young captain's servant or midshipman and it was essential for any young gentleman without patrons or friends on board a ship to make himself useful and gain support. Jeffrey Raigersfield, 'after a good crying when he was alone', did this by 'betaking myself again to climbing the rigging, attending in the round tops, and observing the different shifting and trimming of the sails' with the result that 'the officers appeared much pleased at my quickness, and I very soon became a favourite, not only with them, but with the common sailors likewise.'[29]

If a gentleman and future officer had a rough time, it was even worse for the young boys 'procured for sea service by such organisations as the Maritime Society expressly set up by Jonas Hanaway in 1756 'for contributing towards a supply of two or three thousand mariners for the Navy'. Such boys were recruited by advertisements promising that 'all stout lads and boys who incline to go on board His Majesty's ships, as servants, with a view to learn the duties of a seaman, and are, upon examination, approved by the Marine Society, shall be handsomely clothed and provided with bedding and their charges borne down to the ports where His Majesty's ships lye, with all proper encouragement.'[30] There were age limits of fourteen and a minimum height of four feet, three inches, but such minimum requirements were often forgotten in times of war when the need for naval manpower was at its peak. When he requested twenty lads from the Marine Society for the *Agamemnon* on 6 February 1793, Nelson promised that 'the greatest care should be taken of them'. The average age of the boys sent to him was fifteen and their average height was four feet eight inches, while most were illiterate. Three of them were unable to adjust to naval life and were discharged at their own request within three weeks, but the others were engaged as servants.

In order to ensure that the boys were fit for service before being sent to sea they were medically examined by a surgeon, at whose lodgings they were scrubbed, disinfected and treated for 'the various distempers which are the constant consequences of poverty and nastiness', such as the 'trots', scurvy and the 'itch' (scabies). They were also kitted out with a felt hat, two worsted caps, a kersey pea jacket, waistcoat, shirts, drawers, trousers and shoes so that they could go on board ship in a clean condition with less chance of carrying the louse which could spread typhus. Those boys recruited by the Marine Society who were not in good physical condition were looked after, given any necessary care and fed up by the Marine Society until they were considered seaworthy. They were also given religious instruction as 'religion makes the steadiest warriors.'[31] Some of their critics, though, believed that once at sea the only skills that they would learn would be those of 'blasphemy, chewing tobacco and gaming, from whence they proceed to drinking and talking bawdy.'[32]

Ever since 1703, young vagabonds could be sent to sea as maritime apprentices, a move intended to keep undesirables off the streets as much as to man the navy. However, this could not guarantee a regular supply of men for the naval service, especially not of experienced seamen. The navy, unlike the army which relied upon persuasion and inducement to get men to take the king's shilling, could coerce men into the service. The notorious press gangs roamed the sea ports. Napoleon asked whether 'anything can be more horrible than your pressing of seamen', commenting during his exile on St Helena that their prey was 'every male that can be found, who if they have the misfortune to belong to the *canaille*, if they cannot prove themselves to be gentlemen, are hurried on board your ships to serve as seamen in all quarters of the globe'.[33] The Impress Service, which after 1788 was meant to regularise this iniquitous system of conscription, limited impressment to able-bodied seamen, fishermen or waterman between the ages of 18 and 55, but abuses were common. Along the Thames in 1771 'it has been a common practice for the press gangs to seize abundance of honest tradesmen indiscriminately, and carry them to the rendezvous houses, where they extort money from them to let them go again.'[34] It was not easy for a victim of the press gang to prove his age and men with no sea experience could be seized from their beds. A child who had been kidnapped from his father's coach office in Portsmouth in 1807 and 'has not the most distant recollection how he was enticed away, but remembers he was put aboard the *Royal William* and afterwards sent to the sea in the *Laurel*', returned home from twenty-five months in a French prison in 1812 to find his father dead, the son having been 'given up for lost'.[35] Men exempt from impressment, including foreigners, apprentices, customs-house officials, militia volunteers and the crews of outward-bound merchant ships had to carry a certificate of protection at all times, but in times of national emergency such as March 1803 when invasion seemed imminent, such exemptions were suspended. At Plymouth 'the different press gangs with their officers literally scoured the country on the eastern roads and picked up several fine young fellows' and from 'the gin shops at Dock, several hundreds of seamen and landmen were picked up and sent directly on board the flag ships.'[36] Landsmen unfit for service at sea did not make good sailors.

Impressment alone was not enough to ensure an adequate supply of naval recruits in time of war and in 1795 the passage of two Quota Acts required every county and port to supply their quota of able-bodied men for the naval service in return for a bounty. Such quotas were inevitably filled with landsmen and also criminals. William Hotham, commanding *Adamant*, complained that 'the scheme of quota men was a new and injudicious one; and threw a whole mass of population into the fleet, whose habits were altogether strange to the seamen of it, the admixture with who was unnatural and prejudicial.' He was especially scathing about this being 'a common problem with the London Police when they got hold of a confirmed rogue but lacked sufficient evidence to convict him, to send him on board any ship known to be in want of men, in order effectually to dispose of him.'[37] The seamen and marines themselves were contemptuous of such recruits, particularly 'Lord Mayor's Men, a term given to those who enter to relieve themselves from public disgrace, and who are sent on board by any of the city magistrates, for a street frolic or night charge.' Such men were mocked by the sailors 'who generally cut the tails from their coats, and otherwise abuse and ridicule them.'[38]

Despite the emphasis on impressment and conscription to maintain the strength of the navy, many seamen enlisted voluntarily, whether lured by the romance of the sea or enticed by their lack of prospects on land. Some impressed men indeed bowed to the inevitable and agreed to volunteer. Others were listed as volunteers even if they had been pressed. George Price, aged twenty-three, rated as a landsman on board *Speedy* and listed as a volunteer, had actually been impressed in Deptford in November 1803 from an East Indiaman about to set sail for China. He 'was very unwell at the time they took me on board the *Speedy* brig, and there I got so bad that they was obliged to send me on board the *Sussex*, hospital ship lying at Sheerness.' He wrote to his brother, an inn keeper in Southwark, that 'I did not know where I was, no more than you did, and in that state I lost every article belonging to me, even the shirt off my back. Now I will leave you to guess what miserable state I am now in.'[39]

Conditions on the receiving ships were dreadful for volunteer or impressed man alike. For William Robinson in May 1805, 'it was the first time I began to repent of the rash step I had taken' in volunteering to serve in the Royal Navy, causing him to conclude that 'whatever may be said about this boasted land of liberty, whenever a youth resorts to the receiving ship for shelter and hospitality, he from that moment must take leave of the liberty to speak or to act; he may think but he must confine his thoughts to the hold of his mind, and never suffer them to escape the hatchway of utterance'. After a doctor had examined him and pronounced him 'seaworthy', Robinson was sent down to the hold to spend a night 'with my companions in wretchedness, and the rats running over us in numbers.' The journey from London to the Nore in the Admiral's tender was no more comfortable as the men had to spend the following day and night 'huddled together for there was not room to sit or stand separate; indeed we were in a pitiable plight, for numbers of them were seasick, some retching, others were smoking, whilst many were so overcome by the stench, that they fainted for want of air.' Gratings had been put over the hold and a guard of marines placed around the hatchway 'as though we had been culprits of the first degree or capital convicts.'[40] When the officer on deck realised that the men in the hold were 'overcome with foul air' he ordered that the hatches should be taken off but by now 'when daylight broke in upon ... a wretched appearance we cut, for scarcely any of us were free from filth and vermin.'[41]

Indeed the physical appearance of many recruits was shocking. Daniel Goodall was appalled at the sight of the men he could expect to serve with while waiting to be assigned to a ship at Greenock in 1801:

A more ruffianly, villainous-looking set of scamps I have rarely had the ill-fortune to fall amongst. True they were seen to the very worst advantage, for they were dirty, ragged and reckless. Many bore marks of violence received in resistance to the press gang, and the moody sullenness stamped on the faces of most of the victims of Government urgency was in the last degree forbidding. Traces of deep debauchery were visible on the faces of the majority, and altogether the picture was such that I had a strong feeling of having made a very serious mistake in the choice of a vocation. This impression did not, however, last long and a more careful survey of my companions showed me that there were some honest men amongst them, and led me to the inference that the greater part of the physical material I saw before me would improve by time and favourable circumstances.[42]

The fourteen year-old Daniel Goodall had been indignant when as a volunteer he was 'handed over to the tender mercies of a corporal of marines, whose duty it was to conduct me to that purgatory of naval neophyte, the press-room as the dog-hole in in the hold of the tender is called' and that 'no distinction was made between those who were forcibly deprived of their freedom and those who surrendered of their own free will their liberty of action for the time being.' Once in the hold, he was 'hustled' where he was repeatedly 'seized and violently shoved forward' until 'I was ready to drop between the pain of my bruises and sheer exhaustion' only for the cry to go around 'up with him again and hustle him.' Eventually one man took pity on him and found him a place to sleep in the 'floating hell'.[43]

In 1790, *The Times* had suggested that confining the volunteers and impressed men in the holds of tenders was unhealthy and instead recommended that 'there should be large roomy houses for them on shore, where the air might have free circulation, and where health could not be forced away by the stench of putrified air.' The building of such facilities at Tower Hill, Deptford and Greenwich would 'rebound to the humanity of the Government, whose duty it is to provide in the most comfortable manner for these men who are torn from their families to do the most dangerous part of the public duty.' Instead the men 'are crammed together like so many slaves from Africa, and used, not as the men on whose fidelity and courage the existence of this country depends, but as if they were the veriest felons that ever received sentence of transportation'. Inevitably, 'deaths and diseases are the consequence of the bad treatment these poor fellows receive before they get on board the fleet.'[44]

Such a call for change reflected the concerns of a number of naval surgeons about the dangers of typhus being taken from land to sea. The physician James Lind referred to the guardships and pressing tenders from which the men came as 'seminaries of contagion to the whole fleet'.[45] Coming on board in filthy clothing, the new sailor brought with him the lice that spread the bacteria that cause typhus (also known as gaol fever), characterised by a prolonged fever, diarrhoea, headaches and delirium, rashes 'consisting in small livid spots, like flea-bites, dispersed over the skin', with haemorrhaging, often 'to terminate in death.' It was the 'most common fever' of the

Channel fleet in 1806.[46] Robert Robertson, a naval surgeon, contracted it 'by inspiration, by inhaling the morbid effluvia into the lungs' in a confined place containing infected clothing, and treated himself with heavy doses of cinchona bark.[47]

It was a disease that quickly spread in crowded conditions – and 'there is no situation where so large a number of human beings are confined in so small a space as in a man of war'.[48] Although there was as yet no understanding of the cause of the infection, the source of the contagion in the Navy had long been recognised as the impressed seaman. Gilbert Blane noted that 'a single infected man, or even part of his clothing, may spread sickness through a whole ship's company', and 'when the cause of the sickness of particular ships is traced to its source, it will generally be found to have originated from taking on board infected men at Spithead, or wherever else the ship's company may have been completed'.[49] James Lind placed the blame firmly on 'such idle fellows as are picked from the streets or the prisons.' From them came 'a disease of contagious nature, the produce of filth, rags, poverty and a polluted air, which subsists always in a greater or less degree in crowded prisons, and in nasty, low, damp, unventilated habitations loaded with putrid animal streams'.[50]

Lind's proposals for preventing the infection of healthy ships were hardly original, similar ideas having been put forward at the beginning of the eighteenth century by the surgeon Patrick Campbell in his pamphlet *Occasions of Sickness in Fleets and Ships of War which come not within the verge of Physick or Surgery at Sea, but come wholly under the Cognizance of Great Officers on Shore and Principal Officers at Sea*, and were to be argued for by other naval surgeons.[51] Lind urged the necessity of using quarantine ships, the fumigation of clothing and the provision of a ship's uniform. He suggested that 'the most effectual preservative against this infection, during a press, would, perhaps, be to appoint a ship for receiving all ragged and suspected persons, before they are admitted into the receiving guardship'.[52] Here all impressed men would be stripped of their clothes, bathed and given new clothes and bedding before being allowed on board the guardship. The quarantine ships would be equipped with 'soap, tubs, and proper conveniences for bathing, and with a room on deck for fumigating of clothes.'[53] Any filthy rags, especially those coming from such wells of infection as Newgate and other prisons, would be destroyed. Any clothing that could be cleaned or fumigated with brimstone would be returned to the men.

The rags in which the impressed men arrived on the guardships harboured lice and any attempts 'to keep these ships sweet, well-aired and clean' were useless 'for the purest air cannot cleanse rags from contagion.' Lind himself had witnessed 'a thousand men confined together in one guardship, some hundreds of whom had neither a bed, nor so much as a change of linen'. Many of them had been committed to his care at the naval hospital at Haslar still wearing 'the same clothes and shirts, they had on, when pressed several months before'.[54] At a time when four members of the bench, including the Lord Mayor of London, had died from typhus at the Old Bailey in the Black Assize of 1750 supposedly spread from the 'polluted clothes' of Newgate prisoners, Lind warned that 'still greater danger may be apprehended from such sources of infection in a ship'.[55] The solution was to supply clean clothing to the impressed men, whether they came from prison or the street.

Lind went further than merely advocating the supply of seaman's clothes, known as slops, and suggested that 'if the seamen in His Majesty's service were put into an uniform sea-habit, with some little moveable badges, or variations, if judged necessary, by which it might be known to what ship they belong, each man would at first go clean and neatly clothed on board His Majesty's ships, and by the proper care of the officers, in frequently inspecting their apparel, be kept so constantly'.[56] Gilbert Blane also believed that 'it would certainly be for the benefit of the service that a uniform should be established for the common man as for the officers.'[57] Thomas Trotter, an opponent of impressment, also believed that the men should be given a uniform that would offer them self-respect and make it more difficult for them to desert. He proposed a uniform of 'blue jackets, white waistcoats, white trousers and a small round hat or cap'. He later elaborated on this uniform with the suggestion that the waistcoat could be trimmed with blue tape, the shirt should be striped with a black silk neckcloth, buttons with the letters R.N. embossed on them and a narrow belt around the hat bearing the name of the ship. Such a uniform would 'increase attachment to the service and its commanders, and with these all the virtues of good discipline' as well as inculcating the 'personal delicacy and cleanliness' so important for the health of the men.[58] It was a view shared by Rear-Admiral Richard Kempenfelt, who believed that 'to keep the seaman properly clothed and clean, they should be uniformed, which 'might contribute something to check desertion' and 'keep the men in a more decent appearance' since 'at present their appearance in general is a disgrace to the service, very shabby and very dirty'.[59]

However, despite naval officers having enjoyed the distinction of uniforms since 1748, it was not thought necessary to introduce a uniform for able bodied seamen until the mid-nineteenth century, mainly because of the expense involved. The purser was allowed to issue free slops to destitute men newly boarding the ship, but after the first month the cost of all clothing issued was to be deducted from pay and entered into a Slops book. Trotter considered that 'the navy slops are really made in a form that no sailor, who has any taste in dress, will put them on.'[60] It was not just the style of the slops that made them unpopular; they were also often inadequate in quality. Benjamin Caldwell, captain of the *Agamemnon,* believed that much of the clothing supplied to the men was too skimpy and too small for them, especially trousers which 'should be much thicker and larger, as the least shower goes through them'. He believed that in a cold climate trousers made of *fear-nought*, a coarse woollen cloth, should be allowed and changes of clothing made available for when the men got soaked when reefing topsails in rainy weather such that their wet trousers stuck to them. Flannel trousers were considered better in wet weather, while Caldwell observed that 'it is commonly remarked that the men who wear the thickest linen shirts are the most healthy'.[61]

The importance of flannel as a healthy material for wearing next to the skin was not universally recognised by all naval surgeons who, while accepting it being worn by the sick, opposed its use for men who perspired heavily or got wet and failed to wash themselves before steaming themselves dry in their hammocks. Thomas Trotter considered the practice of wearing flannel next to the skin as 'filthy and unwholesome' and urged that, 'clothe them as warm as you please

... in the name of cleanliness give them linen or cotton next the skin'. Despite this, Admiral St Vincent had ordered that flannels should be worn in cold weather 'and most sincerely exhorts the captains of his ships comprising the fleet under his command to inculcate this doctrine in the minds of their surgeons, who, from caprice and perverse opposition to every wholesome regulation, grossly neglect this important duty'.[62]

Steps were taken by some officers to ensure that new recruits were cleanly and adequately dressed. When 'one Callaghan, a ragged dirty fellow' enlisted as a volunteer on *Terrible* in 1778, lice from his clothing spread among his ship mates and a typhus outbreak was only averted by the prompt action of Captain Mariot Arbuthnot, 'an officer not less distinguished by his naval abilities than by his care for the health of his men', in ordering the destruction of dirty rags, the washing and airing of bedding and the fumigation of the ship.[63] In 1781 Charles Middleton commissioned a 'slop ship', or receiving ship, on which all new men were given clean clothes to avert the danger that 'a single infected man, or even any part of his clothing, may spread sickness throughout an entire ship's company.'[64]

The introduction of the divisional system was to improve standards of naval hygiene. Captain Middleton, later Lord Barham, had introduced such a system on *Ardent* in 1775 when he divided the ship's company into four divisions, each under the command of a lieutenant responsible for regular inspections to ensure that ventilators were working continually, hammocks were neatly stowed in the nettings and that the men were cleanly dressed. The punishment for 'such men as are found to be careless about their clothes, or dirty in their persons' was a few strokes while habitual offenders were 'to be scrubbed in a tub, by order of the lieutenant'.[65] Admiral Howe and Admiral Keith adopted similar divisional systems to that of Middleton as did Prince William in 1788, although the future William IV was perhaps more interested in the smart appearance of his ship than the health of his men.[66]

Although personally close to Prince William, Nelson was as interested in the welfare of his men and ensuring that they were adequately clothed as in maintaining smartness, seeing both as being inextricably linked. Dr John Snipe, Physician of the Mediterranean

Fleet, advised Nelson in 1803 on the importance of warm clothing and urged that the Admiralty should provide free uniforms, including trousers and flannel waistcoats; expenditure which in the long term would reduce the costs arising from sickness from influenza, fevers and rheumatism as 'it would prevent many from being sent to the Hospital, a number of which either die, or are invalided'. Strong shoes and warm stockings would also prevent injuries, ulcers and rope burns to the men's legs and feet, although they would need to be prevented from wearing shorts and going barefooted. Responding to Snipe's warning that 'much of this deplorable waste of men to the service was occasioned by the want of proper warm clothing',[67] Nelson took an interest in the provision of adequate clothing, personally designing and ordering 5,000 frocks and trousers from a Maltese storekeeper, Nathaniel Taylor, in June 1804.[68]

Thomas Hardy, captain of *Victory*, approved of Nelson's orders of clothing from Nathaniel Taylor, commenting that 'the Maltese cotton washes and wears remarkably well'. Less successful was a supply of slop frocks and trousers 'of a very inferior quality' which Hardy received from the supply ship *Diligent* in August 1804.[69] Nelson sent Hardy's complaints about these shoddy and expensive clothes to the Admiralty, together with samples of the inferior frocks and trousers sent from England on *Diligent*, which 'instead of being made of good Russia duck as was formerly supplied ... are made of coarse wrapper-stuff', and examples of his own superior purchases from Malta. The result was that Hardy was able to order 395 Maltese frocks and 857 pairs of Russian duck trousers for the crew of *Victory*. Nelson also considered that the increased cost of the inferior slops, now selling at 2d each for a frock and 3d for a pair of trousers, 'will no doubt occasion murmur and discontent'. His own opinion was that a contractor supplying inadequate slops 'ought to be hanged'.[70]

Nelson's concern with detail extended to the thick Guernsey jackets he obtained for his men in the Mediterranean in November 1804, although they had previously only been provided for fleets serving on cold-weather stations. Although he was happy with the quality of the material used, he believed that the jackets were 'considerably too narrow and short to be tucked into the men's trousers', recommending that they should be ten or twelve inches longer 'as they shrink very considerably in washing'. When the abled bodied seamen were on the yards working the sails, their short jackets were liable to be pulled out of trousers which 'exposes them to great danger of taking cold in their loins'. Whilst 'perhaps, the Guernsey jacket, in its present state, might answer the largest of the boys', Nelson believed that if they could be altered these jackets 'certainly would be the best and most valuable slops that were ever introduced into the Service, and be the means of saving many a good seaman's life'.[71]

Not all the seamen were as concerned about healthy, hygienic clothing as their Admiral. Although constantly exposed to the elements, they failed to dress appropriately. Trotter criticised them for being 'too indolent to suit their dress to circumstances, unless they are forced to do it, nor is anything more common than to see them with a pair of thin linen trowsers on in the severity of winter, and a pair of greasy woollen ones in the hottest of weather'[72]. It was no wonder that they were prone to influenza, other fevers and rheumatism. Even Nelson 'took no pains to protect himself from the effects of wet, or the night air; wearing only a thin great coat: and he has frequently, after having his clothes wet through with rain, refused to have them changed, saying that the leather waistcoat which he wore over his flannel one would secure him from complaint'.[73] Although solicitous that his seamen be adequately dressed, he did not invariably give them the best example in dressing appropriately for the weather himself.

He was also cavalier in his attitude to footwear. His surgeon at Trafalgar William Beatty noted that 'he seldom wore boots, and was consequently very liable to have his feet wet'. If his feet did get wet, Nelson would go down to his cabin and walk on the carpet in his stockings to try to dry them, adopting 'this comfortable expedient' rather than giving his servants 'the trouble of assisting him to put on fresh stockings; which from his having only one hand, he could not himself conveniently effect'.[74] Many of the men, without the luxury of a carpet, to dry their wet feet on, preferred to go barefoot rather than get their shoes and stockings wet. Even officers were observed to go without shoes such as Vice-Admiral Pellew who 'dressed in a short jacket, a pair of trowsers, a small hunting cap and without shoes or stockings', when *Culloden* was caught in a hurricane in the

Indian Ocean in 1809, 'went about infusing courage and fortitude into all'.[75]

Ships' surgeons were concerned that sores on bare feet could be harmful for the men's health. There were also other dangers. When all the glass windows on the *Repulse* were shattered by a huge wave in a storm, Marine Captain Wybourn was concerned that '34 panes of glass was precipitated about the ship in thousands of pieces and it will be a providence if the men, who will go barefoot, do not lame themselves'.[76] Trotter also criticised seaman, whom he considered 'naturally indolent and filthy and are merely infants as to discretion in everything that regards their health', for soaking themselves when washing the decks and continuing to wear wet trousers, shoes and stockings. They 'sit the whole day afterwards, though wet thereby, halfway up the legs, without shifting themselves, to the great injury of their health'. He insisted that they should be forced to take off their shoes and stockings and roll up their trouser legs 'which will not only cause their feet to be dry and comfortable the rest of the day, but necessarily cause a degree of cleanliness which otherwise would be disregarded'.

It was not always easy for the men to keep their clothes clean at sea, although a dirty seaman found sleeping in his clothing and thereby breeding vermin could be punished, 'and if our dress was reported soiled or unclean, then all such were doomed to have their names put on the black list'.[77] Fresh water was too valuable to waste on laundry so the men would have to use sea water. Soap suitable for use in seawater was eagerly adopted by the Royal Navy whose officers were keen to have a soap that would 'possess all the qualities and ... answer its intended purpose equally well as the common yellow or mottled soap does with fresh water.'[78] However, soap had not always been seen as a necessity for nautical hygiene. When every seaman on the sick list in the fleet fighting in the Americas in the 1780s was given half a pound of soap weekly, Gilbert Blane commented that 'the supply of soap was a thing entirely new in the service'.[79] However, despite Blane's advocacy of supplying soap to the fleet, it was not until 1796 that soap for laundry and personal use began to be issued to seamen by order of Admiral St Vincent. However there could be delays in the receipt of supplies from England, so John Snipe would purchase it locally in the Mediterranean ports.[80]

Trotter recommended that 'whenever any payment is made on board, the officers of divisions should take care that men do lay in a sufficient stock of clothes, with soap, and such other articles as may be necessary for them, before they are allowed to squander any of their money in dissipation'. Noting that 'seamen have a custom of dressing themselves to undergo inspection at stated periods, while at other times they are covered with rags and nastiness', he believed that 'they should be compelled to keep their trousers and other clothes clean, how much so ever they may be worn'.[81] Admiralty regulations stressed that 'the Captain is to be particularly attentive to the cleanliness of the men, who are to be directed to wash themselves frequently, and to change their linen twice every week'.[82]

Dental hygiene was neglected, except among the officers, some of whom used toothbrushes and tooth powders. During the blockade of Ferrol in May 1804, Captain Thomas Freemantle on the *Ganges* was 'most distressed about ... the want of tooth powder and brushes for my teeth', asking his wife to send him 'a pretty large assortment well packed up'.[83] When Midshipman Robert James had to share accommodation with ordinary merchant seamen as a prisoner of war at Sarrelibre, he was so horrified when he caught one of them using his toothbrush that he broke it and threw it out of the window only to be told 'I was *vary fulish* to fling it away as he would have returned it to my drawer nicely rinsed'.[84] For most men dental decay and gum disease led to the loss of teeth. When Davy Reed, master of the *Edgar*,' had the misfortune, like many others to lose his teeth', he was sent a parcel containing 'a set of sheep's teeth for David Reed, Esq., with directions for fixing, and a box of tooth powder that, by the smell, appeared to be a mixture of everything abominable'.[85]

However critical surgeons such as Thomas Trotter may have been of the personal hygiene and cleanliness of the British seaman, most British commentators were even more critical of the sailors and ships of other nationalities. George Cockburn boasted of the superiority of the frigate *Lively*, 'our ship is so clean that seasickness (which, I think, in nine cases out of ten arises from the dirt and bad smells) is out of the question',[86] compared with a Spanish 70-gun ship he observed at Cadiz which contained 'such dirt, filth and misery I could not conceive'.[87] When the surgeon James Lowry was captured on the *Swiftsure* in the

Mediterranean in 1801, he noted that 'the French have very bad discipline amongst their men: hence the superiority of our fleet at sea. The men are very dirty, the smell not of the most fragrant kind'.[88] Going to sea with the British Navy, whether as an enlisted or pressed man, had its terrors, but other navies were considered to have even worse standards, and all were prey to infection in new climes.

# 2
# Feverish!

Nelson prided himself on having survived several bouts of fever despite his body's frailty, boasting that 'I am here the reed among the oaks: all the prevailing disorders have attacked me, but I have not the strength for them to fasten upon. I bow before the storm, whilst the sturdy oak is laid low.'[1] It was undoubtedly an exaggeration and characteristic piece of self-dramatization, but Nelson's experience of illness encompassed most of the diseases that afflicted the navy of his day: malaria scurvy, dysentery, possibly yellow fever and perhaps tropical sprue. Much of his concern for the welfare of his crews was to come from Nelson's own struggles with disease and wounds. He knew that epidemics could debilitate a navy and devastate its fighting capability. He also knew the meaning of suffering from sickness, yet there was something remarkably robust about Nelson's constitution which allowed him to overcome the effects of various fevers and tropical diseases which afflicted him in his youth and lingered on throughout his life.

Nelson was first stricken with a serious illness, probably malaria, during his time as a midshipman on *Seahorse* in the East Indies. After having served eighteen months on the East Indies station, he returned to Bombay with a severe fever. All Nelson knew was that it was a 'life-threatening illness' that reduced him 'almost to a skeleton'. For a time he lost the use of limbs and his brown hair turned almost grey.[2] On 14 March 1776, he was discharged from the *Seahorse* and sent home on the *Dolphin* with Captain James Pigott, whose 'kindness at that time saved my life'.[3] His health slowly improved on the voyage back to England, but he did have doubts about his future as he recovered and

'I felt impressed with an idea that I should never rise in my profession' only to vow that 'I will be a hero, and confiding in Providence, I will brave every danger'.[4] When he got home, he was fit enough to take an immediate position with the *Worcester*. Nevertheless, he was to be plagued with recurrent bouts of the illness throughout his life.

In time his attacks of malaria were to become almost common place and something that Nelson was to accept as his fate. As a lieutenant on *Lowestoffe* in 1777, he was to be troubled by severe chest pains and occasional febrile attacks which left him so weak that on a cold night, while leading a rendezvous party to press men into service near the Tower of London, Nelson's legs gave way and he had to be carried back on piggyback to the tavern where the rendezvous was based by Midshipman Joseph Bromwich.[5] In 1780, by now promoted to his first command on the frigate *Hinchingbroke* and stationed in the insalubrious West Indies where disease ensured rapid promotion prospects, Nelson was again so ill that his doctors advised him to leave Jamaica. A number of his acquaintances including the former master and coxswain of the *Lowestoffe* and Captain Joseph Deane of the *Ruby* had recently died of fever and Nelson was struck down with his 'old complaint in the breast'. Although 'it is turned out to be the gout there', he had twice been 'given over' to 'that cursed disorder' in the previous eight months, and it is more than possible that he was actually suffering from recurrent attacks of malaria.[6]

More often than not Nelson knew when he was suffering from the ague, as malaria was known. In March 1784, his special day, when 'last Friday I was commissioned for the *Boreas* in Long Reach', was spoiled for him since 'I am sorry to say, that the same day gave me an ague and fever, which has returned every other day since, and pulled me down most astonishingly.'[7] In 1787, he was so ill on returning to England after his marriage to Fanny Nisbet, that he had a puncheon of rum ready for his body should he die during the voyage.[8] Before the wedding he had been so sickly that Prince William Henry, who made fun of his friend when 'poor Nelson is head and ears in love', thought that 'he is in more need of a nurse than a wife. I do not really think he can live long.'[9] In 1794, after he was wounded at Calvi, he wrote to Admiral Hood that 'this is my ague day, and I hope so active a scene will keep off the fit. It has shaken me a good deal; but I have been used to them, and so don't mind them much'.[10] He was not the only one to suffer from the ague as 'the climate here, from July to October, is most unfavourable to military operations. It is now what we call the Dog-days, here it is termed the Lion Sun; no person can endure it: we have upwards of 1000 sick out of 2000, and the others are not much better than phantoms. We have lost many from the season, very few from the enemy'.[11] Ill-health alternated with periods when 'my health was never better', as he wrote to his wife on 27 January 1795.[12] Two months later he recorded that 'I do not know when I have been so ill, as during this cruise but I hope a good opening to the Campaign will set me quite to rights'.[13] Indeed when he was inactive, he was more likely to suffer from illness but 'when I am actively employed, I am not so bad. My complaint is as if a girth were buckled taut over my breast, and my endeavour, in the night, is to get it loose'.[14]

Nelson's time on the Jamaica station was not conducive to his good health and he was to suffer serious illness during the expedition to San Juan in Nicaragua in 1780 at the end of his time there. He only narrowly escaped being bitten by a poisonous snake and believed he had been poisoned by drinking water from a spring into which branches of the machineel apple, used by the Indians to make a poison for the tips of their arrows, had been thrown. The Duke of Clarence, believed that Nelson's already delicate health had suffered a 'severe and lasting injury' as the result of this poisoning.[15] Whether or not he drank enough for there to be any lasting effects from the contaminated water, Nelson certainly was laid low by persistent diarrhoea and 'a fever which destroyed the army and navy attached to that expedition' during the siege of the castle of San Juan in April 1780. Both Nelson and his surgeon Thomas Dancer went down with fever on the same night 'that in the *Hinchingbroke*, with a complement of two hundred men, eighty-seven took to their beds in one night and of the two hundred, one hundred and forty-five were buried in mine, and Captain, now Admiral, Collingwood's time; and I believe very few, not more than ten, survived of all that ship's crew'.[16]

This infection has been variously identified with dysentery, tertian malaria, typhoid, yellow fever and tropical sprue. The afflicted men suffered from 'cold, hot and sweating fits' every other day, Some of the sick had boils on their bodies or pustules on their lips and extremities that 'generally indicated a crisis or solution of the fever', others showed 'a universal yellowness' shortly before they died, and in mature cases a bloody flux and 'obstructions of the spleen' developed sometimes accompanied by disorientation and derangement.[17] Traditionally it has been interpreted as yellow fever, but Thomas Dancer did not think that these were typical symptoms of that disease when he was treating the men and distinguished between yellow fever and the intermittent fevers he saw in Nicaragua.[18] Nor did he report any incidence of black vomit usual among sufferers from yellow fever. It has also been argued that tropical sprue, an intestinal disease caused by a lack of vitamin C and folic acid could have been the cause of the sickness.[19] Nelson later observed that 'the fever which destroyed the crews of the different vessels invariably attacked them from twenty to thirty days after their arrival in the harbour', which would fit in with an incubation period for the disease.[20] Tropical sprue is characterised by weakness, a sore tongue, indigestion, weight loss, anaemia and diarrhoea. Dancer only observed diarrhoea and dysentery in the later phases of the disease whereas they are considered to precipitate sprue. For it to have been the cause of the sickness at St Juan, it would have been necessary for the seamen to have been in a pre-scorbutic condition, but the men were reported to be 'in general good health and in great spirits'.[21] Dancer thought that 'in the beginning it was dependent on climate and affecting only individuals' but that it had later become 'evidently contagious and affected everyone who came within the infection'.[22] Typhoid, tertian malaria and bacillary dysentery have been put forward as more likely identifications of the diseases.[23] That there is so much disagreement about the nature of the infection that destroyed the San Juan expedition shows the difficulties of any retrospective diagnosis from historical data.

The fevered Nelson was recalled to the fleet headquarters at Jamaica, upon his appointment as Captain of the *Janus*, 'an effect which providentially withdrew him, when in a most precarious state of health, from a scene of death' on 24 April 1780.[24] He was so sick when he arrived to join his ship at Port Royal, near Kingston, where the fleet was stationed, that 'they were obliged to take him on shore in his cot; and in this manner he was conveyed to the lodging-house of his former black nurse, Cuba Cornwallis, a well-known and respectable negress, who had saved the lives of many naval officers'.[25] Admiral Parker and his wife took him into their quarters and nursed him. The only person who could persuade him to take any medicine was the youngest daughter of Admiral Parker, whom Nelson called his 'little nurse'.[26] On returning to duty, he soon fell ill again. The surgeons who examined him reported that as a result of his 'repeated attacks of tertian and quartan agues, and those now degenerated into quotidian, attended with bilious vomitings, nervous headaches, visceral obstructions and many other bodily infirmities, and being reduced quite to a skeleton, we are of the opinion his remaining here will be attended with fatal consequences' and 'would therefore recommend an immediate change of climate as the only chance he has for recovery'.[27] He was sent back to Europe on the *Lion* with Captain William Cornwallis, 'whose care and attention saved my life'.[28] Declaring that 'it is the climate that has destroyed my health and crushed my spirits. Home, and dear friends, will restore me',[29] he spent his convalescence at the fashionable spa town of Bath.

During his long convalescence Nelson's left arm was paralysed and he continued to suffer from diarrhoea. The paralysis seems to have been caused by peripheral neuropathy as a result of his illness. In January 1781, he was confident of recovery after having been bed-ridden and wrote that 'although I have quite recovered the use of my limbs, yet my inside is a new man, and I have no doubt but in two or three weeks, I shall be perfectly well'.[30] He was over optimistic when in February he reported that 'my health, thank God, is very near perfectly restored, and I have perfect use of all my limbs, except my left arm, which I can hardly tell what is the matter with it. From the shoulder to my fingers' ends are as if half dead, but the surgeons and doctors give me hopes it will all go off.'[31] However by mid-March: 'I have relapsed very much'[32] and 'I have entirely lost the use of my left arm, and very near of my left leg and thigh'. By this stage he was back in London and under the care of the surgeon Robert Adair, who 'gives me hopes a few weeks will remove my disorder.'[33] His account with the apothecary Robert Winch for ointments, vial drops and decoctions mounted up to almost £9 in only two months.[34] By August 1781 he was well enough to take command of the frigate *Albemarle*, though in October he was 'so ill as hardly to be kept out of bed'.[35] It was during the voyage to Quebec that Nelson and his crew suffered from scurvy, though the colder climate of Canada was to be more congenial to Nelson and his health than the feverish Tropics; he declared that 'health, that greatest of blessings, is what I never truly enjoyed until I saw fair Canada' and that 'the change it has wrought is truly wonderful.'[36]

Nelson was concerned when he had any fever and in May 1804 claimed that 'the health of this fleet cannot be exceeded; and I really believe that my shattered carcass is in the worst plight of the whole fleet.' Although his doctors had told him that he was suffering from 'a sort of rheumatic fever', he was worried because he had 'felt the blood rushing up the left side of my head' and suffered with 'violent pains in my side and night sweats, with heat in the evening and quite flushed'.[37] His faith in his surgeon George Magrath relieved his worries. Nelson was also anxious about pains in his breast, which the surgeon William Beatty dismissed as 'the consequence of indigestion, brought on by writing for several hours together', though 'the attack alarmed him as he attributed it to sudden and violent spasm'.[38] Nelson recovered from these spasms very quickly with exercise and in his last days 'His Lordship's health was uniformly good with the exception of some slight attacks of indisposition which never continued above two or three days nor confined him in any degree with respect to exercise or regimen.'[39] These spasms have been interpreted as signs of effort syndrome or soldier's heart, a condition caused by the stresses of war, an interpretation which cannot be proved and has been challenged.[40] It is not surprising that there should be so much uncertainty over the exact nature of Nelson's illnesses and their precise diagnosis when there was little understanding of, or differentiation between, fevers in the late eighteenth and early nineteenth centuries. A modern doctor is likely to interpret the symptoms in a different way to his or her predecessors. All that is certain is what his doctors and he observed and thought.

The term 'fever' could be used to cover a wide variety of illnesses and these tended to be classified according to their pathological behaviour. James Lind recognised three types of fever: remittent fever, with irregular intermissions; continual fevers with no intermissions ; and, intermittent fever, with regular intermissions between the bouts of fever. Intermittent fevers were divided into quotidian fevers, with bouts of fever, every day and tertian fevers, with bouts of fever every other day.[41] George Cleghorn further divided tertian fevers into simple and double tertians.[42] Theories of disease were largely concerned with symptoms rather than causes, but generally the dogma of miasma held sway, that diseases arose from bad air. Cleghorn believed that 'distempered bile' or an attempt by the body to rid itself of 'noxious humours' caused tertian fevers,[43] while Lind attributed the outbreak of fever in Portsmouth in 1765 to excessive heat and standing water, which conspired to release the 'putrid moisture in the soil'.[44] Lind also believed that 'the fever may be communicated by contagion, but this contagion is very slight unless co-operating with bad air, and in a ship is often very greatly checked, if not wholly destroyed, by going out to the open sea'.[45] Fever was linked to the environment on land. The concern with fevers was linked to the maintenance of British interests, especially in the 'Hot Climates', the Tropics.

The Tropics were notorious for infection. Around half of all Europeans who travelled to tropical climates in the eighteenth century died of microbial infections within a year of arriving there, many of them from mosquito-borne malaria and yellow fever as well as from dysentery and smallpox. Europeans had long been familiar with malaria but now encountered a more virulent form of the ague or intermittent fever than they had previously known. James Lind warned that 'the recent examples of the great mortality in hot climates, ought to draw the attention of all the commercial nations of Europe towards the important object of preserving the health of their countrymen, whose business carries them beyond seas' and stressed that 'unhealthy settlements require a constant supply of people, and of course drain their mother country of an incredible number, and some of its most useful inhabitants.'[46] Thomas Trotter was confident not only that Europeans were congenitally unsuited to life in hot climates but that their health would degenerate and their manliness be undermined by laziness, dissipation and an addiction to luxury and leisure induced by the Tropics.[47] Other doctors, such as John Hunter, believed that Europeans would adapt gradually to such climates, becoming resistant to disease and even darkening in complexion over a number of generations.[48] Lind accepted that 'if any tract of land in Guinea was as well improved as the island of Barbados, and as perfectly freed from trees, shrubs, marshes, etc the air would be rendered equally healthful there, as in that pleasant West Indian island.' However, he still advised that 'the best preservative against the mischievous impressions of a putrid fog, a swampy, or of a marshy exhalation, is a close, sheltered and covered place; such as the lower apartments in a ship, or a house in which there are no doors or windows facing these swamps'.[49] Gilbert Blane believed that 'the duties of wooding and watering are so unwholesome that negroes if possible should be hired to perform them'.[50] Black men were considered more resilient to tropical diseases and working in such climates than Europeans. By the 1790s it had become accepted that Europeans were unsuited to labouring in the tropics but trade and colonial development meant that a naval presence there was unavoidable.

Malaria attacks tended to begin with a chill followed by a bout of fever then concluded with a sweat, subsiding fever and a general sense of relief. A pattern of alternating cold and hot fits, was used to differentiate malaria from other fevers. Malaria was classed as an intermittent fever. It was observed by Robert Robertson on the sloop *Weasel* in the Gambia in July 1769 when Seaman David Clency 'was seized with a chilliness, which was succeeded by a violent headache, a sickness at stomach with a reaching to puke, severe pains in all his bones, particularly in his loins, and of great thirst'. This 'paroxysm ended in a profuse perspiration towards morning; after which he continued perfectly cool and easy' until another bout of 'paroxysm' returned. Robertson classified this illness as an intermittent fever because 'there was a total cessation of the fever and symptoms between the paroxysms'.[51]

Malaria was also responsible for loss of life among sailors and marines in the Caribbean, India and the Mediterranean as well as in Africa. Leonard Gillespie as surgeon of the *Majestic* and physician to the hospital in Martinique noted that malaria was a major killer in the West Indies between 1794 and 1797.[52] After witnessing the high rate of mortality caused by a combination of malaria, dysentery and typhus among the army and navy participating in the 1809 Walcheren expedition to destroy the shipyards of Antwerp, Midshipman

Frederick Marryatt considered that 'Walcheren, with its ophthalmia and its agues, was no longer a place for a gentleman'.[53]

Most naval surgeons believed that malaria had a miasmatic cause. Lind thought that this explained why the marines who exercised upon the beach at Southsea in the lingering night airs and early morning fogs were susceptible to malaria, and 'half a dozen of them at a time were frequently taken ill in their ranks, when under arms,' as were the seamen manning the guardships in the muddy, stagnant parts of Portsmouth Harbour.[54] Robertson believed that it was dangerous for seamen to remain overnight on marshy, low lying shores, after observing an outbreak of fever among a weeding and watering party, concluding that 'I therefore think it cannot admit of a doubt, that their lying ashore was the sole cause of their sickness'.[55] James Lind offered advice on how infection could be avoided in tropical climates which became the basis of most preventative measures against malaria. He advised that ships should anchor as far from shore as possible on pestilential coasts, preferably in the open sea and to the windward to avoid miasma. Any gun ports that might be exposed to noxious land breezes should be kept tightly shut and the crew should avoid the open decks as much as possible, especially at night. Any sailors who had to sleep ashore were to be sheltered in tents and huts close to fires which would purify the tainted air with the heat and smoke.[56] Intended to offer protection against miasma, Lind's advice was actually effective for avoiding mosquito-borne infections.

Seamen and marines who went ashore in places where there was a danger of tropical diseases were prescribed Peruvian bark, which contained quinine, mixed with spirits or wine and water before they left the ship and on their return to protect them against malaria.[57] On the *Spencer*, seven gallons of spirits and two gallons of wine were mixed with Peruvian bark and issued over five days in October 1804 to the 272 men sent ashore on the coast of Sardinia.[58] It was the New World that had provided this the first effective remedy for malaria when cuttings from the cinchona bark were taken from a Peruvian tree and carried back to Europe in 1632. This bark was quickly recognized as being able to provide relief from certain intermittent fevers. It was promoted by the Jesuits and for a time there was a Protestant reaction against a Catholic cure though it very quickly came into demand as a powerful remedy for the ague and was soon a standard in most pharmacopoeia. By 1808 Peruvian bark in wine was widely used as a prophylactic against malaria in maritime medicine but many doctors continued to believe that 'bloodletting is the best general practice in tropical fevers' since cinchona tasted bitter and its side effects included vomiting and diarrhoea. It was not until 1820 that quinine was isolated from cinchona bark by the French physiologist François Magendie in collaboration with the pharmacist Pierre-Joseph Pelletier.[59]

Lind was a strong advocate of Peruvian bark, arguing that 'it is certain, that the bark, when good in its kind, and judiciously administered, has often completed a cure, when every other remedy had proved unsuccessful'.[60] As a result of the recommendation for its use by Lind, Robert Robertson, Gilbert Blane, Thomas Trotter and Leonard Gillespie, cinchona bark was the most popular treatment for malaria adopted by the Royal Navy. Blane argued that it should be used as a preventative measure as well as a remedy, since 'nothing is more advisable than to take some doses of Peruvian bark, after clearing the bowels with a purgative' in order to 'prevent the effects of this bad air'.[61] Not all naval surgeons agreed. Francis Spilsbury on the sloop *Fortune* thought that it was wasteful 'to give our men bark in wine; a glass before they went, and another when they returned, under the idea of preventing fever.' He condemned it as a 'hocus-pocus mode of driving away fever'.[62] Robert Robertson had by contrast ensured on the *Rainbow* that 'the waterers get the tincture of bark in the morning'.[63] Robertson later attempted to find a way of overcoming the bitter, unpleasant taste of Peruvian bark by mixing it with treacle, brown sugar, or honey[64] and later devised a Peruvian bark ginger bread, *Panis Cinchonae Aromaticus*, which could be baked in advance and transported in tin canisters.[65]

Nelson authorized the issue of a dose of Peruvian bark mixed with spirits, wine or water to all of his seamen going ashore on wooding and watering parties in the Mediterranean in 1803, both on leaving and returning to their ships, on the advice of John Snipe. As Snipe believed that infection was caused by impure air and that noxious effluvia were contained in green, unseasoned wood, he also recommended that all wood taken on board should first be smoked.

His insistence that only the purest water be taken from the head of the springs and that casks should be carefully maintained were also observed.[66] Nelson's orders were obeyed. On the *Spencer* in October 1804, when the ship was taking on fuel and water at Agincourt Sound, Sardinia, the surgeon, William Beatty, prescribed over seven gallons of spirits and two gallons of wine mixed with bark for 272 men sent ashore over five days.[67]

Yellow fever has been described as a 'disease whose behaviour at sea was a baffling enigma'[68] until the role of *Aedes aegypti* mosquitoes in transmitting the virus was firmly established by Walter Reed in 1900. Its symptoms were recognizable by a red tongue, flushed face, and reddening of the eyes, high fever, bleeding into the skin and damage to the liver and kidneys, and it was most common at the height of summer. It was known by a variety of names in the nineteenth century, including 'coast', 'jungle', 'ardent' and 'bilious' fever. Some men called it the 'black vomits' because sufferers became feverish and spewed up a dark, bloody liquid, while their eyes and skin became jaundiced. The infection was also known as 'yellow jack' after the yellow quarantine flag flown on the ships. There was no absolute agreement as to whether or not it was a contagious or non-contagious disease. Those who believed it to be non-contagious did so on the grounds that it was thought to be a variant of a remittent fever like malaria, which was seen as caused by a specific location and did not spread between individuals on a ship. In 1829 when McKinnal, the surgeon on *Sybille* attempted to show that it was non-contagious by drinking a toast to his fellow officers from a wine glass of black vomit from a sufferer, he suffered no ill effects, but it was possible that he had served in a tropical station long enough to have acquired an immunity. However the high rate of mortality among French naval surgeons during an epidemic at San Domingo in 1802, when 208 out of 300 doctors died from yellow fever, had supported the contagionist view that it could devastate a ship.[69]

The high mortality rate associated with yellow fever meant that a posting to the West Indies, where it was prevalent, was especially dreaded. The wartime movement of refugees and the influx of susceptible European soldiers and sailors coupled with higher than normal temperatures and rainfall in the years from 1793 to 1798, caused outbreaks of epidemic proportions in the West Indies. Leonard Gillespie believed that Admiral Jervis had lost a fifth of the men in his fleet to the disease in 1794. As Physician of the hospital at Martinique, Gillespie reported 14,000 deaths from yellow fever.[70] In 1794 it made 'lamentable havoc' among the crew of Midshipman Frederick Hoffman's ship at Port Royal, Jamaica, when 'six were either carried to the hospital or buried daily.' Fifty two seamen, four midshipmen, one of the lieutenants and the captain's clerk all died. There were another thirty cases of the fever on board when the ship went to sea as 'the surgeon thought the pure sea-breeze might be the means of preserving their lives.'[71] Sadly, once the outbreak of yellow fever had passed, Hoffman's ship succumbed to scurvy with 140 seamen 'obliged to keep to their beds' because their 'legs, hands, feet and gums became almost black and swollen to twice their natural size'.[72] However generally, it was believed that 'the sea is without doubt the healthiest place in a tropical climate' because 'the breeze, pure, fresh and invigorating, untainted by pestiferous effluvia, and uninterrupted by obstructions, revives the drooping frame from the effects of heat or laborious avocations.'[73] James Prior, surgeon on *Nisus* in 1811 believed that 'the best preservative is to keep embarked' as it was only on the ship in unhealthy climates that 'we may often bid defiance to the grim fiend – Death, and his ruthless agents, marsh and animal effluvia'.[74]

James Veitch, surgeon of the naval hospital at Antigua, noted 'the rapidity of convalescence and restoration to health, after the cure of yellow fever, and instances, of men relapsing, were not known at the Hospital at Antigua; particularly, where we had the good fortune to receive the patient early, and we consequently had an opportunity of thoroughly subduing the fatal movements of this disease; by decisive evacuations.' However, when patients were 'admitted to the Hospital, who were improperly denominated convalescent, and whose treatment had not been managed with a decisive hand; and where determinations to internal organs, of a chronic nature, had taken place, these often suffered relapse, but such relapses could not be called Yellow fever; they were symptomatic and yielded to mercurials.'[75] For the treatment of these patients with a frequently recurring yellow fever, Veitch used a combination of purging, bleeding and mercury.[76]

Thomas Downey, sailing to the West Indies in 1795, found that 'with respect to the treatment of the disease, I was much at a loss'.[77] Although Leonard Gillespie and other naval authorities relied on bark mixed with lemon juice or wine, demulcent drinks and tepid baths for the treatment of yellow fever, other experts believed that cinchona bark, while effective against malaria, had no effect upon yellow fever. Such military medical officers as Robert Jackson, Colin Chisholm and, Nelson's friend and fellow combatant in Nicaragua, Benjamin Moseley, together with the Philadelphian physician Benjamin Rush, recommended bleeding. Jackson and Rush were also exponents of cold effusions. Chisholm advocated the use of mercury. Thomas Downey, after attempting to assess the merits of all of these treatments, placed most trust in calomel.[78] The use of purgatives and emetics to relieve vomiting and anti-inflammatory agents to induce perspiration and encourage remission of the fever, was a complete contrast to the emphasis of French physicians in the West Indies on letting the disease take its course and keeping the sufferer comfortable with rehydrating drinks, warm baths and careful nursing.[79] Downey, who had attempted to assess the best way of treating the disease was invalided home himself in 1796 but took the place of the surgeon on the *Daedalus*, which was full of yellow fever sufferers. He fell ill himself after two days without sleep while tending the sick but continued his work for his patients and 'saw them at intervals when I had strength to be supported to their cots'.[80]

Feared as yellow fever was because it was a killer, dysentery was 'by far the most loathsome' of the diseases to which a ship's company was prey because of 'the constant doleful complaints from the various violent pains of the bowels; from gripes, and tenesmus; from the continual noxious fetor about the sick, as well as from that of the necessary buckets'.[81] On the *Rainbow* in the West Indies in 1773, 'the dysentery still continued to rage amongst, the people, attacking young and old; but none of the officers were seized with it'. This the surgeon Robert Robertson did not find surprising 'if it be considered that they lived better in every respect, and were not exposed to so many hardships as the people were'.[82] The attendants of the sick also went down with the 'bloody flux', as dysentery was known. Robertson thought that 'what renders the dysentery on board of ships most distressing, is, that no certain method of curing it has yet been discovered.'[83]

Quarantine remained the tried and tested means of ensuring that infectious diseases could be controlled. Britain had been a late adopter of quarantine but in 1711 an outbreak of plague had prompted quarantine legislation on vessels entering British ports from infected areas. Parliament responded to an outbreak in Marseilles with further legislation which remained in force until another Act of Parliament introduced new regulations in 1753. An Order in Council could require the Customs officials of a port to quarantine ships arriving from named destinations.[84] Ships arriving from the plague-ridden coasts of Africa and the eastern Mediterranean were escorted to an isolated anchorage where they would be kept under watch for forty days. When the vessel was 'on station' (at the quarantine anchorage), a Customs officer held up a 'Quarantine Testament' or 'Plague Bible' at the end of a long pole for the ship's master to swear an oath that there was no sickness aboard his vessel.[85] He also had to fill in a questionnaire recording the ports the ship had visited, the origin of the cargo, the number of people on board, the length of the passage and whether there had been any sickness or deaths among the crew and passengers during the voyage.[86] No one was allowed to go onshore during this period of quarantine, any breaches of this regulation being punished with six months imprisonment and a £200 fine.'[87]

Nelson was well aware of the importance of quarantine to prevent a devastating spread of infection to his fleet. When a virulent epidemic of yellow fever broke out in southern Spain in late 1804 and early 1805, spreading to Gibraltar where it devastated both the garrison and civil population, Nelson imposed strict quarantine, since 'the greatest precaution is necessary to prevent the fever now raging at Spain and at Gibraltar from getting into the Fleet.' He decreed that 'ships are particularly desired not to board on any account vessels coming from Gibraltar, Cadiz, Malaga, Alicante, Cartagena or any place where the fever has been'. He even forbade anyone to board his ships who had been in contact with ships from the afflicted ports. Any French or Spanish prisoners were segregated from their captors to prevent the spread of infection.[88] The port of Gibraltar was not reopened to British ships until 12 January 1805.[89]

The French and Spanish fleets suffered a loss of experienced mariners as a result of the epidemic of yellow fever that was raging through southern Spain, and indeed did not have in place any effective measures against scurvy or other sea diseases. In the West Indies in 1805 the Spanish fleet had been vulnerable to yellow fever and malaria and Vice-Admiral Gravina had feared that 'had we remained there a month longer, I believe that we should have lost half our crews and it might have been impossible for us to return to Europe'.[90] The French fleet was in no better shape and scurvy and other diseases put many sailors on the sick list, the situation not being helped by an inadequate diet as a result of poor victualling. At Cadiz, the hospitals could not cope with the men landed and 'not in a state to support any fatigue, all having symptoms of scurvy'.[91] The Spanish navy was unable to replace losses from disease and desertion with experienced sailors after yellow fever had rampaged through southern Spain the previous year with 9,326 deaths in Malaga alone.[92] When Villeneuve sailed to meet Nelson at Trafalgar, there were 1,731 sick in the Combined Fleets of France and Spain.[93]

# 3
# Sea Surgery

Wounds were to prove a far more serious health hazard than fevers for Nelson at a time when generally it was disease which killed more men at sea than injuries from battle. In many ways he was very unlucky in battle, almost accident-prone in suffering injuries which led to the loss of sight in his right eye and the amputation of his right arm.[1] Yet, rather than detracting from his allure, these injuries enhanced his heroic status and did nothing to impede his career, a contrast with the fate of wounded ratings who became the objects of charity. No one would ever have considered Nelson to be disabled or infirm.

It was at the siege of Calvi in Corsica on 12 July 1794 that Nelson attained his iconic one-eyed status, or rather, to be strictly correct, blindness in one eye as he never actually lost the eye despite popular misconceptions. Its French defenders had little hope of success even though they occupied a formidable defensive position which made a last-ditch defence possible. Not without cost to his men, Nelson had established an advanced battery some 750 yards from Fort Mozzello. The mate of a transport ship had holes ripped through his thighs by French grapeshot and shells, with two crown coins from his pocket being driven through one of his legs into the other. A seaman from the *Agamemnon* and three soldiers were also killed. Captain Serocold, described by Nelson, as 'a gallant good officer and as able a seaman as ever went to sea', was hit behind the ear by grapeshot as he encouraged the men hauling the final cannon into its place. Serocold's friend Captain Hallowell helped to carry the injured man to the more peaceful banks of a small stream where he died.[2] The battery in place, Nelson, ever reckless and bold in battle, had commanded it from the front and had come close to injury. On the second day of fire an enemy shell had burst among the hundred and so people gathered around General Charles Stuart and Nelson in the centre of the advanced battery, but no one had been seriously hurt.[3] Nelson had previously suffered 'a cut on the back' during the siege of Bastia, but had not considered it serious.[4] All was different on 12 July when a chance blind discharge smashed into the merlon of Nelson's battery. He and his companions threw themselves face down to the ground, but for Nelson this was too late. His face was covered with blood. Michael Jefferson, the surgeon's mate on the *Agamemnon*, cleaned the wound, but there were lacerations around the eye and part of Nelson's right eyebrow had been blown away.

Nelson himself characteristically dismissed his injury as 'a very slight scratch towards my right eye which has not been the slightest inconvenience' and believed that 'the blemish is not to be perceived unless told.'[5] Within four days, he had lost the sight in his eye. It did not incapacitate him and he wrote to Admiral Hood that 'I got a little hurt this morning' though this was 'not much, as you may judge by my writing'.[6] Hood was less optimistic and wrote that 'he speaks lightly of it, but I wish he may not lose the sight of an eye'.[7] Nelson, however, congratulated himself that 'the surgeons flatter I shall not entirely lose the sight, which I believe for I can clearly distinguish light from dark. It confined me, thank God, only one day'.[8] By January 1795, he had recognized that his sight was lost and acknowledged that 'my eye is grown worse and is almost total darkness; and very painful at times; but never mind, I can see very well with the other'.[9]

Without any firm contemporary diagnosis of the nature of Nelson's eye injury at a time when there were no diagnostic ophthalmic instruments, it is impossible to be certain as to what actually caused Nelson's loss of sight. He himself referred to the skin surrounding the eye as having been 'cut down' and to the eye being hit but not perforated.[10] The immediate loss of vision has been attributed by later medical experts to a detached retina, swelling and watering caused by concussion, or to a vitreous haemorrhage within the cavity between the iris and lens. Damage to the optic nerve may also have caused optic atrophy, or else secondary glaucoma had developed with a corneal oedema which would have been responsible for loss of vision and continued pain.[11]

Despite having downplayed his eye injury at the time, Nelson was subsequently concerned that his injury should be recognised, and, 'not any notice having been taken in the public list of wounded at the siege of Calvi of my eye being damaged', he asked Lord Hood to 'take such measures as you may judge proper that my Sovereign may be informed of the loss of an eye in his service'.[12] His claims were supported by two, certificates, one signed by John Harness, Physician to the Fleet, and Michael Jefferson, surgeon on *Agamemnon*, and the other by William Chambers, Surgeon General to the Forces in the Mediterranean. Harness and Jefferson confirmed that Nelson had received 'a wound of the iris of the right eye, which has occasioned an unnatural dilation of the pupil, and a material defect of sight' while Chambers recorded that the eye was 'so materially injured that in my opinion, he will never recover the perfect use of it again.'[13] Nevertheless, there were 'doubts which had arisen respecting the damage my eye had sustained' which made it 'impossible to say whether it was such as amounted to the loss of a limb' though Nelson stressed that 'a total deprivation of sight for every common occasion in life is the consequence of the loss of part of the crystal of my right eye'.[14] He considered that the taking of Corsica had cost him '£300, an eye and a cut across my back and my money I find cannot be repaid me'. Bitterly he commented that 'nothing but my anxious endeavour to serve my country makes me bear up against it; but I sometimes am ready to give it all up'.[15] After attending a private court of the Surgeons' Company, he was awarded an annual pension of £763 16s for a wound 'fully equal to the loss of an eye'. His comment was that 'it was only for an eye; in a few days I shall come for an arm, and in a little time longer, God knows, most probably a leg!'[16]

Superficially, Nelson's right eye appeared normal, which led to rumours that he had exaggerated the extent of his injury for financial gain. Nevertheless in October 1804 *The Times*, ostensibly 'for the satisfaction of those of his Lordship's admirers who are not personally acquainted with him', claimed that 'Lord Nelson "is not blind of either eye"' and that Nelson had himself claimed that 'he could see best with what he called his worst eye'. The report was correct in its correction of the popular impression that 'the gallant Lord Nelson has lost one eye', but was incorrect in claiming that, though 'he for a short period lost the sight of one eye', this very soon had 'been happily restored'.[17]

There are many apocryphal stories arising from Nelson's insouciance about the loss of sight in one eye and how he turned it to his advantage. At the battle of Copenhagen in 1801, notable as the only one of Nelson's naval engagements in which he was not wounded, when ordered to disengage by Admiral Sir Hyde Parker, he is said to have remarked to his flag captain, 'You know, Foley, I have only one eye. I have a right to be blind sometimes' before lifting his telescope to his right eye and remarking 'I really do not see the signal.'[18] In the negotiations with the Danes after the battle in the royal palace, he is also reputed to have murmured ' Though I have only one eye, I see all of this will burn very well' as a not-all-that-veiled threat in order to obtain the desired agreement.[19]

Despite a widespread belief that Nelson covered his blind eye with an eye patch, this was something Nelson never wore nor indeed needed to wear. Even though most of his portraits flatter the image of the naval hero, none of them give any indication of an eye problem and superficially the eye looked normal. In later years he wore a green eye-shade made by Emma Hamilton and sewn into his hat.[20] This was depicted in a posthumous portrait by Arthur Devis and the clothing supplied for Nelson's effigy in Westminster Abbey also contained a hat with a patch providing shade from the strong light such as he had worn in life. However, it has not stopped modern depictions of him with an eye patch, including on a toby jug of a half-length bust of Nelson in the uniform of a vice-admiral purchased by Queen Mary in 1952 and donated by her to the National Maritime Museum.[21]

The strain on Nelson's left eye convinced William Beatty that eventually he would have gone blind had he not been killed at Trafalgar.[22] In January 1801, Thomas Trotter treated Nelson for trouble he was having with his good eye and his fear that a membrane that was growing over the pupil would result in total blindness. Various quack remedies were recommended to Nelson, but Trotter merely 'prescribed a dark room and bathing the eye every hour with cold spring water, which in 24 hours had a surprising effect, and in two days more the inflammation was entirely gone.'[23] A pterygium, a benign growth of the conjunctiva probably caused by exposure to sunlight, dust and wind, was also growing at the inner side of both eyes, visible and notable enough to be represented in portraits of

Nelson. Trotter recommended that Nelson should shade his eyes from bright sunlight and in 1801 Nelson accordingly had written to ask Emma Hamilton to make him 'green shades for my eyes' which were troubling him so that 'my eye is like blood; and the film so extended that I only see from the corner farthest from my nose'. He was sitting in a darkened room, eating only the simplest of food, abstaining from wine and porter and bathing his eyes in cold water every hour, yet, despite his 'fear it is the writing has brought on this complaint', was writing to his lover, 'the only female I write to'.[24] Other correspondents were informed 'I am almost blind'[25] and to 'pity the sorrows of a blind and (in constitution) old man'.[26]

Good eyesight was important at sea and was recognized as such by naval commanders. Admiral Peter Rainier chose to have himself portrayed by Arthur Devis wearing an ungainly-looking pair of spectacles of moulded iron with straight sides and tortoiseshell 'Martin's margins' around the lenses to protect against sideways glare, reflecting the need for visual aids in some cases despite the inconvenience of wearing such glasses at sea where they could mist over and the iron frames rust.[27] With advancing age many admirals and captains conceded the need to help their vision by using spectacles rather than the telescope they usually preferred to be depicted with. Cuthbert Collingwood lamented in 1802 that 'I am not short sighted, but I do not see as I did formerly, and sometimes can scarce read without spectacles'.[28]

Glasses could be obtained easily from the same shops that sold telescopes in an age when the spectacle maker, using his optical skills, made the lenses for spectacles, microscopes and telescopes. The stock of the optician's shop in Carthusian Street off Charterhouse Square, London, owned by John Marsh in 1805 consisted of barometers, thermometers, spectacles, reading glasses, silver pencil cases, pocket knives and trinkets.[29] C. Lincoln, an optician in Leadenhall Street stocked more scientific merchandise, including mathematical, astronomical and surveying instruments, reflecting and achromatic telescopes and microscopes, aximuth compasses, achromatic perspective-glasses, theodolites, sextants, quadrants, globes, hydrometers, military telescopes, concave and convex mirrors, opera and reading glasses, spectacles, eyeglasses, scales and rulers.[30] At such an optician's shop a naval officer could not only buy navigational equipment but also personal aids to better vision while he did so.

Indeed opticians led the way in the development of improved telescopes and navigational instruments. John Dollond, optician to George III and the Duke of York, had developed an achromatic telescope objective, patented in 1758, which was later improved upon by his son Peter. The firm of Peter and John Dollond supplied optical instruments for James Cook's second voyage and the telescopes produced by the firm were in such demand that 'a Dolland' became a synonym for a telescope.[31] The London spectacle maker Archibald Blair worked on the problem of trying to improve the performance of refracting telescopes with his father Robert Blair, a former naval surgeon who had become interested in navigational instruments while serving in the West Indies and in 1785 was appointed to the newly established role of Regius Professor of Practical Astronomy at the University of Edinburgh until his appointment in 1793 by the Admiralty as First Commissioner of the Board for the Care and Custody of Prisoners of War, where he was a strong supporter of the use of limes and lemons to combat scurvy. Archibald Blair believed in the superiority of the lenses he and his father had produced, and declared in 1827 that telescopes they had made over twenty years earlier were still in good condition.[32]

There was little that could have been done to restore Nelson's sight, though he himself sought out treatment. In 1799, while at Palermo, he wrote that 'I am undergoing a course of electricity which I begin to think will give sight to my blind eye.'[33] There is no other record of Nelson's eye treatment with galvanism, the use of electricity to stimulate the contraction of muscles, but, according to the London-based, Neapolitan-born doctor Tiberius Cavallo, 'inflammation of the eyes, the throwing of the electric fluid by means of a wooden point, is constantly attended with great benefit; the pain being quickly abated and the inflammation being generally dissipated in a few days'.[34]

Luigi Galvani, Professor of Medicine at the University of Bologna, following his observation in 1786 that severed frog's legs twitched when subjected to an electric charge, believed that animal electricity was a vital force. Despite Alessandro Volta's rival interpretation of electricity as a physical rather than biological phenomenon, Galvani's nephew Giovanni Aldini promoted the idea of galvanism by demonstrating the effects of electrical currents on corpses throughout Europe. In 1803 he used this electro-stimulation technique on the corpse of an executed criminal George Foster in London, causing one eye to open, the right arm to move and motion in the legs and thighs. Soon the idea of using galvanism to reanimate nerves in the human body as well as the dead became popular.[35] For Nelson to attempt to restore the sight in his eye using galvanism was a sign of his openness to new ideas in contemporary medical science.[36]

Michael la Beaume claimed a number of successful treatments of eye problems with galvanism, including 'a gentleman, whose blindness was occasioned by a defective energy of the optic nerves from intense application to minute objects, but whose health was tolerably good,' and who was, 'after a tedious course of Galvanism topically applied, restored to useful sight but not to his former visual powers.' In another case 'a middle-aged man, whose sight was nearly lost from syphilitic inflammation, was soon restored by the administration of Galvanism to the system'. Meanwhile another patient whose right eye was 'nearly destroyed by a ball thrown from a racket' and one whose eye was 'very seriously injured by a wine-bottle thrown at his head' apparently had their vision restored to them by 'the local application of Galvanism' which la Beaume claimed 'not only removed the chronic inflammation, but gave tone to the organs of sight, and fully restored the visual powers'.[37]

Ophthalmology was in its infancy as a specialty in Nelson's time, but was to assume greater importance as a result of Napoleon's Egyptian campaign at the beginning of the nineteenth century. A purulent and extremely contagious eye infection that could cause blindness, 'Egyptian ophthalmia' or trachoma became a major problem affecting both the French and British armies and navies. As a result of the virulence of this eye condition, a number of ophthalmic hospitals were established in London, Edinburgh and Dublin, most notably the London Dispensary for Curing Diseases of the Eye and Ear, subsequently better known as Moorfields Eye Hospital.[38] The Navy sent its ophthalmic cases to the Royal Eye Infirmary after it opened in 1805.[39] The fear that every blind soldier or sailor might become a charge on the government gave an added imperative to study the causes of the disease, which was suspected as having a connection with *ophthalmia neonatorum*, caused by infection of a child with gonorrhea at birth.[40] More attention was now given to a study of the anatomy of the eye and its diseases. James Wardrop's 1808 study of ophthalmic pathology, *Essays on the Morbid Anatomy of the Human Eye* was one of the first such studies prompted by this threat to the efficiency of the British armed forces.[41]

Nelson's eye injury did not deter him from playing an active role whenever he saw action thereafter and at the battle of Cape St Vincent he received an internal abdominal injury on 14 February 1797 which left him with a hernia and future digestion problems. He was struck by flying debris which left him 'bruised but not obliged to quit the deck'.[42] Ralph Miller, captain of Nelson's ship *Captain* reported to his father that 'my noble Commodore was struck in the side by the splinter of a block and would have fallen had not my arms supported him', for which Nelson thanked him with the gift of a topaz and diamond ring.[43] Nelson himself initially dismissed the injury and merely noted that 'among the slightly wounded is myself, but it is only a contusion and of no consequence, unless an inflammation takes place in my bowels, which is the part injured.' Nine days after the battle he complained that 'my hurt at the moment was nothing, but since, it has been attended with a suppression of urine, but the inflammation has gone off, and I am fully recovered.'[44] Although he made no mention of the injury in his letters to his wife Fanny, he did inform the Duke of Clarence ten weeks after the accident that 'my health is getting so indifferent from want of a few week's repose, and the pains I suffer in my inside, that I cannot serve, unless it is absolutely necessary, longer than this summer.'[45] The effects of this wound continued to affect him for the rest of his life and he was to frequently complain of 'a violent pain in my side'.[46] In November 1804 he moaned to Lady Hamilton that 'my cough is very bad, and my side, where I was struck on 14th February is very much swelled; at times a lump as large as my fist, brought on, occasionally, by violent coughing'.[47] For the resulting digestive problems he was given magnesia and peppermint to sooth his stomach when aperients such as rhubarb worsened the problem.[48] Generally a hernia, or rupture, was treated with warm baths and a grain of opium every eight hours together with attempts at reduction. If this failed, immediate surgery was recommended as it was believed a delay of 36 hours would lead to inevitable mortification and death. A recurrent hernia would result in discharge from the service.[49] Nelson's, while a recurrent problem, was not serious enough for this.

Much more serious was his wound during the unsuccessful landing at Santa Cruz, Tenerife, on July 24 1797, when only quick thinking by his stepson Josiah Nisbet in applying an improvised tourniquet to the wound caused by grapeshot shattering his right elbow saved his life though not his arm.[50] Ironically, Nelson had tried to dissuade Josiah from joining the landing party with the argument: 'you must not go, supposing your poor mother was to lose us both, what will she do?'. Fanny indeed almost lost her husband who was shot in the very act of stepping from the boat. Nisbet caught the blood in his hat and stopped the blood flow by grasping his step-father's right arm despite finding that 'the revolting of the blood was so great that Sir H. said he could never forget it'. He then improvised a tourniquet from two silk necker-chiefs, one borrowed and one his own, and tied up the arm with it.[51] Such improvised tourniquets were recommended by the physician Gilbert Blane who believed that the men should carry their own home-made tourniquets into battle', 'a garter or piece of rope-yarn' in order to bind up a limb in case of profuse bleeding; and that 'if it be objected that this, from its solemnity, may be apt to intimidate common men, officers should at least make use of some precaution.'[52] For Josiah it was a rare and notable use of initiative. Nelson acknowledged to Fanny that 'Josiah under God's providence was principally instrumental in saving my life'.[53] The nearest ship was the *Seahorse* but Nelson refused to board it for fear of disturbing the pregnant Betsy Freemantle, whose husband Thomas, captain of the *Seahorse,* was still involved in the fighting. It was a fortunate decision as Freemantle too was injured in the arm but received unskilful treatment that left the wound slow to heal. On arriving back at the *Theseus,* Nelson refused the offer of a chair, insisting on walking up the side of the ship since 'I have yet my legs and one arm'.[54]

The other arm was to be amputated.[55] Nelson himself was in no doubt that this would be necessary and, 'with his right arm dangling by the side, while with the other he helped himself to jump up the ship's side, and with a spirit that astonished everyone, told the surgeon to get his instruments ready, for he knew he must lose the arm and the sooner it was off the better'. Midshipman Wiliam Hoste, for whom Nelson 'has been a second father to me', praised him for the way in which 'he underwent the amputation with the firmness and courage that have always marked his character'.[56] The amputation was carried out by the twenty-eight year-old surgeon Thomas Eshelby, assisted by twenty-four year-old surgeon's mate Louis Remonier, a French Royalist *émigré* who had been a surgeon at Toulon before joining Admiral Hood's fleet. They found a 'compound fracture of the right arm by a musket ball passing a little above the elbow, an artery divided'. There is no record of Nelson having been given spirits or a leather pad to bite on to help him manage the pain of amputation, the only things available in a pre-anaesthetic age. He was held down by a couple of seamen, one of whom fainted and had to be replaced by the chaplain. His arm was 'taken off very high, near the shoulder' by Eshelby using a circular motion to cut through the soft tissue and then taking up his saw to cut the humerus bone. Bleeding was controlled with a screw tourniquet around the top of the arm, which was slowly released as ligatures were tied. Remonier, 'according to the practice of French surgeons, advised the use of silk instead of waxed thread for the ligatures'.[58] Once the amputation was done, 'opium was afterwards given'.[59] Nelson complained of 'the coldness of the knife and was later to instruct George McGrath on the *Victory*, 'whenever there was a prospect of coming to action, to have a hanging stove kept in the galley for the purpose of heating water, in which to immerse the knife, in the event of his being the subject of an operation, and on which he always calculated.'[60] When asked if he wanted the amputated limb to be embalmed, Nelson told the surgeon to 'throw it in the hammock with the brave fellow that was killed beside me.'[61] Nelson's attitude was generally fatalistic and he accepted that 'my mind has long been made up to such an event' when reassuring his wife and father that they 'will not think much of this mishap' which was 'the chance of war'.[62]

Generally amputations were carried out with the patient seated and his body, limb and the part to be amputated held down. The surgeon, who had first marked the place, would then fix a tourniquet to the artery. The assistant holding the limb would then draw up the skin tightly and 'apply the tape circularly around the limb to guide your knife in the incision which you are now to make with the amputating knife, standing between the patient's legs'. The surgeon would cut through the flesh 'circularly' while his assistant drew up the flesh 'as much as possible to open a passage to the bones, that they may be cut off a little higher than the incision, and that the flesh may afterwards wrap over them'. The surgeon was expected to 'work the saw upon both bones after they have been partly entered by the teeth and cut through them as speedily as possible, but be careful to have both bones divided at the same time without splintering them.' Once the limb was amputated, the assistant would relax the tourniquet to show the surgeon 'by the starting forth of the blood' where the ends of the arteries were so that they could be ligatured and secured with a 'surgeon's knot'. All of this was given without anything to deaden the pain, although laudanum might be administered afterwards.[63]

Although his life had been saved, Nelson continued to be in great pain. He 'rested pretty well and quite easy' after the operation, but the opium given to him caused constipation and he had to be given a laxative of senna and jalop five days after the operation. He was also placed on a light diet of tea, soup, sago and lemonade. By 1 August he 'continued getting well very fast' and the 'stump looked well; no bad symptoms whatever occurred. The sore reduced to the size of a shilling; in perfect good health'. However, there was a problem with the ligatures, one of which had 'not come away'.[64] By 20 August, Nelson was suffering from 'twitching pains at times' and when he arrived back at Portsmouth on 1 September he 'would not suffer the ligature to be touched.'[65] The pain could have been caused by sepsis, but Nelson thought that a nerve had been taken up with the ligated artery, noting in October that 'my poor arm continues quite as it was, the ligature still fast to the nerve, and very painful at times.'[66] The belief was that 'some mistake was made in taking up one of the arteries, in consequence of which the Admiral suffered the most excruciating torture for several months.'[67]

At that time it was common surgical practice to leave the ligature ends long and hanging out of the wound after amputation in order that, as suppuration occurred and the ligatures separated by necrosis and granulation, they could be gently pulled until they came away after two to four weeks. A different method was proposed in 1786 by Lancelot Haire, assistant surgeon at Haslar Hospital, who recommended that arterial ligatures should be cut short because 'the ligatures sometimes became troublesome and retarded the cure.' By cutting the ligatures short, he claimed to 'have seen stumps healed in the course of ten days' and without 'the patient being sensible of pain' when the ligature 'made its way out by a small opening'.[68] This new method of ligature helped when David Fleming, surgeon on *Tennant*, carried out the first success- ful ligation of a carotid artery on 17 October 1803. A rating on the ship, Mark Jackson, who had attempted to cut his throat, burst his carotid artery in a violent fit of coughing, so Fleming cut down and tied the carotid which 'put an effectual stop to any further loss of blood' in a new procedure of which Fleming 'had never heard of such an operation being performed'.[69] Whether or not Haire's method of short ligatures would have helped Nelson more than Eshelby's use of time-honoured long ligatures can never be known.

Phantom pains in the right arm were also put down to the ligaturing. Nelson's brother William asked a local Norfolk surgeon in Swaffham about 'the apparent pain in your right hand' and was assured that 'it was a sure sign of a nerve being taken up with the artery, indeed he says it is hardly possible to avoid it, as there are so many and such small ones that you must now have patience and all will do well, but he thinks that the ligature had better not be forced too much'.[70] Nelson had to endure the agony. In the midst of the national rejoicings following the battle of Camperdown, Nelson, who regretted not having had a role in the victory, 'retired to his bed-room after a day of constant pain, hoping with the assistance of laudanum to enjoy a little rest'. His house in Bond Street was unlit and the London mob demanded to know why it was not celebrating the naval victory. When told that 'Sir Horatio Nelson, who had been so badly wounded, lodged there and could not be disturbed', the leaders of the mob withdrew and 'that universal sympathy for the health of Nelson which pervaded even the minds of the lowest of his countrymen was clearly shown, no subsequent visit being paid by the mob, notwith- standing the tumult that prevailed.[71] Meanwhile Nelson 'suffers a great deal of violent pain and takes opium every night' but was 'impatient for the healing of the wound that he may go to sea again'.[72]

Nelson had to accept and adapt to the loss of his arm. He told the Duke of Clarence that 'I assure your Royal Highness that not a scrap of that ardour with which I have hitherto served our King has been shot away.'[73] Hoping to continue his career, he was to put on a brave front to his royal friend, but was more despondent before his wife, confiding that 'I shall not be surprised to be neglected and forgot, as possibly I shall no longer be considered as useful',[74] echoing his comment to Lord Sat Vincent that 'a left-handed Admiral will never again be considered as useful'.[75] Nevertheless, he was able to dress with the help of a servant and Lady Spencer gave him a special fork-knife, manufactured so that one of the four prongs had a cutting edge, enabling him to feed himself with one hand. His shirts were in future to be made with short right sleeves and cuffs that could be drawn over the stump by a tape. His armchair was adapted to have a pad on which the stump could be placed. Within two days of his injury, he was using his left hand to write letters. By the end of March 1798, he was able to return to sea. He was also able to jocularly refer to his stump as his fin, which became agitated when he was angry. The stump also ached and alerted him to changes in the weather allowing him to use his fin as almost a personal barometer.[76] Already by December 1797, ever the loyal churchman and devout Christian, he was able to send a letter to the Vicar of St George's Hanover Square stating that 'an officer desires to return thanks to Almighty God for his perfect recovery from a severe wound, and also for many mercies bestowed upon him.'[77]

A year and six days after the loss of his arm, he was again badly wounded in the head at the Nile on 1 August 1798 when a piece of langridge, rough metal fired as anti-personnel shot, tore open his forehead leaving a flap of skin hanging down over his good eye.[78] Temporarily blinded by the blood, he collapsed into the arms of Captain Edward Berry, crying 'I am killed! Remember me to my wife!'[79] Carried to the cockpit of the *Vanguard,* he insisted that he take his turn among the wounded waiting for attention, but his wishes were disregarded for once by the surgeon Michael Jefferson who, after probing the wound, declared that there was no 'immediate danger' from this 'wound on the forehead over the right eye' with 'the cranium bared for more than an inch, the wound 3" long'. The edges of the wound were brought together and the skin kept in place by adhesive strips. Later, the dressing was replaced and another sticking plaster applied with lint. Opium was administered to deaden the pain and aperients given to counteract the resulting constipation. By 1 September Jefferson considered that the wound had 'healed perfectly', but, 'as the integuments were much enlarged, I applied every night a compress wet with a discutient embrocation for nearly a month, which was of great service'.[80] Nelson hid the ugly scar by brushing his hair forward from this time on.[81]

Although Jefferson had discharged him from the sick list on 1 September 1798, Nelson continued to suffer from his injury and felt that 'my head is ready to split' and that 'if there be no fracture my head is severely shaken'.[82] Despite obvious concussion following his wounding, Nelson had withdrawn from the cockpit as soon as he was treated in order to make room for the other casualties of the battle. That night, Jefferson had to perform three amputations, deal with the loss of a man's eye and attend to thirty other wounded. He had already dealt with twenty-seven casualties before Nelson was brought down to the cockpit. Richard Craden, a twenty-one year-old landsman, was the first casualty to be treated for a compound fracture of his left leg, to be followed by Philip Murphy, brought down to the cockpit with his skull laid bare and his right eye missing, and John Tripp had a wound in the abdomen and his right forearm almost torn off. Of the 589 on board the *Vanguard*, seventy-six men were wounded and thirty killed.[83] Disobeying Jefferson's orders, Nelson went back on deck to view the 'most grand and awful flagship of the French flagship *L'Orient* exploding.' It was this moment of going back on deck to see the French flagship explode, with his head bandaged and his hand on his heart, that Nelson chose to have painted probably as a love token gift for Emma Hamilton during his convalescence in Naples.[84] Very much Nelson is the lovesick hero rather than the seasick seaman.

Edward Berry believed Nelson 'to be out of danger tho' his wound is in his head' and 'he has been sick' after the battle, but noticed that he was unusually irritable, could not sleep and was unable to compose himself. On 3 August he remarked that 'he is now more easy than he was this morning, the rage being over'.[85] Nelson himself complained that 'my brain is so shook with the wound in my head that I am sensible I am not always so clear as could be wished'[86] and even in July

1799 considered that 'as to myself I have been long sick and tired out'.[87] Margaret Parker, whose husband Sir Peter Parker had commanded Nelson in the West Indies and 'ever regarded you as a son', was 'very uneasy about the wound in your head and would have you quit a station that must retard your recovery.'[88] She advised him that 'quiet is the only remedy for a blow on the head' and warned him that 'a few months relaxation and a cold climate will soon fit you for another enterprise but should you continue in constant exertions of both body and mind, years, not months, will be required for your recovery.' It was advice which Nelson considered wise but 'my health is such that without a great alteration I will venture to say a very short space of time will send me to that Bourn from whence none shall return' and 'after the action I had nearly fell into a decline. I am worse than ever'. Yet, even though he knew that 'nothing but the air of England, and peace and quietness can perfectly restore me',[89] he was unable or unwilling to leave Naples and Emma Hamilton with whom he had started an affair during his convalescence.

The battle-scarred, one-armed, half blind hero may have had an allure for Emma Hamilton, but the toll taken on Nelson's health by his wounds can be seen in a portrait possibly commissioned by Sir William Hamilton in Naples in 1799 from a local artist, Leonardo Guzzardi. His face is drawn, haggard and emaciated, while his cocked hat is angled to avoid any contact with the scar above his right eye. The painting is not an idealised portrait of a naval hero but of a man in ill-health and weighed down by war. Wearing a rear-admiral's full dress uniform and the ribbon and star of a Knight of the Bath, the St Vincent naval medal on a blue and white ribbon round his neck, and the Turkish chelengk on his hat, Nelson is shown in full glory standing woodenly and in a bizarre attitude on the deck in front of a naval gun. His left hand is outstretched with his index finger pointing to a scene from the battle of the Nile, while his empty right sleeve is hooked up to a waistcoat button. It is not a prepossessing image, but reflects the hero's ill-health at the time it was painted.[90] At first sight Nelson had never looked impressive. Prince William Henry, Duke of Clarence, dismissed him as 'the merest boy of a captain I have ever beheld' on first meeting him in 1782.[91] After his numerous wounds, he was even less pleasing in appearance, being described after the battle of the Nile as 'a little man with no dignity and a shock head' and by Sir William Hamilton as 'a little man and far from handsome'.

In looking older than his years, Nelson's lot was no different than that of his seamen. Gilbert Blane observed that 'a seaman at the age of forty-five, if shewn to be a person not accustomed to be among them, would be taken by his looks to be fifty-five, or even on the borders of sixty' and 'in consequence of what they undergo, they are in general short lived, and have their constitutions worn out ten years before the rest of the laborious part of mankind'.[92] In *Persuasion,* Jane Austen satirised the popular perception of sailors who are 'all knocked about, and exposed to every climate and every weather, till they are not fit to be seen' by confounding the vain Sir Walter Elliot's prejudices about sailors being 'the most deplorable looking personage you can imagine' by describing Admiral Croft as 'a very hale, heart, well-looking man, a little weather-beaten to be sure, but not much' and Captain Frederick Wentworth for whom his years at sea 'had only given him a more glowing, manly, open look, in no respect lessening his personal advantages'.[93] Nelson, however, may have gone to sea as a fresh-faced boy, but life at sea weathered him like his shipmates.

More idealised is a drawing of Nelson having his head wound dressed by the surgeon's mate Samuel Cotton in the cockpit of the *Vanguard,* while the surgeon Michael Jefferson attends a leg wound with his chest of surgical instruments beside him in a rare almost contemporary representation of a cockpit in action.[94] If anything the scene is perhaps too orderly. The cockpit became the scene of intense activity for the naval surgeon during a battle. The surgeon Robert Young on *Ardent* at the battle of Camperdown on 11 October 1797 was 'employed in operating and dressing till near four in the morning, the action beginning about one in the afternoon.' During the battle over 90 wounded were brought down to the cockpit and 'the whole cockpit deck, cabins wing berths and part of the cable tier, together with my platform, and my preparation for the dressings, were covered with them. So that for a time, they were laid on each other at the foot of the ladder, where they were brought down.' With no mates to assist him because the recent naval mutinies had driven many out of service and assailed with 'melancholy cries for assistance ... from every side by wounded and dying, and piteous moans and bewailing from pain and despair', Young felt overwhelmed and 'so great was my fatigue that I began several amputations under a dread of sinking before I should have secured the blood vessels.' However he had to 'preserve myself firm and collected, and embracing in my mind the whole of the situation, to direct my attention to where the greatest and most essential services could be performed.' His first priority was to distinguish between men who needed more urgent attention but who were not as clamorous as 'some with wounds, bad indeed and painful, but slight in comparison to the dreadful condition of others' who were 'most vociferous for my assistance.' He also needed to maintain morale and 'I cheered and commended the patient fortitude of others, and sometimes extorted a smile of satisfaction from the mangled sufferers, and succeeded to throw momentary gleams of cheerfulness amidst so many horrors' while using his surgical skills to handle those horrors. His patients included men whose thighs had been taken off by cannon shot and others blackened by the explosion of a salt box. Fifteen or sixteen dead bodies had to be removed once the battle was over before Young could get to the operating and dressing materials he had prepared before the action. Yet, he could claim satisfaction in saving the lives of many of the wounded under his care.[95]

The surgeon usually operated during naval engagements in the cockpit on the orlop deck, normally the living quarters of the midshipmen, master's mates and assistant surgeons. Below the waterline, it was an area regarded as safe from enemy gunfire. Cramped, badly ventilated and dimly lit, it was not the ideal place for surgery. If the cockpit was too small, the surgeon might have to ask the captain to have a platform erected in the cable tier on which sailcloth could be laid for the reception of the wounded. Otherwise the platforms for performing operations were to be placed as close to the hatchways as possible, and 'let there be fixed a chest of proper height to perform your operations upon, and on another just by lay your apparatus'. Often mess tables or chests were lashed together to form makeshift operating tables. Buckets and tubs were also conveniently placed near the operating table with 'a bucket of water to put your sponges in, and another empty to receive the blood in your operations; a dry swab or two to dry the platform when necessary; a water cask full of water near at hand in readiness for dipping out occasionally'.

Linseed oil, lime water, ceruse, olive oil and compresses of cold vinegar were readied for the treatment of burns. Also essential were 'wine, punch or grog and vinegar in plenty'. The surgeon's and purser's own beds were to be reserved for the reception of wounded officers, but the surgeon was expected to promise to all his patients 'in the softest terms to treat him tenderly and to finish with the utmost expedition'.[96]

It was difficult in the heat of battle to carry out any form of triage, but some surgeons did attempt to assess the severity of the wounds that were coming down to the cockpit and deal with the most serious cases first, but usually there was little time to do this and more often than not it was a case of men being treated in order of arrival. William Robinson, serving on the *Revenge* at Trafalgar, noted that 'the rule is, as order is requisite, that every person shall be dressed in rotation as they are brought down wounded, and in many instances some have bled to death.'[97] At the battle of Camperdown, George Magrath, surgeon on the *Russell*, had little choice but to juggle priorities among the injured seeking his attention. Henry Spence, a twenty-five year-old seaman, had been injured when 'a large cannonball from the opponent's ship struck him a little above the ankle joints and carried away both legs', but while he examined Spence's legs Magrath was interrupted by a more urgent case when 'another man came to the cockpit with profuse haemorrhages from a large artery that was divided by a splinter. I was therefore necessitated to leave Spence (previously applying the tourniquet) to staunch the man's bleeding.' Spence was later laid on the operating table to have his legs amputated and 'lucky it was that he bore it so well, as a shot at this time came into the cockpit and passed the operating table, close, this startled all the women who formed the chief of my assistance.' Once the operation was over, Spence was bandaged up, given a cordial and laid on a platform erected for the accommodation of wounded men in the cable tier, and only when the action was over was he put into a cot. When first brought into the cockpit, he had seemed a hopeless case: Magrath commented that 'the man's legs were amputated in the heat of action, which I am happy to say did not retard the case, indeed when he was first carried to the cockpit there were little hopes of success.'[98] A good surgeon needed to be quick and incisive. This, unfortunately, was not always the case. Sir William Dillon complained about his surgeon that 'although an excellent scholar, being nearsighted with a defect in one of his eyes we did not place much reliance in his abilities at amputation'.[99]

Not all amputations were as successful as that performed by George Magrath on Henry Spence. When a seaman had the calves of both his legs shot away in an unsuccessful attack on the French fleet in the Basque Roads in 1809, one of his legs was amputated but he begged the surgeon to leave him the other and 'very coolly observed that he should like one leg left to wear his shoes out.' When the second leg was amputated, he exclaimed 'now to the devil with all the shoe-makers, I have done with them'. Despite his humour, fortitude and his apparent good progress, 'from lying in one position for such a length of time, his back mortified, and he breathed his last, much regretted by all his shipmates'.[100] In a battle between the frigates *Macedonian* and USS *United States* in 1812, Samuel Leech, a boy seaman, saw 'a man bearing a limb, which had just been detached from some suffering wretch' and the surgeon and his mate 'smeared with blood from head to foot: they looked more like butchers than doctors.'[101] One of their patients John Wells had his arm amputated and observed that 'I have lost my arm in the service of my country; but I don't mind it, doctor, it's the fortune of war'. He somehow managed to remain 'cheerful and gay', optimistic that he had received only a slight injury, but he was given too much rum by his messmates, rapidly developed a fever and very soon died; Leech believed that 'his messmates actually killed him with kindness.'[102]

Cannon balls and chain shot caused serious wounding, while smaller missiles such as musket and pistol balls and grape shot could also lodge in the body and do considerable damage. Wooden splinters would also be flying around after the ship had been hit by a cannon ball. Probes and probe scissors were used to explore the wounds for foreign bodies, and balls and other debris were grasped and removed with bullet forceps or a scoop.[103] Where possible, amputation was avoided. When 20 year-old John Evans, a seaman on *Lion*, was shot through both hands while boarding a Greek ship, the surgeon James Young 'extracted all the loose portions of the fractured bones, reduced as nearly as possible into site all the fractured ends of the metacarpal bones' and 'applied simple dressings with proper splints and band-ages'. In this case 'in the right the ball entering the back part of the hand passed in an oblique direction and shattered the metacarpal bones of three fingers making its exit through the palm—in the left the shot entering nearly at the articulation of the first phalange of the thumb with the trapezium passed quite through and totally destroyed the joint—having splintered all the bones of the thumb it passed out between it and the forefinger'. The operation was successful and Evans was 'quite recovered except the use of his left thumb.'[104]

A particular clinical condition recorded by surgeons during battle was 'wind of a ball', which the surgeon William Turnbull defined as 'a peculiar accident very common in engagement at sea. If a cannon ball in its flight passes close to any part of the body, that part is rendered livid and benumbed for some time.' He believed it to be 'most dangerous when it approaches the stomach, and has in such cases proved instantaneously fatal, without the least visible mark of injury' although often 'tumours or marks of violence are conspicuous'.[105] Gilbert Blane explained the phenomenon as 'perhaps owing to the compression and tremor of the air in consequence of its resistance to the motion of the ball'.[106]

Burns from the accidental explosion of loose gunpowder were common in battle, especially when the wads that held the shot and gunpowder in place were not wetted when firing cannons, which 'prevents their inflaming and blowing back when they fight the fair weather side of the ship; a circumstance which, without this pre-caution, gives occasion to a number of accidents by the burning parts catching the loose powder or setting fire to the cartridges'.[107] David Morris, a thirty year-old seaman on *Leviathan* at Trafalgar, and Andrew Pheling were both burnt 'by an explosion of one of the main guns, the breach of which flew out'. Pheling, 'burnt in the face, neck and thighs', survived and returned to duty after a month. Morris, 'severely burnt over his forehead, face, neck and over the whole of the breast and belly', was not so lucky. Given opium and various oint-ments, he was also bled and given an enema by the surgeon William Shoveller, but died within a fortnight.[108]

The success of a surgeon was not only in how he performed during battle but in whether or not his patients survived and thrived once the conflict was over. On *Victory* at Trafalgar, Beatty and his assistant surgeons, Neil Smith and William Westenburg, dealt with about 100 officers and men wounded during the battle, examining wounds, locating and removing splinters and other foreign bodies, performing amputations and tying arteries. Beatty alone amputated nine legs and two arms.[109] The rows of shattered men lying on the orlop deck were so overwhelming that the surgeon of the schooner *Pickle*, Simon Gage Britton, had to be brought aboard to help with the casualties and remained there for three days.[110] It was difficult to keep the wounded comfortable aboard ship. On the way to Gibraltar, *Victory* was caught in a storm; wounded men lying on the deck were rolled along the ship, those in hammocks were pitched against each other and the bulwarks, some were thrown down to the decks, and wounds were reopened. Despite this, the high survival rate of the casualties was remarkable and reflects an impressive quality of surgical care. On the decommissioning of the *Victory* in early January 1806, Beatty reported that no more than six of the 102 convalescents had died, five on board and one in the hospital at Gibraltar. All the others under his charge had recovered from their wounds except for five men who had been left at Gibraltar and five who had been transferred to the hospital ship *Sussex*. The high number of eight of the eleven amputees survived their operations. Of the men who died following their amputations, loss of blood had been the cause of death for two of them and only the twenty-two year-old seaman William Smith died from infection after his leg was taken off at the thigh. There were surprisingly few deaths from infected wounds among the other casualties who did not undergo amputation; Alexander Palmer, twenty-one year-old Midshipman, died of tetanus after being struck in the thigh by a musket ball, and twenty-two year-old landsman Henry Cramwell died of gangrene after suffering severe contusions from splinters.[111]

The picture was not so rosy when British naval surgeons witnessed the results of the work of their counterparts in the French and Spanish navies. After the battle of Cape St Vincent, the Spanish ships were 'full of dead bodies, some with their heads off, and others both their legs and arms off, and the rest knocked all to pieces, and their entrails all about, and blood running so thick we could not walk the decks in parts without going over our shoes in human blood, which was a deplorable sight and too shocking to relate.'[112] William Shoveller, the surgeon on *Leviathan* at Trafalgar was not at all impressed by the condition of

Spanish prisoners taken aboard, many of them 'with tourniquets on their different extremities, and which had been applied since the action, four or five days elapsing, consequently most of the limbs in a state of mortification or approaching it.'[113] Shoveller had to intervene to try to do something to save the lives of these men. The seaman William Robinson was similarly scathing about the 'the scene of carnage horrid to behold' on a captured Spanish ship with the dead bodies 'in a wounded or a mutilated state' piled up in the hold and 'the heart-rending cries of the wounded' on a French ship where the doctor, 'having lost or mislaid some of his instruments, was reduced to the necessity of resorting to the use of the carpenter's fine saw, where amputation was needful.'[114] It was preferable to be wounded on a British vessel. Survival in any degree of fitness was more likely. Yet after Trafalgar, Collingwood was praised as being 'not less distinguished for your humanity than for your valour in battle', for offering to exchange wounded prisoners of war with the Spanish as 'humanity and my desire to alleviate the sufferings of these wounded men' so that they 'may be taken proper care of in the hospitals on shore'.[115]

British naval surgeons prided themselves on having developed considerable skill at speedy battle surgery and it was in battle that reputations were earned or lost. For them and their patients, a job was well done if lives were saved and health restored, although for many death or permanent disability was the result of battle despite all that the surgeon could do for them. Robert Young on *Ardent* could congratulate himself after the battle of Camperdown when his surviving patients were 'conveyed on shore in good spirits, cheering the ship at going away, smoking their pipes and jesting as they sailed along, and answering the cheers of the thousands of the populace who received them on Yarmouth key.'[116] This was the true mark of successful surgery at sea.

# 4

# Surgeons at Sea

Considering Nelson's personal medical history of illness and injury, it would be too easy to conclude that he knew only too well the limitations of the doctors who had treated him and would have had little regard for the medical practice of his day. Indeed he prided himself that 'one plan I pursue, never to employ a doctor, nature does it all for me and Providence protects me'.[1] Despite this boast to his friend, the Duke of Clarence, and his claim that 'as usual, my health is got up again: after the doctors telling me, they could do nothing for me, dame Nature never has failed curing me',[2] Nelson had no choice but to consult regularly a large number of different doctors, both at sea and ashore, about his myriad of health problems.[3] He was also well aware of the importance of maintaining the health of the men under his command and the part played in that by naval surgeons.

A naval surgeon was expected to be a jack of all trades. Whereas on shore, there was a division in the status and roles of different types of medical practitioner, at sea the surgeon did it all and had complete responsibility for the health of the crew. The elite physicians ashore held medical degrees entitling them to use the title of 'doctor' and were members of the College of Physicians. The other two types of doctor of the time were of lowlier status and organised themselves as members of trades rather than of professions. The apothecaries dispensed medicines for most ailments, while the surgeons treated boils, sprains and fractures and performed amputations. The surgeons had learned their craft through an apprenticeship for between three and seven years to a master surgeon like any other craftsman and were members of a livery company, the Company of Surgeons, rather than of a professional body. Among them the naval surgeon was considered the lowest, not even worthy of full membership of the Company that would have at least entitled them to attend a sumptuous livery dinner. Ships of the Royal Navy had carried surgeons since the sixteenth century, but they were not classed as officers despite their often high level of education. John Bell, surgeon to the Yarmouth Naval Hospital considered that 'to the life of a navy surgeon there are, God knows, no seductions' and 'nor will men ever delight in a profession which is not made respectable, honourable and useful'.[4]

For many naval surgeons, the decision to begin a career at sea was a consequence of relatively disadvantaged social origins, not a lack of intellectual ability. The surgeons of Nelson's navy came from a variety of backgrounds throughout the British Isles, although perhaps three-quarters of them were Scottish, Irish or Welsh at a time when perhaps the majority of medical practitioners were English. Some were the sons of apothecaries or surgeons in small towns or ports without the family influence that could be exerted by the better connected physicians and thus had limited vocational prospects. A minority were the sons of clergymen. The majority of them were the offspring of men engaged in commerce, trade or manufacturing. Neil Smith, assistant surgeon on *Victory* at Trafalgar was the son of an Aberdeen merchant. Sir John Richardson was the son of an Aberdeen brewer and magistrate. Yet some of them came from even humbler backgrounds like Daniel McKechnie, the son of a Glaswegian labourer and workman. Many were younger sons for whom there was little other prospect of advancement other than through medicine, but who did not have the option of easier avenues of access into civilian medical practice enjoyed by the majority of contemporary medical practitioners. Through naval service they could acquire the manners and graces of a gentleman by study in their free time and by mixing with officers in the wardroom.[5]

The lack of opportunities facing some naval surgeons when paid off in peace time but with no prospects of setting up in civilian practice led them into areas of medicine that often proved uncongenial. At the end of the American War of Independence, Thomas Trotter, later Physician of the Channel Fleet (1795–1802), had been demobilized from the Royal Navy and had signed aboard the slave ship *Brooks* in 1783–4 simply because he needed a job. What he witnessed there horrified him. The slaves were 'locked spoonways, according to the technical phrase,' below deck and Trotter was unable to 'walk amongst them without treading upon them.'[6] Trotter's evidence before a House of Commons Select Committee in May 1790 was challenged by Clement Noble, captain of the *Brooks*, who claimed that on the voyage in question only 58 slaves had died and implied that this may have been because Dr Trotter was 'very inattentive to his duty' and 'spent a great deal too much time in dress.'[7] It was this experience as a surgeon on board a slaver that made Trotter such a bitter opponent of the slave trade and of any form of colonialism in general. He later deplored the conditions in which naval ratings lived and worked as being little better than those endured by slaves on the notorious middle passage from Africa to the American and West Indian colonies and firmly believed that long periods of service in the colonies, especially in the West Indies, would result in the degeneration of Europeans as their bodies were ill-adapted to service in a hot climate.[8] It was an experience he gained only through lack of a patron.

Patronage could be as important for a naval surgeon as for an officer. Gilbert Blane was the son of a wealthy merchant and had originally gone to the University of Edinburgh with the intention of entering the church. After five years in the faculty of arts he switched to the faculty of medicine, where he was soon elected as president of the students' medical society. Having studied under William Cullen at the University of Glasgow where he obtained his MD, he was introduced by Cullen to the surgeon William Hunter, who in turn recommended him to first Lord Holderness and then to George Rodney as a personal physician. It was as personal physician to Rodney, rather than as a lowlier naval surgeon, that Blane went to sea to the West Indies on board the *Sandwich,* where he distinguished himself for his bravery and medical skill in six naval battles during the War of American Independence. As a reward for going beyond his medical duties and even relaying messages from the admiral to the gunners, he was appointed as Physician to the West Indies Fleet in 1780. At his own expense he compiled a printed *Short Account of the most Effectual Means of Preserving the Health of Seamen, particularly in the Royal Navy* which he distributed to all surgeons in the fleet as a guide to what he expected of them. With the authority of Rodney behind him, he also collected statistics on the morbidity and mortality of the fleet which he used to promote an improved diet and sanitary measures in the West Indies station, which resulted in him being rewarded with a pension.[9]

Blane was to capitalise on his naval connections when he returned to civilian life. He had become acquainted with the Duke of Clarence in the West Indies and, on the strength of this link, was appointed as physician extraordinary to the Prince of Wales in 1785, subsequently becoming physician-in-ordinary to the Prince of Wales' household and later physician to George IV. A recommendation from Lord Rodney helped his election to the post of physician at St Thomas's Hospital in 1783, though he was not to be as popular with his civilian medical colleagues there as he was with his naval ones; Astley Cooper recognized that he was 'a painstaking physician, but he was so cold in temperament, that we called him "Chilblane"'.[10] An invitation in 1795 from Lord Spencer, First Lord of the Admiralty to return to naval service as Commissioner for Sick and Wounded Seamen led to his resignation from St Thomas', a move perhaps not unwelcome to Blane or his colleagues there. After his retirement from naval service in 1802, his expertise continued to be sought by the British government on health in prisons and convict ships. His advice was also sought over the failure of the army medical services to maintain the health of troops on the island of Walcheren off the coast of the Netherlands in 1810. After recommending that the Walcheren expedition should be aborted, he was charged with overseeing the return of the sick and wounded. The award of a baronetcy in 1812 reflected the professional position he had achieved in society.[11]

Patronage also played an important part in the career of the Milanese Augustus Bozzi Granville, who joined the Royal Navy at Lisbon in 1807 aged 24 as acting assistant surgeon of the sloop *Raven*. Having only a limited grasp of English, he was lucky to find that the surgeon 'Francis Johnstone, a Scotchman, spoke English with a certain facility and a pronunciation analogous to that of the Italians' and so 'our own official intercourse on board had been carried on in that language.' When examined in physic at Haslar Hospital to have his appointment confirmed, his examination was also conducted in Latin as his English was not yet proficient.[12] Yet, he was to benefit from the patronage of William R. Hamilton, private secretary to Lord Elgin, whom he had met at Corfu in 1803. After Hamilton's return to London in 1812 as an under-secretary of state at the Foreign Office, he was able to secure Granville's transfer from a small vessel to the frigate *Maidstone*, which was 'likely to yield what sailors look for in war – a good share of prize money'. Then in 1813, Granville's 'Maecenas' arranged for him to be placed on half-pay so that he would be available to 'instruct his two eldest sons, William and Alexander in the Latin language, and to teach them to speak it fluently'.[13]

It is remarkable how loyal Nelson proved to be to many of his naval surgeons. Michael Jefferson, surgeon on the *Agamemnon* from 1793 to 1796, Nelson's first command of a ship of the line, was consulted back in London in the winter of 1797 about the pain Nelson suffered following the amputation of his arm. Jefferson again accompanied Nelson on the *Vanguard* and treated him for his head wound at the battle of the Nile, being rewarded with a shore appointment running the new naval hospital at Malta. However, following his dismissal from that post as a result of his excessive drinking, he forfeited Nelson's patronage, who judged that 'Mr Jefferson got on by my help; and by his own misconduct, he got out of good employ'. Even Emma Hamilton's lobbying to get him a posting on *Victory* in 1804 was useless, and 'he must begin again, and act with much more attention and sobriety than he has done, to ever get forward again; but time may do much, and I shall rejoice to hear of his reformation.'[14] By this time Nelson deemed George Magrath, his surgeon on the *Victory*, 'by far the most able medical man I have ever seen' and appointed him as surgeon to the hospital in Gibraltar.[15]

Candidates, whether with or without patrons, seeking an appointment as a naval surgeon were examined before the Court of Examiners of the College of Surgeons, which met at Surgeon's Hall, Old Bailey, near Newgate in London. Although the examination was not academically rigorous, one candidate Peter Cullen was worried since he 'had been led to believe that the Faculty of London were not so well disposed to candidates from Edinburgh from a spirit of envy'. So he 'made himself thoroughly acquainted with every surgical question or case that could possibly be propounded to him and went confidently in' to face the Court, where 'the examiner proceeded to question him on anatomy, physiology and surgery, some of the more important surgical cases or diseases, and how he would treat them. This Gentleman was quite satisfied with Mr Cullen's proficiency, and taking him up to the centre of the table, where the president bowed to Mr Cullen, and desired him to pay one guinea as a fee.'[16]

This was civilised compared with the popular image of such examinations earlier in the eighteenth century satirised by Tobias Smollett in his 1748 picaresque novel *Roderick Random*, based on his own experiences as a naval surgeon.[17] The eponymous hero of the novel, echoing the experience of his creator, was examined at Surgeon's Hall where the grim-faced examiners told him that 'it was a shame and a scandal to send such raw boys into the world as surgeons' before asking him the farcical question 'If during an engagement at sea, a man should be brought to you with his head shot off, how would you behave?'[18] It was a question to which there could be no answer. Then before he could go to purchase his chest of drugs at Apothecaries' Hall, having already paid bribes to the doorkeeper, cleaner, examiners and secretary at the Surgeon's Hall, Random was unlucky enough to fall into the hands of a press gang on Tower Hill and was appointed second surgeon's mate on the ship *Thunder* to which he was forcibly taken. There, he was shocked by the sick berth where 'I was much less surprised that people should die on board than that any sick person should recover.' In a confined space are fifty 'miserable distempered wretches' who are 'breathing nothing but a noisome atmosphere of the morbid steams exhaling from their own excrements and diseased bodies, devoured with vermin hatched in the filth that surrounded them, and destitute of every convenience necessary for people in that helpless condition.'[19] The sick are summoned to have their sores dressed by a loblolly boy banging a pestle and mortar only to be found fit by the doctor whose greatest desire is to satisfy the captain's wish to have no sick people on board.[20] When Random falls sick with yellow fever, he refuses to swallow one of his colleague's 'diaphoretic boluses' and instead has a blister applied to his neck.[21] He also participates in battle surgery, where the surgeon, 'supported with several glasses of rum', sets to work and 'arms and legs were hewn down without mercy'. Meanwhile the ship's chaplain assisting in the cockpit 'had the fumes of the liquor mounting in his brain and became quite delirious; he stripped himself to his skin and besmirching his body with blood could scarce be withheld from running on the deck in that condition.'[22]

It was a sharply drawn, somewhat outdated picture of the life of a naval surgeon, but it coloured contemporary perceptions. Echoing Smollett's criticisms, the army surgeon Charles Dunnett complained in 1808 that 'I cannot pass over in silence the absurdity of employing such a number of raw apothecaries' boys as hospital mates or assistant surgeons, in His Majesty's army or navy, whose whole education has been acquired, in the course of a year or two, behind the counter of some obscure apothecary or barber-surgeon, nay, in the cockpit of a man of war, as loblolly boys'.[23]

By the time of the French Revolutionary and Napoleonic wars, naval surgeons were expected to have a certain level of professional knowledge and expertise before presenting themselves for examination before the Company of Surgeons. Although they had learned their trade as apprentices to surgeons, they were not uncultured and had to have a basic knowledge of physic and surgery. Most of them would have had a sound grammar-school education, though there were criticisms of the literacy of some naval surgeons. One man whom Charles Dunnett encountered at Haslar Hospital in 1808, 'an assistant surgeon of the Royal Navy, there, who on being ordered to write the case of a sick man he brought from his ship, was under the necessity, after much controversy, to confess he could not write at all.'[24] Despite such complaints of the low standards of education among the recruits to naval medicine, many of them later took the opportunity to gain a medical degree at the University of Edinburgh, where they had to write a dissertation in Latin. A quarter of army surgeons and an eighth of naval surgeons went on to study at Edinburgh when semi-retired on half-pay.[25]

Thomas Trotter did believe that the naval surgeon enjoyed fewer opportunities of maintaining his professional knowledge and equipping himself for a future civilian career than an army doctor, who, being quartered in towns had 'intercourse with polite society' and 'they are not cut off from information to be obtained from books; and their situation affords them opportunities to cultivate acquaintance with literary characters and the general progress of medicine'. By contrast, the naval surgeon confined to his ship all too easily assumed 'a disposition of mind, that unfits him for the exercise of his profession in private practice', especially since 'his naval service, in the prime of youth, had prevented him from making friends and forming connections, that would have been favourable to his future prospects in medical rank and reputation'. For such a man Trotter foresaw his post-naval life as being 'a state of precarious dependence.'[26]

All that was in the future. Once accepted, the successful candidate was appointed as a full ship's surgeon or, more usually, as a surgeon's mate; first, second, or third class. on the recommendation of the Court to which he had just paid his fee. He was also expected to purchase his own instruments and have his instrument chest examined by the Company of Surgeons which then ensured that the chest was locked with the 'seals of the Physician and of the Surgeons' Company to be affixed thereto in such a manner, as to prevent its being afterwards opened, before it comes on board; nor is the Captain to admit any Chest into the Ship without these marks upon it'. This lucrative privilege had been bestowed on the Company of Barber Surgeons by Charles I and had then been granted to its successor Company of Surgeons when that split from the barbers in 1745. Despite attempts in 1715 and 1795 by the Surgeon and Physician of Greenwich Hospital to gain the privilege of examining the chests, this lucrative right was guarded by the College of Surgeons, which retained it on becoming the Royal College of Surgeons in 1800. The examination of the chest guaranteed uniformity in the surgical equipment used throughout the naval service. Whereas the instruments case of an army surgeon was provided by each company, the surgeon had to buy his own instruments, even after 1805 when medicines were provided by the navy for the first time. An allowance was granted to the surgeon for his instruments and medicines, but at £62 for a senior surgeon in 1781 this was never an adequate amount. Few sea surgeons had any pretensions to wealth but were at sea because they could not afford to practice in a more prestigious and lucrative branch of medicine.[27]

It was little wonder that they resented having to pay for their own equipment and medicines, unable even to challenge long established monopolies to find cheaper supplies. The Society of Apothecaries had enjoyed a monopoly over the supply of medicines since 1703. The recommended medications included cordials, emetics like tartar and ipecacuanha, stimulants such as hartshorn and camphor, and such sedatives as tincture of opium and laudanum. There were also drugs used to combat sepsis, contagion and fevers, blistering agents for counter-irritation and mercury for the treatment of gonorrhoea and syphilis.[28] Pastes, ointments, cordials and tinctures often had to be freshly prepared by the surgeon from the materials supplied to him. Even when the Admiralty took over the responsibility of paying first for some drugs in 1796 and then all of them in 1804, the surgeon still had to provide his own instruments. A typical surgeon's chest contained amputating knives, saws, tourniquets, artery forceps, needles, trephines, scalpels, scissors, probes, scoops, ligature thread, lancets, clyster syringes, bougies, splints, cupping apparatus, linen rollers, bandages and a set of pocket instruments. Until 1812, there was also an apparatus for 'restoring suspended animation' and the injection of tobacco fumes 'for the admission of kindly warmth into the internal parts of the body, which in all cases must prove advantageous, but its stimulus seems admirably adapted to excite irritability and to restore the suspended or languid peristaltic motion of the intestines'.[29]

While equipped to deal with battle casualties, most of the surgeon's regular work was less dramatic and more mundane, dealing with accidents and sickness. Much of it was day-to-day drudgery.[30] Rheumatism and influenza alike were treated with bloodletting, purges, emetics and blistering of the skin. When a twenty-four year-old seaman presented himself to the surgeon William Shoveller on *Leviathan* in 1805 complaining of having a 'cough, pain in his breast affecting his respiration and headache and general pains', he was bled, purged and blistered.[31] It was difficult to diagnose sickness precisely and George Magrath felt frustrated when he was unable to identify a mystery sickness which he likened to scurvy and typhus, that affected the crew of the *Russell* in 1801, feeling that 'I am not really in possession of language sufficiently emphatical or expressive to describe the distressed situation of the *Russell's* crew, during the prevalence of this scourge, without feeling and lamenting for the poor sufferers who underwent more human misery than even the imagination can conceive'. He was forced to admit that 'notwithstanding the great advances which of late years have been made in the science of medicine, we are not yet sufficiently acquainted with the laws which govern the system in a state of health'.[32] Lionel Gillespie tried to use natural observation to find such answers and linked 'the restlessness and watchfulness of several patients' when 'one or two were attacked with arthritis' to the weather.[33] The ship's surgeon was on surer ground when dealing with injuries from accidents.

Falls from high in the rigging on to the deck or into the sea were frequent, as were falls down open hatchways. In July 1806, twenty-five year-old Joseph Lawrence on *Canopus* in harbour at Plymouth 'fell from the main deck into the hold in the act of taking his hammock down and fractured the seventh rib of the left side' and was 'immediately bled to the amount of 16 ounces'.[34] Another accident on *Canopus* in October 1806 happened to Stephen Kennedy, who 'in the act of going down the fore ladder when it was blowing hard and the ship rolling very much slipped off and pitched upon a quart bottle on the lower deck which broke and made a very extensive wound in the sole of his right foot'. Gangrene set in but the surgeon did not amputate and by the fourth day the gangrene had extended up the knee and to the groin. Although, Kennedy 'appeared refreshed having had a good night', his pulse was weak and his tongue 'foul'. He 'answers sensibly when spoken to but his eyes have an unusual languor in them', and by the afternoon he was dead.[35]

Minor injuries to the genitalia were all too common on board ship. Scrotal swelling was common in topmen who worked in the high rigging, because of the trauma of sliding down the back stays or lying on the yards.[36] Michael Chris, a twenty-eight year-old sailor, fell down a ladder joining two decks, landing heavily on his perineum with the result that his scrotum became swollen and ulcerated. He was treated with a scrotal support, a variety of poultices and bed rest.[37] When Patrick Wade on *Aboukir* sustained a contusion to his scrotum, he was also sent to hospital for leeches to be applied there to bring down the swelling.[38] Able seaman Peter Ring of *Aetna* reported to the surgeon James Campbell with a swollen testicle after injuring himself whilst furling the mainsail and was cured with purges, fomentations and bleeding.[39] When Benjamin Gagen was kicked in the groin and was unable to make water, he was treated with bleeding and clysters initially, followed by warm baths and opioids, but, when these treatments failed, Robert Tainish, the surgeon on *Theseus*, opined 'I considered this a proper time for the catheter'.[40] A less common injury to the genitalia was suffered by Midshipman Francis Bazze, who was confined to the sick berth of *Alfred* for thirty-nine days after a pistol ball lodged in his scrotum during a duel in Cadiz though he suffered 'no impediment in the action of the member'.[41]

Stones in the bladder were also a common problem. Poultices, the application of hot flannels, cupping, blistering, and bleeding were all tried before a surgeon resorted to the dangerous procedure of lithotomy, known as 'cutting for the stone'. James Williams, aged fifty, stationed in the West Indies on *Alfred*, suffered from the stone and was passing urine like 'soap suds'. He was discharged ashore to the hospital at Port Royal for treatment.[42]

Hernias or ruptures were commonplace among seamen. Turnbull, author of *The Naval Surgeon*, believed that the physical strain of constantly hauling on a rope, working the windlass or lifting heavy weights was the main cause of a rupture. More idiosyncratically, he also identified specific reasons for there being so many hernias in the Mediterranean, blaming the excessive consumption of olive oil and the hot weather, and observing that in Malta 'scarcely any person is exempted from rupture'. He warned that many pressed men would conceal femoral ruptures until nothing could be done and then complain about them so that they could be given lighter work. Turnbull devised his own method of replacing protruding intestines. The patient was to be relaxed by 'the various means of copious venesection; of injections of tobacco smoke, which will take off the tension, as well as prove a laxative; and of opiates, particularly the digitalis if the stomach will retain it'. The intestines were then to be filled 'with tepid water by means of a particular instrument or pump' and then 'when the reduction succeeds, the hernia contents are to be contained by the assistance of a bandage or truss'.[43] Most ruptured seamen were given trusses to keep the protruding organs in place and prevent parts of the intestine from protruding through the abdominal tissue, but these were often ineffective. George Barnes, a twenty-seven year-old seaman on *Leviathan* had a hernia that was 'reducible and supported by a truss; but from his inattention to its application, has allowed the rupture to slip into the scrotum, and his bowels to remain for some days in a state of constipation'. The use of bleeding, enemas, drastic purges and fomentations had no effect and Barnes had to be sent to Haslar Hospital.[44]

Ulceration was a constant problem. Inflamed and painful open sores on the legs were difficult to heal and could result in the loss of a limb if they did not heal. The sick berth of *Gloucester* in 1812 was filled with men suffering from 'hideous ulcers (a general complaint) arising from bruises received in the course of their hard work and exasperated by the damp in which they lie'.[45] Captain Edward Brenton believed that 'the ulcer, when it has once got possession of a ship, is one of the most contagious and serious complaints to which seamen are liable' and remembered hearing that 'during the late year, the *Northumberland* had it to such a degree that I think they were compelled to pay her off, that she might be cleansed from the infection'.[46]

Sharing the same shipboard conditions as their patients, the surgeons themselves suffered from accidents and illnesses, some eighty-five of them dying in service between 1799 and 1815. They were stricken by typhus, tuberculosis, pneumonia, malaria yellow fever, dysentery, hepatitis, ophthalmia and paralysis. They suffered from rheumatism, hernias, fractured limbs and damaged eyesight. In battle they faced the danger of wounding or death. Nor were they free from problems of mental health. A naval surgeon had to be strong to carry out his duties.[47] Robert Young, surgeon on *Ardent* at the battle of Camperdown, was invalided out of the service suffering from typhus and a hernia not long after the battle in which 'I was employed in operating and dressing till near 4 in the morning, the action beginning about 1 in the afternoon', without any assistance from a surgeon's mate, and 'so great was my fatigue that I began several amputations under a dread of sinking before I should have secured the blood vessels'. In battle, 'in the midst of these agonising scenes, I was able to preserve myself firm and collected', but even this exemplary surgeon, 'a man who is at once physician, surgeon and apothecary, upon whom the whole of these characters, the health and lives of so great a number of valuable subjects of the State are often solely depending', could not maintain his own health.[48]

The usual scene of activity for the ship's surgeon was the sick berth. On *Victory* this was to be found in a wing berth on the starboard side of the upper gun deck beneath the forecastle. It was well ventilated and had a skylight to allow in daylight essential for the examination of patients. There was an internal toilet in the roundhouse and convenient access to the heads. Separated from the rest of the deck by moveable canvas bulkheads stretched across wooden frames, the sick berth contained twenty-two cots for convalescents, two urinals, three bedpans and fourteen spitting-pots. It also had its own stove for the preparation by the loblolly boys of such invalid foods as oatmeal porridge and mutton broth. Vinegar and a nitre fumigant powder were used liberally for disinfection. There was a small dispensary in the sick berth, but the main dispensary was located in the relative safety of the orlop deck where the surgeon had his own cabin adjoining it, and which would be adapted for use as a makeshift operating theatre during the heat of battle. The surgeon also had a portable medicine chest for treating officers in their own cabins. Nelson, all too conscious of his own health problems, had his own personal medicine chest, which he always carried with him.[49] The sick berth may seem too small for a ship carrying a crew of 820 men but in normal conditions its beds were rarely all needed. Daily numbers on the sick list averaged between ten and fifteen. On 21 April 1805 there were only ten occupants, four of them having been involved in accidents, two were cases of ulcers, one man was suffering from dysentery, another case had a venereal disease, and two men were sick with 'other complaints'.[50]

Traditionally the sick berth had been no more than a canvas cubicle between two gun ports wherever it could be fitted in until Admiral St Vincent, impressed by the sick berth set up by Captain Adam Markham in 1800 on the *Centaur,* ordered in 1801 that it should be on the upper deck underneath the forecastle. Placed between the two forward guns, it had easy access to the heads. Covered with a skylight and panelled with canvas to keep out smoke from the galley, it was furnished with cots, settees, wash tubs, a stove and its own cooking utensils. There were twenty-two beds. A dispensary was attached to the sick berth. Funds for the mess were provided by the ship's purser, who credited the unused victuals of the sick to a 'sick fund'. The captain and officers in the wardroom sent up wine and delicacies from their own tables. Thomas Trotter considered that this sick berth, a model for others, was 'furnished in a style and delicacy much beyond any ward in our royal hospitals'.[51]

Nelson lost his eye at Calvi.
(© National Maritime Museum,
Greenwich, London, PAD5480)

Queen Mary's 1952 toby jug perpetuates the
unfounded but widespread myth that Nelson
wore an eye patch (© National Maritime
Museum, Greenwich, London,  E5956)

Josiah Nisbett saved Nelson's life, though not his arm, with an improvised tourniquet (Richard Westall, © National Maritime Museum, Greenwich, London, BHC0498)

Horatio Nelson was treated with other casualties in the cockpit of the *Vanguard* after the battle of the Nile. (Charles Heath, © National Maritime Museum, Greenwich, London, PAD5574)

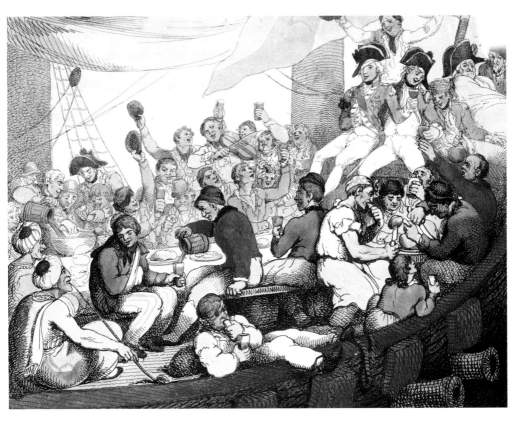

Healthy and wounded alike celebrated after the battle of the Nile. (Thomas Rowlandson, © National Maritime Museum, Greenwich, London, PAF3892)

A love token for Emma Hamilton, a wounded Nelson on deck at the battle of the Nile. (© National Maritime Museum, Greenwich, London, BHC2903)

An ill and wounded Nelson did not cut a dashing figure after the battle of the Nile (Leonardo Guzzardi, © National Maritime Museum, Greenwich, London, BHC2895)

The fatal wounding at Trafalgar for Nelson and his sailors. (Samuel Drummond, © National Maritime Museum, Greenwich, London, BHC0547)

The death of Nelson.
(Benjamin West,
© National Maritime
Museum, Greenwich,
London, BHC0566)

Emma Hamilton as Hygeia, goddess
of health. (© National Maritime
Museum, Greenwich, London,
PAF4385)

William Beatty, Nelson's surgeon at Trafalgar. (© National Maritime Museum, Greenwich, London, BHC2538)

Thomas Trotter, Physician to the Grand Fleet. (© National Maritime Museum, Greenwich, London, PAD3448)

Benjamin Outram's surgeon's chest used at the battle of Copenhagen, essential kit for any sea surgeon. (© National Maritime Museum, Greenwich, London, TOA0130)

Tools of the naval surgeon's trade. (© National Maritime Museum, Greenwich, London, L5058-002)

A rare depiction of an amputation in the cockpit of a ship of
Nelson's navy (© National Maritime Museum, Greenwich,
London, PAD8484)

Lord Howe and casualties from the Glorious First of July,
1794, on the *Queen Charlotte*. (Mather Brown, © National
Maritime Museum, Greenwich, London, NMM, PY7879)

Admiral Peter Rainier was proud of his spectacles. (Arthur Devis, British Optical Association Museum, LDBOA1999.167)

The poor condition of impressed men spread disease in the Navy. (© National Maritime Museum, Greenwich, London, PU4732)

The ship's cook was usually a disabled seaman. (Thomas Rowlandson, © National Maritime Museum, Greenwich, London, PAF4969)

Marines at mess on board the *Pallas*. (© National Maritime Museum, Greenwich, London, PT1993)

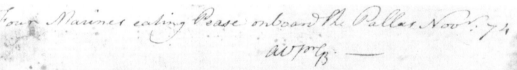

*Four Marines eating Pease onboard the Pallas Nov.r 74*

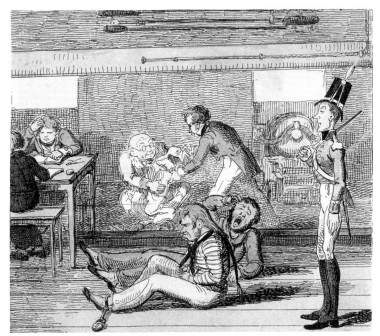

Drunken seamen in irons (© National Maritime Museum, Greenwich, London, PU0157)

Floggings maintained discipline and the surgeon patched up the men . (George Cruikshank, © National Maritime Museum, Greenwich, London, PAD0177)

Recreations on deck kept morale high. (© National Maritime
Museum, Greenwich, London, PAH7339)

The pleasures of Portsmouth Point were drinking and
whoring. (© National Maritime Museum, Greenwich,
London, PX8620)

'Lodgings for single men and their wives' at Portsmouth. (© National Maritime Museum, Greenwich, London, PX8580)

The first permanent British Naval Hospital in the harbour of Port Mahon, Menorca. (© National Maritime Museum, Greenwich, London, PX9694)

Haslar Hospital in 1799. (© National Maritime Museum, Greenwich, London, PAH9738)

A sailor's visit to a quack doctor. (© National Maritime Museum, Greenwich, London, PAG8570)

The Tonbridge Wells spa waters were not to the taste of men used to grog. (© National Maritime Museum, Greenwich, London, PAG8620)

Wounded naval officers enjoyed the Bath races and other pleasures of a spa town. (© National Maritime Museum, Greenwich, London, PX8612)

The Greenwich pensioner had a refuge from his disabilities. (© National Maritime Museum, Greenwich, London, PY3324)

THE GREENWICH PENSIONER

A distressed sailor, wounded and poverty-stricken, discharged from the Navy (© National Maritime Museum, Greenwich, London, PAF3804)

On other ships, sick berths were not so well managed. Thomas Trotter's first sick berth was located in the galley, 'more to stifle contagion with the smoke of the fire than to keep the patient comfortable'.[52] On the *Gloucester*, the sick berth appalled the chaplain Edward Mangin in 1812, when he found it to be 'less than six feet high, narrow noisome and wet; the writhings, sighs and moans of acute pain; the pale countenance, which looks like resignation, but is despair; bandages soaked in blood and matter; the foetor of sores, and the vermin from which it is impossible to preserve the invalid entirely free.' Its location near the heads, rather than being convenient for sick men, merely made it smell all the more and 'whenever it blows fresh, the sea, defiled by a thousand horrible intermixtures, comes more or less into the hospital.' Yet, Mangin realised that being put on the sick list was 'considered an indulgence; as it exempts the sick man from that more dreaded state of toil and servitude to which, when fit for duty, he is necessarily exposed'.[53] Robert Young on the *Ardent* pointed out that 'the surgeon has every necessary article for his practice, but no conveniences for applying them with facility to use.' The storeroom for his lime juice and surgeon's necessaries was usually far too small, and that 'for making up and keeping at hand a regular formula of extemporaneous medicines, for having everything he may want ready of access, his instruments, lint, needles, his lotions, dressings, pills he has no convenience whatever.'[54]

In their work of tending the sick the surgeons and surgeons' mates were assisted by loblolly boys, ratings deemed useless for other duties who had been assigned to help with nursing in the sick berth and were said to be named after the 'loblolly' porridge they served to the bedridden. Some of the women on board ship with their husbands also acted as nurses during the battles. At Camperdown George Magrath relied on 'the women who formed the chief of my assistance.'[55] In the absence of sufficient surgeons' mates, the surgeon needed all the help he could get from whatever source.

The ship's surgeons were conscious of the role their commanders played in promoting health and that they needed such support if they were to carry out their own duties successfully. James Campbell on the *Aetna* in 1808 acknowledged that 'from the very great attention observed by the captain and officers to cleanliness, ventilation, may be attributed the general good health of the *Aetna's* ship's company.'[56] Indeed the attitude of the captain of the ship towards the surgeon and the maintenance of health was vital. On the *Victory* there were only five deaths and two hospital cases between 29 December 1804 and the battle of Trafalgar on 21 October 1805. Of those who died, one man perished of fever, three of consumption and one from a spinal injury. All the men sent to hospital in Gibraltar were consumptive.[57] Beatty believed that Captain Thomas Hardy had been instrumental in maintaining the health of the crew, especially in the avoidance of catarrhal coughs and rheumatic fevers during the winter: 'and this is attributable solely to Captain Hardy's attention to their subordination, temperance, warm clothing, and cleanliness, together with the measures daily adopted to obviate the effects of moisture and to ensure the thorough ventilation of every part of the ship.'[58] Strict discipline was necessary to achieve this. John Snipe, Physician to the Mediterranean Fleet, was a strong exponent of naval hygiene among captains to ensure that the seamen were adequately clothed and fed on 'as nourishing a diet as situation and local circumstances will permit, composed of fresh meat and succulent vegetables', that the ships were well-ventilated, clean and dry, and that sick berths were fit for their purpose, aims only attainable with the co-operation of the naval officers and hinging on 'the improved mode of discipline, which at this moment enables the British fleet to ride triumphant on the seas, and bid defiance to the hostile bands of our combined foes.'[59]

The surgeon played an essential role in providing the observations and statistics upon which a scientific approach to preserving the health of the seaman could be built. Each surgeon was expected to report the state of health of his ship in a standardised logbook, emphasising the accountability of the individual surgeon for his own actions and providing a centralised collection of data by the Sick and Hurt Board which could be used to find the best way to combat disease. This approach had been adopted by other naval surgeons such as Robert Robertson, but Gilbert Blane was to extend it to the entire navy and turn the gathering of naval medical data into an official and centralised procedure.[60] The keeping of such journals helped to foster a professionalism among naval surgeons for: 'from the moment of his entering the service to the date of his leaving it, he is required to submit a daily journal of his practice, giving a minute description of the disorders of the sick, and detailing every variation of symptom and treatment to the superior medical officers'.[61]

Many naval surgeons had an intellectual curiosity and life at sea allowed them to pursue their own interests as explorers and naturalists. Leonard Gillespie, later to be appointed Physician to the Mediterranean Fleet in 1804, used the opportunity offered by his appointment as surgeon and agent to the Naval Hospital at Fort Royal, Martinique in 1796 to study such diverse subjects as the prevalence of infectious diseases in the West Indies, meteorology, geology and statistics. His relationship with Caroline Heiliger, a manumitted, slave of mixed Dutch and African blood, with whom he had two 'quadroon' children, made him sensitive to the issues of slavery and racial prejudice.[62]

There could be time for study and relaxation for the surgeon on quieter voyages. The surgeon James Ker was far from being over-worked on a healthy passage on the *Elizabeth* to the West Indies in 1778. He rose at seven, saw his patients at nine for an hour at most then had time to read in his cabin before taking a walk on deck and reporting to the captain on the health of the ship. Between dinner and supper he amused himself 'variously in reading, writing, card-playing, backgammon, walking or conversation as humour leads' and after supper his time was 'spent in chitchat over our grog drinking.'[63] Leonard Gillespie could enjoy an even more leisurely life in Nelson's entourage on the *Victory* in the early months of 1805. His servant woke him at six o'clock in the morning with a weather report and he would then join Nelson and his colleagues for breakfast before settling down to a day of study, writing and exercise. As Physician and Inspector of the Naval Hospitals in the Mediterranean, Gillespie would only visit the sick berth at the request of the ship's surgeon, George Magrath. Dinner at three o'clock, which 'generally consists of three courses and a dessert of the choicest fruit, together with three or four of the best wines, champagne and claret not excepted; and what exceeds the relish of the best viands and most exquisite wines, if a person does not feel himself perfectly at his ease it must be his own fault, such is the urbanity and hospitality which reign here', was preceded by a band performance, with the meal announced by the tune 'The Roast Beef of Old England'. Following afternoon tea 'Nelson generally unbends himself, though he is at all times as free from stiffness and pomp as a regard to proper dignity will admit, and is very communicative. At eight o'clock a rummer of punch with cake or biscuit is served up, soon after which we wish the Admiral a good night (who is generally in bed before nine o'clock)'. Gillespie, would then read for an hour or socialize with officers in the ward room.[64]

The pay and conditions of naval surgeons before 1805 were inferior to those enjoyed by army surgeons. Regimental surgeons were commissioned officers with the rank of captain, were issued with a uniform and could expect a guaranteed retirement on half-pay, whereby they were on a retainer to be called back to the service if needed. The naval surgeons were classed as warrant officers and did not have a uniform. They had no automatic right to use the wardroom. The surgeon had a cabin off the gunroom alongside the master, purser and chaplain. The assistant surgeons messed with the midshipmen, who were considerably younger than them. Unlike their military counterparts, they had to purchase their own instruments and medicines. The army doctors were paid 10 – 12 shillings a day, while the naval surgeons received a flat rate salary of £5 each month.[65] The naval surgeon could supplement his basic income with extras, such as an annual lump sum varying from £16 to £62 from Queen Anne's Free Gift, 2d a year towards the cost of medicines from each seaman from his annual contribution to the seamen's welfare charity the Chatham Chest, and a share of prize money from captured enemy ships.[66] Prize money was especially valued by any surgeon saving towards his retirement from the service.

During the French Revolutionary and Napoleonic Wars the status of the naval surgeon rose. He was even recognized as being a gentleman. His pay and conditions of service were brought into line with that of army doctors. In 1805 the status of the naval surgeon was raised with the grant of 'similar rank with the officers of the same class in Your Majesty's land forces', although in the naval hierarchy he remained subordinate to the lieutenant of the ship on which he served. A sliding scale of payment was introduced for the surgeon, starting at 10s a day on appointment and extending to 18s a day after twenty years continuous service. After two years of service a surgeon was eligible to be placed on half-pay and would be granted a pension of 15s a day or £373 15s a year after thirty years of service. He no longer had to pay for his own supplies of drugs, but still had to supply his own instruments. The surgeon's mate was promoted to the position of assistant surgeon, but on a fixed daily salary of 6s 6d.[67] There was a new recognition of respectability. In 1813 Jane Austen, whose brothers were naval officers, described a naval surgeon, a minor character in *Mansfield Park*, as 'a very well behaved young man.'[68] Thomas Trotter judged that 'taking the surgeons of the navy list collectively, they may be justly compared to any other body of professional men, some very capable, and others perhaps not. There are many of the number well qualified for the duties of the station, liberally educated and equal to the exercise of the art in any situation.'[69]

This new status was reflected in the introduction of a uniform, consisting of the captain's undress uniform of a coat with blue lapels with a stand-up collar, a white waistcoat and breeches. Buttons bore a plain anchor, while hospital medical officers had 'HS' added to them. The full dress and undress uniforms featured velvet collars and silver-twist embroidery. Physicians were allowed two rows of gold lace on their sleeves. The surgeons themselves had sent a pattern for the uniform with their 1804 petition for them to 'wear a distinguishing uniform'. The physicians and surgeons at Haslar had also asked in 1805 for recognition of 'the claim we have as field officers to wear epaulettes as have been awarded to officers of similar rank in the staff of the army'. A uniform comparable to that of the army doctors was particularly important 'from our being daily liable to meet with army medical officers'.[70] Status was important and a uniform in the army and navy at that time indicated that the wearer was a gentleman in a way that wearing ordinary clothes, even those of a fashionable gentleman could not.

The improvement in the status of the naval surgeon, cemented in 1808 when full surgeons became 'warrant officers of ward room rank', came about as a result of official fear that the Navy had 'suffered materially in the present war from want of surgeons and surgeons' mates', but was equally the result of a campaign by naval surgeons, for an improvement in their conditions and parity with the military medical services. Thomas Trotter had called for reforms in 1790, arguing for more control over examinations of candidates for naval surgeon posts and of drugs by the physicians of the fleet.[71] In 1794, he had again raised the problem with Lord Howe following the battle of the Glorious First of June in which naval surgeons had proved their worth. A petition sent to the Admiralty had resulted in a rise of emoluments to £210 a year, although basic pay remained unchanged and still inferior to that of army surgeons. Surgeons' mates received a pay increase of £1 a month and the number of men eligible for half-pay was increased.[72] The Admiralty was concerned at the shortage of surgeons rather than keen to reward service. A group of surgeons had again petitioned for parity with the army in 1798, but the Admiralty did nothing.[73] Then in 1801, Trotter again petitioned for modest improvements, simplifying the system of emoluments, making all surgeons eligible for half-pay, providing instruments and medicines free and instituting a training programme for potential naval surgeons.[74] In 1802, the wages of all officers were raised, but the surgeons and chaplains got nothing. However, on the renewal of hostilities with France, many surgeons refused to sign up again and it was necessary to take action 'to induce well-qualified and respectable persons to enter the service'.[75] Embittered when army doctors received a considerable pay rise in 1804, another petition was organised by naval surgeons calling for an improvement in their conditions, one which was to be followed by results.

Nelson supported the petition from the surgeons in the Mediterranean fleet with the comment to Henry Dundas, Viscount Melville, First Lord of the Admiralty, that 'as the particular case of so valuable and so respectable a body of men is no doubt well-known to your Lordship, it is not necessary for me to make any comment on the justice of their request.'[76] He was well aware of the importance or retaining the services of such men as his own surgeon, as he explained to Dr Baird, Inspector General of Hospitals in 1804: 'Mr Magrath, whom I admire for his great abilities every day I live, gives me excellent remedies; but we must not lose such men from the service if the army goes on in encouraging medical men, whilst we do nothing. I am sure much ought to be done for our naval surgeons; or how can we expect to keep valuable men? I look to you, not only to propose it, but to enforce it to Lord St Vincent, who must be anxious to preserve such a valuable set of men in the Navy.'[77]

The recognition Nelson gave to the importance of the work of naval surgeons in maintaining the health and efficiency of his fleet was shown in his support of their petitions for improved pay and status. The surgeons themselves appreciated this support and when news of the January 1805 Order in Council introducing the reforms which dealt with their dissatisfaction reached the fleet in the Mediterranean, Leonard Gillespie, as Physician of the Fleet, and the naval surgeons wrote to thank Nelson at 'the earliest opportunity of returning you our most grateful acknowledgements in return for the very prompt and favourable recommendation'. They were in no doubt that Nelson's endorsement of their requests had led to the 'speedy adoption of the present medical establishment' which 'we owe in great measure to your Lordship's efficacious recommendation'. The surgeons believed that these reforms would be answer to the shortage of naval surgeons and that the new arrangement 'holds out so many additional inducements to professional men of experience to serve in His Majesty's Navy.'[78]

At the end of the war and after retirement from the Navy on half-pay like other officers, many of the surgeons who had served in it during wartime settled on shore. In many cases, rather than set up in civilian practices, they referred to live on their half-pay, very comfortably for those men whose long years at sea had given them little opportunity to find a wife and who were ready to settle into a comfortable bachelor existence. A number of men, lacking opportunities at sea, took up positions as surgeon superintendents on convict ships and subsequently on emigrant ships.[79] Others went on to enjoy successful civilian practices. Benjamin Outram was paid off in 1806, studied for a medical degree and then established a successful London practice until his appointment as inspector of fleets and hospitals in 1841. Retirement from naval service for other surgeons meant setting up in provincial general practice away from high society but with a local status. Thomas Trotter, having injured himself and suffered a hernia while climbing the side of the *Irresistible* in order to attend the wounds of the captain during the Quiberon expedition, retired in 1802, got married and set himself up in private practice in Newcastle upon Tyne. There he concerned himself with a variety of medical interests such as inebriation, mental illness and the ventilation of coalmines, and, a member of the Newcastle Literary and Philosophical Society, also wrote plays and poetry.[80]

Wartime service offered other naval surgeons the opportunity to advance themselves professionally and acquire the status of a gentleman.[81] James Clark was the son of the butler to the Earl of Findlater. He had enrolled at King's College, Aberdeen, but had left without gaining a degree, becoming articled to a Banff lawyer before going to Edinburgh to study medicine, where he qualified as a member of the Royal College of Surgeons of Edinburgh in 1809. He had then joined the Royal Navy and, after a year at Haslar Hospital, was appointed as assistant surgeon on the schooner *Thistle*. He was promoted to full surgeon in 1811 and survived the wreck of the *Thistle* off the coast of New Jersey only for his next ship *La Colobri* also to be wrecked at Jamaica in 1813. At the end of the French Wars, Clarke, now aged twenty-seven, was put on half-pay and entered the University of Edinburgh, where he graduated MD in 1817. The following year, after accompanying a patient to France, Switzerland and Italy, Clark visited the Necker Hospital in Paris and was one of the first to adopt Laennec's newly-devised stethoscope.[82] This did not help him in identifying that his next patient the poet John Keats was suffering from tuberculosis when he devotedly attended him during his last few months in Rome. Returning in 1826 to London from Rome, where he had built up a practice among many wealthy English residents, he acted as physician to Prince Leopold, accompanying him on his summer season visits to the German spas, before being appointed as physician to Leopold's sister the Duchess of Kent in 1835. Such an appointment was not welcomed by the Royal College of Physicians, 'the Fellows of which looked on the appointment of a northern graduate very much as the bench of bishops might resent the intrusion of a Dissenter'.[83] Clark insisted that Princess Victoria's window at Kensington Palace should always be kept open when she was out of the room to ventilate the room. In 1837 he was appointed physician-in-ordinary to Queen Victoria and given a baronetcy, dubbing himself the 'wee cock lairdie' of Tillypronie.[84] Prince Albert was to value his advice on medical science and education, although Clark has been criticised for failing to diagnose the typhoid that killed the Prince Consort in 1861.[85]

Naval surgeons varied in ability and in character, but how they were viewed in the wider world perhaps was as nothing when compared with the attitude towards them of the men they treated.

Marine Thomas Wybourn considered that his life at Naples on *Madras* was saved thanks to 'the skill and attention of the mate, a very attractive young man'. The surgeon, however, was 'such a brute that had I not more fortitude than many', rather than saving him he 'would have hastened my end'.[86] William Dillon dismissed the surgeon James Malcolm on the *Defence* in 1794 because 'with all his humane intentions, he unfortunately could not perform the operation of amputating a limb'. Nevertheless, James was otherwise 'a most amiable man' who had been 'the cause of introducing flannel for the use of the seamen in the navy to protect them against the effects of rheumatism'. The assistant surgeon William Yowell had taken on Malcolm's duties and 'he turned out to be a most zealous and able practitioner, or the result might have been very fatal to many' and was so assiduous that he would often go on to the quarter deck at 2 o'clock in the morning for some fresh air before commenting 'I have only two hours to rest myself. After that I must recommence my visits.'[87] It was such men whose conduct raised the status and reputation of the naval surgeon.

# 5
# Poxed!

Nelson memorably declared that 'every man became a bachelor after passing the rock of the Gibraltar'.[1] His own affairs with Adelaide Corręglia at Leghorn and Emma Hamilton in Naples were both conducted in the Mediterranean safe from the attention of his wife though inevitably known to his stepson. Nelson came to view Emma Hamilton as his wife back in England after the death of her husband and his estrangement from his actual wife. Away from home, single and married men found temptations and opportunities difficult to resist. Many seamen suffering from syphilis or gonorrhoea must have regretted, nonetheless, that they had not abstained from sexual relations in port, but equally must have rued that they had not instead remained true to their wives and sweethearts or chaste.

It was not unknown for men to smuggle prostitutes on board ship as well as consorting with them ashore on the rare occasions seamen could leave the ship. The arrival of a ship in port would be greeted by 'swarms of boats' containing young women. For William Robinson these 'bomb-boats' were 'really nothing but floating chandler's shops; and a great many of them were freighted with cargoes of ladies, a sight that was truly gratifying and a great treat; for our crew, consisting of six hundred and upwards, had seen but one woman on board for eighteen months'.[2] It did not take long for the seamen to make their choice of women and bring them on board the ship. These women had been carefully selected by the boatman bringing them to the ship in expectation of a payment of three shillings a girl from his customers on the ship, who had been known to turn away boats containing too many unattractive women: an 'old Charon, with pointer in hand, before they step or board, surveys them from stem to stem, with the eye of a bargaining Jew, and carefully culls out the best looking, and the most dashing dressed'. It was little wonder that Robinson considered it 'a scene somewhat similar to the trafficking for slaves in the West Indies'.

As few men had the benefits of going ashore when in port, the presence of prostitutes on the ship was considered to be necessary to the health and welfare of the seaman for fear that sexual frustration might lead to unrest or 'unclean' acts of homosexuality or buggery. The naval chaplain Edward Mangin admitted that 'this arrangement is asserted to be a necessary evil, and better than allowing the seamen to go and visit their friends and acquaintances ashore; and with reference to the interests of the naval service, this licence may be necessary', but it was an embarrassment for a clergyman which he might accept but could not condone.[3] René-Martin Pillet, a French prisoner of war, observed that 'to deprive the sailor of a wish to visit the land and to prevent the spirit of revolt', it was the British naval custom that 'the vessel is opened to all the girls of a dissolute life, who offer themselves'.[4]

Once on board, the women were taken below to take part in 'the shocking, disgraceful transactions of the lower deck ... where hundreds of men and women are huddled together in one room, as it were in bed ... they are squeezed between the next hammocks and must be witnesses of each other's actions'. The whole scene was described by one prudish witness as 'impossible to describe' except for 'the dirt, the filth and stench; the disgusting conversation; the indecent, beastly conduct and horrible scenes; the blasphemy and swearing; the riots, quarrels and fighting'.[5] These prostitutes were in many cases 'the most pitiable' who from ill-usage had become 'callous, indifferent as to delicacy of speech and behaviour, and so totally lost to all sense of shame, that they seem to retain no quality which properly belongs to woman but the shape and name'.[6] William Robinson, distant from such scenes when describing them in 1836, could only say that his 'constant prayer to heaven is that my daughters may never set foot on a man-of-war'.[7]

Some captains, reluctant to be seen to be condoning vice, would insist that only relatives of the men be allowed on board, so that 'sometimes, for form's sake, a hypocritical captain requires the female visitors to take the title of sister, niece, cousin relation of the sailor they designate, according to the list they send ashore; it is to them a real lottery of age, form and money'.[8] On the *Temeraire* at Plymouth in 1801 Daniel Goodall believed that 'if all had been admitted who set up the claim of connubial right, it would have been a clear case of polygamy for there could not have been less than a proportion of three or four to every man of marriageable age and position on board. As it was no less than three days sufficed to see more than two hundred of the Delilahs of Plymouth settled amongst the crew, not ten per cent of whom could have made out a feasible claim to marital connection with any of the men.'[9]

Prostitutes were even allowed to stay on board ships sailing between ports in home waters, an indulgence also extended to wives. This was not popular with the 'really virtuous females, wives of seamen on board, whose modesty and worth was unsullied amid all the vice and pollution by which they were surrounded'.[10] Edward Hawker stressed that the actual wives and children of the men were 'forced to submit to the alternative of mixing with these abandoned women, whose language and behaviour are usually of the most polluting description, or of foregoing altogether the society of their husbands and parents'.[11]

The prostitutes flocking to the ships were of all ages and had mostly turned to prostitution from necessity. The marine George Watson believed that most of the prostitutes of Portsmouth had been 'previously seduced, and cast upon the world, abandoned by the villains that had caused their ruin'. He found it 'absurd to suppose any truly modest girl, though brought to the greatest extremity of penury and want, would deliberately come hither to join herself to such an unblushing set of wretches as pervade the Point at Portsmouth, where a modest woman would be as hard to find as a mermaid.' He was equally scathing about the prostitutes to be found in other European ports, where 'they are all religious harlots these, in their way, they go on shore uniformly every morning to confess their sins, and get absolution of the priest!'[12] In the West Indies the prostitutes were often slaves 'who brought us fruit and remained on board all Sunday until Monday morning – poor things! And all to obtain a bellyful of victuals', according to mariner John Nicol.

A better class of prostitute preyed on the officers. In 1788 'Miss Devonshire' of Queen Anne Street, Covent Garden, was described in naval terminology calculated to appeal to a naval officer:

This lady is a native of Devonshire, and has only been one of us four months; she is of a fine fair complexion, love tinctured cerulean eyes, fine teeth, and genteel good figure; a charming partner in a dance, a very good companion by the fire side, and dearly loves an agreeable friend and a cheerful glass; many a man of war hath been her willing prisoner, and paid a proper ransom; her port is said to be well guarded by a light brown *chevaux-de-freize*, and parted from Bombay by a very small pleasant isthmus. The entry is rather straight; but when once in, there is very good riding; and when they have paid port customs, they are suffered to slip out very easily, though generally followed by a salute from Crown-point, which hastens their departure by causing the floodgates to open commodiously. She is so brave, that she is ever ready for an engagement; cares not how soon she comes to close quarters, and loves to fight yard arm and yard arm, and be briskly boarded; she is best pleased when her opponent is well armed, and would despise any warrior, who had not two stout balls to block up her covered way, and did not carry metal enough to leave two pounds behind him.[13]

As well as advertising their particular charms, such women would make contact with their wealthier clients in discreet boxes in theatres, opera houses and pleasure gardens. Dashing young officers sought them out in the capital on leave and whenever in port. Prince William Henry complained about Yarmouth that 'I was on shore there but once and had no opportunity of getting hold of a girl. My next excursion was in Yorkshire, where I was going on horseback from Burlington Bay to Hull and intended to lay two in a bed that night'.[14]

Yet, despite the variety of woman who had taken to prostitution, 'these harpies who had preyed upon poor Jack'[15] were all too easily caricatured. The surgeon George Pinckard painted a colourful picture of the 'Portsmouth Polls' and 'Spithead Nymphs:

Imagine something of more than Amazonian stature, having a crimson countenance, emblazoned with all the effrontery of Cyprian confidence, and broad Bacchanalian folly: give to her bold counten-ance the warlike features of two wounded cheeks, a tumid nose, scarred and battered brows, and a pair of blackened eyes, with balls of red; then add to her sides a pair of brawny arms, fit to encounter a Colossus, and set her upon two ankles like the fixed supports of a gate. Afterwards, by way of apparel, put upon her a loose flying cap, a man's black hat, a torn neckerchief, stone rings upon her fingers, and a dirty white, or tawdry flowered gown, with short apron and a pink petticoat; and thus, will you have something very like the figure of a Portsmouth Poll.[16]

It is not a very alluring portrait, but grounded in the reality of the coarseness of the trade these women plied.

The prostitutes 'made a noise more than proportionate to their number, and', as Daniel Goodall noted disapprovingly, 'I am bound to add, they displayed such a reckless disregard of every claim of decency and morality as Jack, even at his worst, could ever hope or would ever attempt to equal'. They behaved in ways that Goodall found un-womanly: 'Smoking was quite a prevalent fashion amongst the dear creatures, and as for swearing, they seemed to take quite a peculiar delight in uttering "the oldest oaths the newest kind of ways", and those ways the most revolting it is possible for even the vilest to imagine. The coarsest seamen on board far outdone by those damsels'.[17] They also smuggled alcohol on board and brought with them disease.

On some ships it was the practice of the surgeon to examine the women boarding the ship for signs of an infection with a venereal disease. Any woman found to be infected would be 'sent out of the ship'. However, moralists who wanted to ban immoral women from naval vessels entirely rather than to see sensible measures taken to prevent the spread of venereal disease, found it praiseworthy, 'to the honour of the assistant surgeons in the navy, that some have resisted this order of their captains'.[18]

Even naval surgeons who knew the dangers of catching a venereal disease were not risk averse when fiddlers and whores proved seductive. Surgeon James Lowry, like other young men in Nelson's fleet, delighted in the female company he encountered in Naples and Sicily during his seven years' service between 1798 and 1805. Despite noting that many noble women suffered from syphilis and gonorrhoea as a result of their practice of taking lovers, including the Princess of Butero who reputedly died of syphilis in 1802, he was not discouraged from making his own romantic conquests where ever he could and was no stranger to the bordellos of southern Italy.[19] He found that 'masquerading is a very convenient and suitable way for intrigue with the ladies or in other words criminal connection'.[20] He had been made aware of the problem of sexually-transmissible diseases on his first posting to the hulk *Bedford,* where 'we had on board 400 prostitutes and of course out of such a number many were diseased.'[21] Nor was he unfamiliar with the brothels of Portsmouth visited by naval officers after long voyages before returning home to their wives and despite 'knowing if he would have connection with his wife would communicate the contagion'.[22] Yet, despite his fascination with the subject, he never admitted to having contracted a disease himself.

It was not only women who spread sexually transmissible infections to their partners, although it was women who were usually blamed and vilified. Men could pass the infection on to partners of either sex. Homosexuality was a criminal offence at sea and men found practicing it were court-martialled. They could be reported by their own shipmates who were often shocked when 'something was carried on that was not right'. In 1796, John Morris was sentenced to death after Seaman Thomas Hall reported that he had observed 'two men under the cable, one lying down on his belly and his trousers down. I saw another man towards his feet and came close to them. I could plainly perceive that one of them had his privates out and his two hands hold of Savage's jacket'. William Savage was obviously seen as the victim of Morris and was acquitted of having committed homosexual acts.[23] In 1800 on *St George*, a marine informed the master-at-arms of a homosexual encounter he had witnessed. When the master-at-arms grabbed hold of one of the men, Thomas Hubbard by the neck, he 'found that George Hynes was under him naked on his belly'. Hynes tried to 'slue himself on one side in his hammock' only to reveal 'Thomas Hubbard's yard come from between the backside of George Hynes.' Holding him fast by the collar, the master-at-arms yanked Hubbard from his coupling and 'made him button his trousers up.'[24]

Darkness may have given men the opportunity to commit 'unnatural acts' but in at least one court martial, the accused were acquitted because of it being too dark for the witnesses to have seen what they were doing. The Maltese seaman Francisco Falso and John Lambert were accused of sodomy after being found 'laying down and both their trousers down' in the galley of the *Prince Frederick* late at night in August 1798. Thomas King, a waister, had 'heard a bustling on the bench, but did not know what it was, being so dark. I walked up to it, and touched a man's naked flesh with my hand'. Another sailor Thomas Ellis was dozing in the galley at the time and could see nothing untoward especially as 'I had no suspicion of anything of the kind'.[25]

Such sexual encounters were necessarily conducted in close proximity to other seamen. Officers and warrant officers, though, had much more privacy. It was among such grades of men that most reported attacks on young ships' boys took place. The first lieutenant on *Hazard*, twenty-two year-old William Berry, 'remarkably well made and as fine and handsome a man as is in the British navy', was charged in October 1807 with an 'uncleanness' and a 'horrid and abominable offence' against Thomas Gibbs, 'a boy belonging to the ship'.[26] Gibbs had complained of being abused by Berry for some time, but the only witness was 'Elizabeth, alias John Bowden', a girl who had disguised herself as a boy in order to join the ship. Elizabeth Bowden had 'looked through the keyhole and I saw Thomas Gibbs playing with the prisoner's privates'.[27] Berry, who had been engaged to be married on his return to port, was hanged for the offence of sodomy, having 'seemed very penitent and perfectly resigned' in his last days and dying as 'a young gentleman, in the bloom of life, for a crime not fit to be named among Christians.'[28] His victim Gibbs, although probably over sixteen, was taken to be no more than fourteen years of age and accordingly was considered blameless. Had he been older, he would have shared his abuser's fate despite having been forced against his will.

It was essential for the discipline of the ship that any 'unnatural acts' should be swiftly punished, but the seamen did not like the shame that could be brought on their ships by a public execution for the offence. In 1798, two men were court martialled and 'executed for sodomy' on the *St George*, but the seamen mutinied because 'an execution for such a horrible offence would bring shame on the ship'. Admiral Lord St Vincent responded by bringing forward the original execution to a Sunday morning immediately before prayers and also executing the leaders of the mutiny, of whom 'the whole seven have been proved to be the most atrocious villains'.[29] Part of his squadron was engaged in skirmishes with Spanish gunboats at the time so that 'the inside division of line of battleships was engaged by the gunboats, the other division had their pennant up at the mizzen peak for prayers, and the other division had the yellow flag hoisted, a-hanging of two men, all at one time on a Sunday morning.'[30]

Nelson was shocked in 1796 when he learned that Charles Sawyer, captain of the frigate *Blanche*, had preyed upon two young midshipmen whom he summoned to his cabin; he felt both sympathy and revulsion such that 'indignation and sorrow are so mixed in my mind that I know not which predominates!' He had loaned books to Sawyer and had great respect for his abilities. Yet, he could not ignore the charges brought against Sawyer. A seventeen year-old midshipman accused the thirty year-old captain of having 'hauled me down in his cot and put my hand on his privates' and 'when I got up he made me promise that I would not tell anyone of it'. Sawyer had also tried to make the boy share a hotel room with him at Leghorn. A black seaman had testified that 'the captain had frigged him and he had frigged the captain' while the coxswain described Sawyer as 'a man-fucking bugger'. Sawyer had attempted to defend himself by threatening his accusers that unless 'matters could be accommodated' he would destroy their careers. Found guilty of using his position to commit homosexual acts, he was dismissed from the service.[31]

Deprived of female company, some of the men had little relief other than 'to box the Jesuit and get cockroaches', an expression used at sea for masturbation, 'a crime, it is said, much practised by the reverend fathers of that society'.[32] Other outlets for sexual frustration were less innocent. John Sherwood was sentenced to a hundred lashes when found copulating with a sheep on *Milford* in 1800. Isaac Wilson on the sloop *Orestes*, however, was luckier when found 'lying down all his length in the goathouse and with his trousers unbuttoned and his shirt out before and behind' after the goat had made 'such a noise, I thought she was dying' and the court accepted his excuse of having fallen asleep in the goat house when drunk and that the goat had trampled on him rather than he having assaulted it.[33] When William Bouch was found lying with a pig on *Hotspur* in June 1812, the surgeon was immediately summoned to examine him on the spot of the act of bestiality and reported that 'I could not see if he was entered into the pig as he was laying upon her belly, but I conceive from the way he drew back, the pig's grunting at the time and his remaining perfectly quiet, that he was in the pig'. The unfortunate animal was thrown overboard into the Bay of Biscay while Bouch was sentenced to 300 lashes, loss of pay and a year in solitary confinement in the Marshalsea Prison.[34] Bestiality may have had other health dangers but it was sex between humans that was responsible for spreading syphilis and gonorrhoea among the men that posed a serious problem for their health and naval efficiency.

Nelson, despite his reputation as the greater lover of Lady Hamilton and his other affairs of the heart, seems to have escaped contracting the pox (syphilis) or the 'itch', although he suspected on one occasion that he may have caught something. Still in his early twenties, Nelson had complained of a 'fleshy excrescence' on his gums that was painful when he shaved. He had consulted a naval surgeon at Haslar Hospital 'who assured him the case was venereal, and had prepared him to go through a mercurial course'. Before starting this treatment, Nelson had met the Chevalier Bartholomew Ruspini, a dentist touting a tincture he had concocted, who removed the benign papilloma from his gum with a scalpel, 'and the cure was completed in a few days without any application other than the tincture'. Ruspini saw Captain Nelson again two years later 'when his perfect state of health confirmed my prognosis and convinced the hospital surgeon of his mistake.'[35]

Nelson may not have had a venereal infection, though at first he thought he had, but these were rampant throughout the navy in his time. The clap, dose or strain, as gonorrhoea was commonly called, was diagnosed by a milky discharge from the penis but could be asymptomatic. It was generally treated at sea in the eighteenth century with bleeding, purging, fomentations and astringent injections.[36] It was associated with the much more serious sexually transmitted infection of syphilis, otherwise known as the great pox, which had first struck Europe virulently in the sixteenth century following the exploration of the Americas. Primary syphilis, when the disease is at its most infectious, is characterised by chancres (ulcers) on the genitals and by buboes (swelling of the lymph glands). If left untreated, the secondary stage of the illness develops and is marked by extensive rashes, fever, general exhaustion and aching bones. This may be accompanied by alopecia resulting in a moth-eaten appearance to the scalp. There may then be a latent period before tertiary syphilis develops in a third of untreated cases.

In the eighteenth century, it was thought by a number of surgeons and physicians that the two diseases were actually the same infection and that gonorrhoea was merely the first stage of syphilis. The London surgeon John Hunter had tried to demonstrate this by infecting himself with a discharge from a patient that he thought was suffering from gonorrhoea. He then observed that he himself had developed syphilis. Unfortunately, the man from whom he had obtained the discharge for his self-experimentation had probably been suffering from both separate infections. It was not until the specific bacteria causing the two diseases were identified in the late-nineteenth and early twentieth centuries that it was proved that different bacteria caused the infections, the gonococcus in the case of gonorrhoea and the spirochaete in that of syphilis.[37]

Many men adopted a 'devil may care' insouciance towards syphilis and gonorrhoea. At Spithead in May 1778 the captain of marines on the *Russell* 'has a girl on board, the same that communicated this disease, and, although he is well aware that she is injured, he still continues to sleep with her, notwithstanding I have put him in remembrance of what mischief she may do him.'[38] A very similar case had been reported by the surgeon Lionel Gillespie on the *Racehorse* where there were 'four prostitutes who have affected three or four persons, two with gonorrhoea and the rest with chancres – yet these women are seemingly well in health, are in good spirits and having been turned over from their first paramours are entertained by others who seem to remain unaffected by any syphilitic complaints.'[39] Even a man dying of syphilis was willing to risk being infected again. William Thompson on *Unité* in 1808 was confident: 'I'll get well soon, time enough at any rate by the time we go again to Malta and then I'll have another rattle'.[40] Prince William, Duke of Clarence, later as William IV known as the Sailor King, had as a bluff young naval officer indeed sighed in vain for the type of girl who 'would not clap or pox me every time I fucked'.[41]

The commonest and most effective treatment involved the use of mercury. It was a commonplace that a night with Venus would be followed by a lifetime of Mercury. This could be applied as an ointment rubbed into the joints pills, liquors or as a fumigation. The drawbacks of treatment with mercury were such unpleasant side effects as profuse sweating, corrosion of the membranes of the mouth, gum ulcerations, loosening of the teeth and erosion of the bones. In many ways the treatment and its side effects were not only as unpleasant as the disease itself, but were also very similar. It was little wonder that man seamen preferred not to report sick, which would have meant losing pay and the stigmata to 'have the word "venereal" appear against their names at the pay table' as well as facing a painful treatment. Instead they 'concealed their complaints or quacked themselves until their constitutions were often ruined'. The result was that their primary symptoms disappeared without treatment despite 'all the disadvantages of a sailor's duty and irregularity of living'. However, the infection was latent within the body and 'at subsequent periods, of various duration, secondary symptoms broke out with terrible violence, and our naval hospitals were filled with the horrible victims of syphilis treated without mercury.' When, naval surgeons were able to administer mercury at an early enough stage, 'secondary symptoms almost disappeared from our fleets and hospitals'.[42]

Seamen would present themselves to the surgeon with a variety of syphilitic symptoms. Jason Darling, a twenty-three year-old able seaman on *Albion* had developed chancres of the glans and prepuce and a swelling in the groins some ten days after 'seeing a girl' which left him with difficulty in walking. He was treated with a mercurial ointment, lunar caustic.[43] Marine Thomas Cocksley on *Seahorse* had been ill for eleven months with a venereal ulcer of the groin and fistula in his anus before he was seen by a new ship's surgeon Thomas Eshelby, who believed that he had been overdosed with mercury and had little choice but to send him to Haslar for treatment.[44] D. Parry, surgeon on *Adventure* made it his policy to always treat syphilitic chancre and buboes with mercury, but advocated bed rest and a cooling regime of milk and barley water in which wine, spices, onions and meat were excluded from the diet for feat that they would inflame the body.[45] The men were also warned against 'amorous dalliance with women, obscene books and whatever else inflames the fancy'.[46]

Nevertheless, many men preferred to use quack treatments available from mountebank medical practitioners on shore rather than appeal to their surgeon. These patent cures were easier to take but totally ineffective. Many of the advertisements for them preyed on fears by listing the symptoms, such as 'the gonorrhoea or running of the reins, shankers, buboes or swellings in the groin, pains in the head, arms, shoulders and legs, or ulcers in the mouth, throat, scabs, itch, and breaking out over the whole body', so that it was possible to make the reader convinced that he suffered from the disease.[47] What was offered was a painless alternative to the conventional use of mercury and extravagant promises of 'an Herculeanean antidote against the pox'[48] or an undertaking that 'all injuries sustained by mercury where the parts are not perished' are 'faithfully repaired with the blessing of God'.[49] The patient did not have to be confined to bed and there were no side effects, such as excessive salivation, swollen gums, loose teeth and a foetid smell. These patent cures, often based on guiacum, sassafras and sarsparilla, such as Isaac Swainson's Velno's vegetable syrup, Keyser's pills and Kennedy's Lisbon diet drink were easily obtained over shop counters and could be shared with shipmates once obtained. Wessel's Jesuit Drops were advertised with the guarantee that 'in His Majesty's navy, these drops have for near 100 years past maintained their character as a specific for the scurvy, gravel, dropsy, stranguary, weakness and obstruction, in the urinary passage, and general debility, but particularly for their absolute and speedy cure on the first attack of the venereal disease'.[50] Such a general remedy was of little value for any of the conditions it claimed to treat, and certainly a seaman with a venereal disease would have been best advised to seek out the help of the surgeon. Sometimes they had to do so when their self-treatments went wrong. Ship's cook Jason Hull, and seaman Jonathan Squire on *Albion* had attempted to cure themselves of venereal disease by injecting substances urethrally and had to present themselves to the surgeon with swollen testicles.[51]

Until 1795 men reporting to the ship's surgeon for treatment were fined 15s for their cure, usually with mercury. The fine had originally been 15s for a marine and 30s for a seaman, but this invidious distinction was reduced to 15s per man for all on board the ship. The surgeon was allowed to keep this fine as a perquisite of his job. As a result many men resorted to quack cures, shared questionable medicines with their messmates and only reported sick to the surgeon when 'the most excruciating and dangerous symptoms had super-vened.'[52] The surgeon Robert Robertson on *Rainbow* in 1773 believed that 'seamen on board of His Majesty's ships are so desirous to save their fifteen shillings, that by taking medicines of each other's prescriptions, and putting off time, three out of every four who complained on board the *Rainbow* had *lues venera*.'[53] The fine was unpopular with the men who, even if they reported the disease in its early stages, did not always pay the surgeon, merely offering a note of hand for payment when a ship was paid off and the men received their pay which was never honoured. The surgeons asked that the fines be stopped from the men's pay just as the purser stopped money for slops and tobacco.[54] Thomas Trotter's recommendation that this fee should be abolished was implemented in 1795 and 'thus terminated a perquisite illiberal from its institution, inhuman in its practice and impolitic from its continuance. It forms an epoch in naval improve-ments, for hundreds of seamen have annually fallen victims to its effects.'[55]

# 6

# Morale and Mania

For Nelson, the health and morale of his men were closely interlinked. It was not only in regard to his attention to provisioning, clothing and health care that he demonstrated his concern, but also in ensuring that their morale and spirits remained high, he showed the importance he placed on mental as well as physical health. Life at sea could be monotonous drudgery and it was important to introduce as much variety as possible to stop seamen becoming bored; with boredom could come a mutinous mood. The link between psychological well-being and physical health was appreciated and it was recognized 'on account of the known effect of melancholy and a discontented temper, in producing scurvy and other maladies, that every means should be employed and encouraged to promote gaiety and good humour.'[1] Thomas Fremantle, on *Neptune* during the blockade of Cadiz in 1805, complained that 'the very sad sameness makes all days like one day, and as the song says, only for prayer day we never know Sunday, the fact is a sea life under present circumstances, is really a life of misery and ennui'.[2] Nelson realised the importance of keeping his men continuously busy and entertained. In 1804 rather than maintaining a long blockade of Toulouse he changed 'the cruising ground' in the Western Mediterranean so that he would avoid 'the sameness of prospect to satiate the mind'. Sometimes the fleet cruised around Toulon, Villefranche, Barcelona and Rosas, and then would run around Menorca, Majorca, Sardinia and Corsica, 'and two or three times anchoring for a few days, and sending a ship to the last place for onions, which I find the best thing that can be given to seamen'. He believed that 'our men's minds are always kept up with the daily hopes of meeting the enemy'.[3]

Nelson made positive attempts to keep the men entertained and amused, and 'the promoting cheerfulness amongst the men was encouraged by music, dancing and theatrical amusements; the example of which was given by the Commander-in-Chief in the *Victory*, and may with reason be reckoned among the causes of the preservation of the health of the men'.[4] He was not alone in doing this as it was acknowledged to be 'a certain mode, under proper regulation of keeping Jack out of mischief, and in health and spirits'. On the *Temeraire* in 1802, 'our captain would pipe all hands to amusement'. The officers were encouraged to join in 'the general amusements' and 'regular sets for dancing were formed with as much decorum, but with far more freedom, than in the stateliest ballroom'. Those men who 'preferred a rollicking jig or hornpipe in presence of a more select circle, could find plenty of fiddlers among their shipmates only too glad of the opportunity to display their skill in extracting sound from catgut'.[5] Similarly on *Culloden* in 1804, Rear-Admiral Sir Edward Pellew and Captain Christopher Cole 'both well knew the advantages of cheerfulness in a ship's crew, and embraced all opportunities of bringing it into play', so that 'in the evening the instrument of Black Bob, the fiddler, was in almost constant requisition giving spirit to the evolutions of those who were disposed to trip it a little on the light fantastic toe'. At the same time 'invigorating and enlivening games were going on in all quarters, and if there happened to be more dancers than could get conveniently within the sound of Bob's fiddle, the Admiral's band was ordered up.'[6]

Not only admirals but the wealthier captains would also have their own bands. The captain on *Macedonian* 'procured a fine band, composed of Frenchmen, Italians and Germans, taken by the Portuguese from a French vessel' and these musicians 'consented to serve on condition of being excused from fighting and on a pledge of exemption from being flogged'.[7] The pressed American seaman James Durand also 'joined the musicians thinking it easier to play an instrument in the ship's band than to do ship's duty' and accordingly 'for three weeks while we chased French privateers, my chief work was blowing on a flute'.[8] Such bands would entertain the captain during his mealtimes and would play on deck when the ship entered or left port. Nelson would be entertained by his band on *Victory* before dinner, always being played in to the strains of 'The Roast Beef of England'.[9] They would also play for dances on board ship to which the local gentry were invited when in port, though not all the guests found such balls enjoyable, the ladies invited to such an event on *Imortalité* in 1802 complaining to a midshipman that 'the lieutenants – alas! for poor human nature! – were both tipsy, and so redolent of onions were your own messmates, that they were quite unapproachable.'[10] Samuel Leech on *Macedonian* found the bands an asset to ship life and considered that 'on the whole, their presence was an advantage to the crew, since their spirit-stirring strains served to spread an occasional cheerful influence over them'.[11]

In the absence of a band, the men would make their own music with a fiddle or a flute and would sing and dance jigs and reels. The hornpipe became known as the seamen's dance. Although not allowed to sing sea shanties while working in case they failed to hear orders, the men had their hard labour at the capstans hauling in the anchor cables enlivened by tunes played on the fiddle or flute. Many of the songs popular with the men were bawdy, with 'the poet you might see employed composing sea-songs or odes on naval exploits; sometimes also smutty or amorous rhymes to gratify the youthful midshipman and other lusty members of his auditory'.[12] A man with a good singing voice was popular with his shipmates who enjoyed impromptu concerts. A good singer on *Macedonian* was missed by his fellows when he deserted as he was 'quite popular among them for his lively disposition and his talents as a comic singer, which last gift is highly prized in a man of war'. Finding that he had merely escaped to a merchant ship delivering gunpowder to his former ship, he gave himself up and was pardoned to the joy of his friends who insisted that 'seated on a gun, surrounded by scores of men, he sung a variety of favourite songs amid the plaudits and encores of his rough auditors'. It was 'by such means that 'sailors contrive to keep up their spirits amidst constant causes of depression and misery', so much so that 'but for these interludes, life in a man of war, with severe officers would be absolutely intolerable; mutiny or desertion would mark the voyages of every such ship'.[13]

Despite the men having spent the day doing hard physical work, it was thought healthy for them to spend their evenings exercising themselves through dancing. Sampson Hardy, surgeon on *Maidstone*, observed that 'there also appeared a disposition in the people to intermittent fevers, the effects of which I could easily remark were in a great measure obviated by the salutary exercise of dancing which was encouraged in the ship's company every evening, Captain Mowbray kindly allotting the space under the half deck on the starboard side for that purpose'.[14]

As well as music, the sailors would also be entertained by the occasional theatrical performances put on for them by their officers. On the *Temeraire*, 'independent of the numerous sea games wherewith we diversified our dancing, the midshipmen got up very enlivening, if not critically correct, dramatic entertainments, which their audiences, more inclined to be pleased than critical, always took in the best spirit possible, and thus afforded encouragement to the perseverance on the part of the young gentlemen'.[15] The midshipmen enjoyed the diversion that amateur dramatics offered to them and on the *Amelia* anchored off Coruna, 'our middies, by way of contributing their quota to the general amusement, got up a dramatic representation, to which everybody of importance in the place was invited, for they judged rightly that nautical amateurs would be regarded as quite a novelty, if not a treat'. There were some wives of seamen on board who 'lent their aid in getting up the young gentlemen in their parts and in supplying some needful articles from their wardrobes'. The acting ability was not high and one of the cast, the schoolmaster, 'endeavoured to brace himself with a tumbler or two of grog' which gave him the courage to deliver the prologue 'with an emphasis, accent and gesticulation most wonderful and amusing' until he fell over and 'one of the middies rushed out half-dressed, and, seizing the schoolmaster by the collar of the coat, dragged him off, still seated, and roaring lustily at the unlucky prologue, amid shrieks of laughter'. Members of the audience were sure that 'the best of the joke was that our foreign visitors, though they joined in the general mirth, seemed to take it for granted that it was all in due course.'[16]

Despite the amateurishness of such performances, they were seen as important means of impressing dignitaries in foreign ports, and some of them could be quite professional. Vice-Admiral Cuthbert Collingwood was proud that 'we have an exceedingly good company of comedians, some dancers that might exhibit at an opera, and probably have done so at Sadlers Wells, and a band consisting of twelve very fine performers. Every Thursday is a play night and they act as well as your Newcastle company'. Collingwood invited a Moorish envoy from the Governor of Tetuan to one of these performances and 'the astonishment which this man expressed at the assembly of people, and their order, was itself a comedy.' In particular, 'his admiration of the ladies was quite ridiculous; and he is gone to his prince fully convinced that we carry players to sea for the entertainment of the sailors; for though he could not find the ladies after the entertainment, he is not convinced that they are not put up in some snug place till the next play night.'[17]

Other amusements, such as buffet the bear, leap-frog and wrestling kept the men happy during the time that 'in fine weather, when the retreat from quarters was beaten, the band was ordered up for those who preferred the amusement of dancing'. On the *Phaeton*, 'everyone was at liberty to amuse himself as he thought fit, the quarter deck being alone kept sacred' and 'this temporary relaxation of the bonds of discipline was as much enjoyed by the captain and officers as by the crew themselves'.[18] Other men took the opportunity of having time for leisure to make or repair their clothes and shoes and 'those who are not employed sewing or mending, you'll see them either learning to read or write, or cyphering, or instructing others'. For others it was the opportunity for 'relating awful stories of what happened in awful times, while their hearers are listening with respectful silence'.[19] Some listeners found these tales to be 'of things most rare and wonderful; for your genuine old tar is an adept in spinning yarns, and some of them, in respect to variety and length might safely aspire to a place beside the great magician of the North, Sir Walter Scott'.[20] Others were bored when 'the same anecdotes or stories were repeated over and over again, with little or no variation, and the listeners were like children, who, when once you have told them a story, do not like the smallest deviation, either in word or deed, from the original text' and sighed that 'if I have heard the story of a distinguished admiral and the midshipman's pig once, I have heard it a thousand times'.[21]

Animals on the ship also provided a diversion and a focus for affection, Captain Thomas Pasley was perhaps unusual in his fondness for the livestock onboard, mourning the death of 'my favourite pet sheep, who has been my companion to and from the Cape of Good Hope'.[22] Thomas Fremantle was more usual among officers in his choice of pet, admitting that 'if it was not for my poor little dog that I worry all day and who is so good that I allow him to sleep in my bed, I should be more miserable than I am'.[23] He also planned to cheer himself up with other pets popular with officers as 'I mean to buy a parrot at Gibraltar and perhaps a monkey to amuse myself'.[24] When the *Salisbury* left Newfoundland in 1785, 'the Admiral having given permission for any person that pleased to take home a dog, seventy-five were actually embarked'. One 'Newfoundland dog of great size' on the *Barfleur* gained a reputation for lifesaving, and 'did the cry for assistance reach his ear, Boatswain would instantly distinguish it from the amidst the hubbub of the multitude, prick up his ears, jump overboard and swim to the person who appeared to require his assistance'. As 'this noble quadruped had saved many lives', it is little wonder that 'Boatswain was not only the pet and delight of the middies' berth, but equally enjoyed the goodwill of the whole crew'.[26] More dangerous was Bruin, a bear on Abraham Crawford's ship who was 'petted and kindly treated by the sailors' yet, when provoked by a cook, bit another sailor's hand's 'that hung below the stool upon which he had stretched himself to take a nap after dinner, and before it could be released from the brute's jaws, the man's hand was much lacerated, and one of his fingers had to be amputated'.[27]

Anything to alleviate the boredom was welcomed, but astute observers such as Samuel Leech realised that 'these things are often resorted to, because they feel miserable, just to drive away dull care.' Leech considered that, as on the slave plantations of the American South, 'in a man of war, where severe discipline prevails, though cheerfulness smiles at all times, it is only the forced merriment of minds ill at ease, minds that would gladly escape the thraldom of the hated service to which they are bound.' Despite this 'a casual visitor in a man of war, beholding the song, the dance, the revelry of the crew, might judge them to be happy.'[28]

This was a complete contrast with the low morale aboard those ships involved in the Spithead Mutiny of April 1797, which no one could have considered happy, least of all those in the sick berths. The surgeon Peter Cullen noted that 'the sick themselves showed something of a mutinous spirit and at first were rather insolent.'[29] On *Sandwich*, this insolence was linked to the overcrowding of the ship with its sick crew, 'in general very dirty, almost naked, and in general without beds', whose recovery was hampered by 'their own bad habits, but oftener to the foul air they breathe between decks; besides being frequently trod upon in the night from their crowded state.'[30] Thomas Trotter reflected that 'the founders of the mutiny were all men about middle age, married and had children' and were not linked to political discontent or radicalism, but were more concerned about practical matters;[31] the 'original cause of the mutiny was a seaman's grievance, and not to be charged to the levelling doctrines of the times'.[32] Indeed when at Spithead he 'remonstrated with the delegates, as the leaders of the mutiny styled themselves,' over their criticisms of conditions on the hospital ship *Medusa*, 'they seemed abashed: and when they saw the comforts that were provided for them in *Medusa* they were astonished. These complaints concerning the sick were therefore never more heard in the service.'[33]

Surgeons critical of conditions gave support to the 1797 mutinies. William Redfern was transported in 1801 for his part in the Nore mutinies of 1797 when, as the nineteen year-old surgeon's mate on the *Standard*, he had urged the mutineers to unite. His sentence of death was commuted to transportation on account of his youth and he then worked as an assistant surgeon at the Norfolk Island penal settlement. After being pardoned in 1803, he continued to practise as a surgeon and in 1808 joined the Colonial Medical Establishment at Sydney where one of his achievements was the building of a new general hospital.[34]

Some officers believed that the 1797 mutinies had been encouraged by the introduction of a cheap one penny prepaid postage rate for the seamen which had been introduced in 1795, since 'giving encouragement to a an extent of epistolary communication never known before and palpably injurious to discipline and order' gave the opportunity for 'ill-disposed men' to use the post to 'institute comparisons and test the different modes officers had of preserving their authority 'in the opinion of Captain William Hotham.[35] Without the subsidised mail the men would have had even less contact with their families than they did, reinforcing the sense of isolation which went with monotony and boredom. Marine Lieutenant John Fernyhough complained that 'sometimes I fancy myself deserted by all the world, every ship brings letters to all except myself'.[36] Marine Captain Thomas Wybourn only received two letters from home in ten months and welcomed that 'at last an opportunity offers itself to send letters to England which we have been looking for this long time. I fear you will think it long since the date of my last, but I assure you no ship has sailed for England, and to send by land might cost 16 shillings, which would exceed by at least 15 times the value of my scrawl'.[37] When a mail bag did arrive, 'the men crowd around as the letters are distributed, and he was pronounced a happy fellow whose name was read out by the distributor; while those who had none, to hide their disappointment, would jocularly offer to buy those belonging to their more fortunate messmates'.[38] For the many men who were illiterate 'and either altogether deprived of the privilege of intercourse with their friends or were dependent on the kindness of others to read or write for them', there was a further sense of isolation.[39]

Reading was a diversion for officers and a few educated seamen. A committed Anglican, Nelson, along with his fellow commanders, distributed among his crew copies of the Bible and prayer books published by the Society for the Propagation of Christian Knowledge. In his view, 'a ship where divine service is regularly performed is by far more regular and decent in their conduct than where it is not'.[40] On some ships there might even be small libraries 'to improve our mental faculties when we had a few leisure moments from ship duty and naval tactics'.[41] The emphasis was on providing improving literature rather than books for entertainment or relaxation which might have given imaginative insight into worlds beyond the confines of the ship.

Shore leave, which might have been expected to give some respite from the enclosed world of the wooden walls and a view of other worlds and cultures, was rare. When in port, the emphasis was on 'the usual routine of business going on in the fleet, all bustle, confusion and hurry to get water, provisions, repair ships, set rigging to rights, painting'. Thomas Wybourn pitied 'the poor sailors, fagged to death from daylight until after dark and frequently all night, and when all is complete, they are the only class not permitted to enjoy a few hours on shore. So much for the brave fellows who are so conspicuous in their country's cause – how these undaunted men submit is a matter of astonishment.'[42] It was the fear that men might desert which kept them confined to their ship by their officers. Tattoos had become popular among sailors after James' Cook's voyages to the Pacific and were encouraged by naval officers as they helped them to identify deserters.[43] Similarly very few sailors could swim, which shut off a healthy form of exercise to them and made them vulnerable if they fell overboard or were in a shipwreck, but stopped them absconding from their ships when in port. When the opportunity did come to go ashore, many a seaman was 'like an uncaged bird, as gay and quite as thought-less'; and 'these indulgences were abused for purposes of riot, drunkenness and debauchery'.[44] At Halifax, Nova Scotia, two marines got drunk on 'calibolus', a local brew of rum and spruce beer, followed by three pints of neat rum; they both died from alcohol poisoning.[45]

Most seamen, faced with a fairly monotonous diet and poor quality drinking water, found solace in alcohol. A fondness for drink indeed was considered to go along with life at sea. Recruiting posters for the Royal Marines in 1810 announced that 'all men of respectable character, good countenance and robust health who do not exceed twenty five years of age and are full five feet six inches high, can enjoy a glass of grog or are fond of a jovial life, have now the opportunity of enlisting in that gallant corps the Royal Marines.'[46] Gilbert Blane recognized that 'there is a great propensity in seamen to intoxicating liquors, which is probably owing to the hardships they undergo, and to the variety and irregularity of sea life. But there is reason to think that all sorts of fermented liquors, except distilled spirits, are conducive to health at sea.' He ascribed this this to the circumstance that 'as the solid part of sea diet is very dry and hard, and as the salt it contains is apt to excite thirst, a freer use of liquids than at land is necessary, particularly in a hot climate.'[47] He especially recommended that the men drink porter and spruce beer for their anti-scorbutic qualities and wine because it seemed to preserve the French fleet from scurvy, but he complained that 'the abuse of spirituous liquors is extremely pernicious everywhere, both as an interruption to duty, and as it is injurious to health.' He was especially opposed to the drinking of rum in the West Indies 'both because the rum is of a bad and unwholesome quality, and because this species of debauchery is more hurtful in a hot than a cold climate'.[48]

Until 1740 the men had been served their daily half pint of spirits undiluted, but then Admiral Edward Vernon, appalled by 'that formidable Dagon, drunkenness', had ordered that, 'whereas the pernicious custom of the seamen drinking their allowance of rum in drams, and often at once, is attended by many fatal effects to their morals as well as their health, which are visibly impaired thereby… besides the ill consequences arising from stupefying their rational qualities, which make them heedlessly slaves to every passion,' the daily allowance of half a pint for each man was to be mixed with a quart of water in 'one scuttled butt kept for that purpose and to be done upon the deck'.[49] Sensibly this was served twice a day to prevent the men from downing their allowance in one go, and was known as 'grog' in reference to Vernon's nickname of 'Old Grogram', given to him for his habit of wearing an old grogram boat cloak. However, this did not prevent men from saving up their allowances and drinking it in one go; while 'some of the hardest drinkers, however, would at times take what might be called a sober fit, and would then save their allowance day by day for weeks together in bottles, when they would either sell it to those who could purchase of them or assemble their chosen friends for a carouse – too frequently ending with confinement in irons and a parade at the ship's grating afterwards'.[50] Men, desperate for alcohol would also smuggle drink aboard. Thomas Trotter despaired that 'singular stratagems had lately been devised for carrying liquor into ships' and that 'vessels in the form and dress of a sugar loaf, and other articles, the small guts of animals, and bladders formed into the most fantastical shapes, and covered with silk or cotton, to be concealed in different parts of the female dress, have all been detected'.[51]

Attempts were made to reduce the opportunities for drunkenness and debauchery in the home ports. Admiral St. Vincent deplored that seamen found 'their only gratification in getting beastly drunk with ardent spirits in the lowest brothels, from whence they return to their ships with their blood in a state to receive every disorder arising out of such practices'.[52] Thomas Trotter, whose doctoral thesis had been on drunkenness, denounced the irresponsibility of the indiscriminate issue of gin shop licences by magistrates in Plymouth, and, with the support of St Vincent, action was taken by the Home Secretary the Duke of Portland, leading to the closure of two thirds of the 300 public houses in Plymouth.[53]

Alcohol was responsible for the many accidents at sea which took up so much of the daily routine of many surgeons, such as falls from the high rigging or through open hatchways. Lord Keith deplored the effects of alcohol as 'it is observable and deeply to be lamented that almost every crime except theft originates in drunkenness, and that a large proportion of the men who are maimed or disabled are reduced to that situation by accidents that happen from the same abominable vice.'[54] Doctors also associated intemperance with the destruction of the digestive system and liver, and with the development of scurvy and malignant diseases.[55] The penalty for drunkenness on board ship was thirty-six lashes, with persistent offenders being given forty-six or sixty lashes. Hardy on the *Victory* made a determined attempt to control immoderate alcohol consumption with 135 out of a total of 225 floggings in 1805 being for drunkenness.[56]

Strict discipline was enforced on board even the most contented of ships as any relaxation could impede the smooth running of the ship and make it ineffective in action. Offenders had their legs bound in irons, considered by many to be 'a severe and degrading punishment', before being brought before the captain where 'if any officer speaks in their favour, they are acquitted or their punishment is mitigated'.[57] However if they were found guilty by the captain, they would be flogged. Having first been ordered to strip, the man was 'then seized to a grating by the wrists and knees; his crime is then mentioned, and the prisoner may plead, but in nineteen cases out of twenty, he is flogged for the most trifling offence or neglect.'[58] Guarded by a marine, the man being punished would be flogged with a cat-o'-nine-tails, 'a most formidable instrument in the hands of a strong, skilful man', by the boatswain's mate until 'the lacerated back looks inhuman; it resembles roasted meat burnt nearly black before a scorching fire'.[59] The surgeon would have to tend to the injuries, but it was a lesson to all offenders that insubordination would not be tolerated. How often men were flogged depended on the strictness of the captain and how often the men committed offences. George Jackson thought that Captain Edward Hamilton on the *Trent* ran an efficient ship, but these qualities had all been promoted at no small sacrifice of humanity 'as 'the cat was incessantly at work'. Discipline was so strict that 'no sailor was allowed to walk from one place to another on deck, and woe betide the unfortunate fellow who halted in his run aloft, unless expressly bidden to do so for some particular purpose.'[60] Some captains were more lenient. On *Temeraire* four men charged with drunkenness were spared punishment when news of victory at the battle of Copenhagen was received and 'the Captain, after reading them a very severe lecture, told them, to their own great pleasure and the contentment of their mates, that he should overlook their offence for that time, so as not to mar the rejoicings for the success just announced, but that he should consider himself bound to inflict a double allowance if he ever found them before him again charged with the same or any other offence.'[61] He was as good as his word. What mattered was fairness when it came to maintaining discipline and good morale.

Nelson did not flinch from flogging when it was necessary, however affable he may have been to the men under his command and however concerned he may have been for their mental and physical welfare. On board *Boreas* between May 1784 and July 1787 he had flogged 86 out of 334 men, representing 25.7 per cent of his ship's company, at a time when the average contemporary percentage of men punished on board British warships on the same station was nine per cent.[62] The *Victory* was also a flogging ship, with a high punishment rate that owed as much to Nelson as to Hardy with 225 floggings in 1805.[63] Yet Nelson also reproved a lieutenant commander, H. Shaw, who had flogged all his men for not revealing the identity of a miscreant since he was unable to 'approve a measure so foreign to the rules of good discipline and the accustomed practice of His Majesty's Navy.'[64]

An officer who paid attention to the welfare of all on his ship would always be popular. Robert Hay thought of Cuthbert Collingwood that 'a better seaman, a better friend to the seaman, a greater lover and more zealous defender of his country's rights and honour, never trod a quarter deck'. Hay could not 'recollect a single instance of a man being flogged while he remained aboard' but asked himself the rhetorical question, 'was discipline neglected then?' to which his answer was that 'there was not a better disciplined crew in the fleet.'[65] Collingwood, like Nelson, was well aware of the importance of maintaining morale, through keeping his men occupied, visiting the sick berth and keeping a close watch on the health of the ship. He instructed Captain Clavell of the *Ocean* to 'cherish your men, and take care of your stores, and then your ship will be serviceable.'[66] He found it difficult to reconcile his evangelical religious beliefs with excessive discipline, and 'I cannot, for the life of me, comprehend the religion of an officer who could pray all one day, and flog his men the next.'[67] Generally, his approach was to rely on flogging as little as possible and to regard excessive flogging as 'big with the most dangerous consequences, and subversive of all real discipline'.[68]

This was not advice which Nelson's royal fiend and patron Prince William Henry, later Duke of Clarence, would have agreed with. He was notorious for his fondness for the lash and his high-handed discipline as captain of *Pegasus*. A martinet with regard to discipline, he could be loutish in manner and high-handed with other naval officers, despite his friend Nelson declaring that 'in his professional line, he is superior to two-thirds, I am sure, of the list; and in attention to orders, and respect to his superior officer, I hardly know his equal'.[69] Sent to sea at the age of thirteen, the prince was lacking in courtly graces but knew only too well his own importance. Despite his later bluff, down to earth reputation as the 'Sailor King', William IV as a young man was not popular with his crew. A midshipman on *Pegasus* complained that his 'strictness' in enforcing discipline amounted 'almost to torture'. He preferred to be 'respected and feared', unlike some of his contemporaries.[70]

The attitude of Nelson and his captains towards the health and welfare of their men can be compared with that of the captain of the ship *Leander* during Francisco de Miranda's 1806 expedition to liberate the Spanish colonies in South America and establish a Venezuelan Republic, who 'showed an inhumanity which we should wonder at to find in a cannibal' and was 'a wretch who could answer the calls for relief from those lingering under disease and want, frequently with curses'. His attitude towards the sick on the ship was callous and he even deprived them of fresh water, which he reserved for himself, his dog 'and a portion of the sailors with whom he was making a party', on the grounds that 'it was uncertain whether the sick would live or die; and if the latter happened, attention would be lost on them.[71] Miranda, who despite his adventurous life in the armies of Spain and France was more of a visionary, *El Precursor*, than a commander of men, and whose 'greatest battles were fought with his pen', had failed to take any action when faced with complaints about the conduct of this man, stoking up resentment on the *Leander* which helped neither his cause of independence nor morale among his forces.[72] He was also criticised for not visiting his wounded men or those sick with yellow fever, but preferring to stay in the comfort of his own quarters, 'picking his teeth in silence' and sharing better food with his close associates and his dog than his men enjoyed.[73]

Good leadership did matter. Thomas Trotter believed that the superiority of the British navy came from 'that courage which distinguishes our seamen' which 'though in some degree inherent in their natural constitutions, yet is increased by their habits of life, and associating with men who are familiarized to danger, and who from national prowess, consider themselves at sea as rulers by birth right.'[74] It was a sentiment that would have been agreeable to Nelson, whose concept of an officer's duty was to obey orders, honour the King and hate all Frenchman, a xenophobia which he expressed when he wrote 'I trust Almighty God will, in Egypt, overthrow these pests of the human race'.[75] It also chimed with the concern he had for maintaining the morale of his men and their mental health.

Nelson himself was prone to bouts of depression and not always able to maintain his own morale. Although generally, he had a high opinion of himself, having claimed to his wife when still a post-captain that 'one day I will have a long *Gazette* to myself. I cannot, if I am in the field of glory be kept out of sight'[76] and that there would be 'not a kingdom or a state where my name will be forgotten', in his moments of depression he could complain that 'I am become a burden to my friends, and useless to my country.' When sent home from India suffering from malaria, the eighteen year-old Nelson had 'felt impressed to an idea that I should never rise in my profession' and 'after a long and gloomy reverie, in which I almost wished myself overboard, a sudden glow of patriotism was kindled in me, and presented my King and my Country as my patron'. Thenceforward 'a radiant globe' was suspended in Nelson's mind eye, which saved him from further suicidal thoughts.[77]

There was a streak of hypochondria in Nelson linked with his depression. He had warned his uncle in 1786 that 'my activity of mind is too much for my puny constitution. I am worn to a skeleton'.[78] He described himself in 1799 as 'worn out, blind and left-handed'.[79] In 1801 he believed himself 'even at death's door, apparently in consumption'.[80] During the blockade of Toulon in 1804, he moaned that he 'suffered very much from anxiety'[81] and that 'my health does not improve, but because I am not confined to my bed, people will not believe my state of health.'[82] Racked with a perpetual cough, troubled with seasickness and suffering from toothache while on service in the English Channel off Boulogne in 1804, he informed Emma Hamilton that 'nothing can be more miserable and unhappy than your poor Nelson. My heart is almost broken.'[83] He bemoaned that' I have such dreadful pain in my teeth that I cannot hold up my head'.[84] In 1805 he complained that 'I can neither eat, drink or sleep' and that he had lost so much weight that the rings on his fingers were falling off.[85] Beatty believed that 'he possessed such a wonderful activity of mind, as even prevented him from taking ordinary repose, seldom enjoying two hours of uninterrupted sleep,[86] and on several occasions he did not quit the deck during the night.' Devoted to their commander and patron, Nelson's officers and men did their best to cheer him up; in the Baltic 1801, 'all in the fleet are so truly kind to me that I should be a wretch not to cheer up. Foley has put me under a regimen of milk at four in the morning; Murray has given me lozenges; Hardy is as good as ever, and all have proved their desire to keep my mind easy'.[87]

Yet, despite this concern with morale and keeping the mind easy, the Royal Navy had a poor record in dealing with the mental health problems of the navy. Gilbert Blane claimed that insanity was seven times more common among seamen than in the general population and that one in a thousand sailors would exhibit signs of madness, disregarding those men showing signs of mania who were quietly discharged. This was ascribed to such physical causes as intoxication and the head injuries common on board ships. Gun crews were affected by shock and blast in battle which upset their mental balance. Significantly there was a high proportion of officers among the cases of insanity, with fifteen officers and one hundred and twenty-five seamen being confined to asylums in 1813, which would be a proportion of roughly one officer to eight men in an asylum at a time when the proportion of officers to men in the navy as a whole was approximately one to twenty.[88]

It was claimed that the majority of the inmates of London asylums following the battle of the Glorious First of June came from the navy.[89] Indeed the horrors of battle could have an effect on an entire crew. On the *Russell* at the battle of Copenhagen in 1801, the crew were already low in morale with 70 cases of scurvy before action commenced. During the battle the men showed signs of nervous exhaustion 'with sunken eyes and dejected countenances'. This mood affected other men since 'they came forward trembling and groaning, and at every groan the hearts of all those who beheld them forgot their courage; their nerves slackened, their hands shook, and the instruments of labour fell from their grasp'. The *Russell* was lucky to have no fatalities and only six men were wounded, but the mental exhaustion of the crew was soon followed by an outbreak of sickness.[90]

There was little that the surgeon could do when it was shock rather than wounds that he was faced with. On the *Revenge* in action against the French in 1809, a lieutenant was taken down to the cockpit covered with blood having been struck on the breast by shot which had 'knocked a man's head completely from his shoulders' and then 'knocked down by the force of the head striking him.' It was assumed by the surgeon that he had also been wounded as he was 'very much besmeared with the blood from the man's head', but when the surgeon unbuttoned his waistcoat and examined him he could detect no injury. The only treatment possible was to leave the lieutenant to recover his composure himself before returning to his duties, but 'it was some time before that fit of composure went off, for he very prudently had no notion of going on deck again, while men's heads were flying about, and doing so much mischief.'[91]

Nelson was involved in some cases of insanity affecting the men under his command. He was called to the Old Bailey in December 1787 as a witness to the character of James Carse, cooper on the *Boreas*, charged with the murder of a prostitute when drunk. Nelson testified that Carse was 'the quietest soberest man that I ever saw in my life', unlike some of his shipmates, as 'seamen, I know perfectly, when they come home, the landlords will furnish them with raw liquors' and 'I saw myself thirty or forty men from that ship that were as mad as if they were at Bethlem, and did not know what they did.' He ascribed Carse's uncharacteristic behaviour to a fever brought on by sunstroke, claiming that 'at the island of Antigua, I think it was, he was struck with the sun, after which time he appeared melancholy, I have been affected with it. I have been out of my senses. It hurts the brain.' Carse was found guilty but eventually pardoned thanks to Nelson's intervention.' [92]

Nelson showed great sympathy in 1797 when two men on *Swiftsure* were suspected of pretending to be mad to obtain a discharge. He believed their lunacy was genuine, and 'I hope, for the poor men's sakes, that they are imposing on me; but depend on it, that God Almighty has afflicted them with the most dreadful of diseases'.[93] He thought that there was hope for the younger of the two men 'as he has intervals of sense, his countenance is most interesting', and he was prepared to pay £50 to send him home 'to place him in some proper place for his recovery'. He found that 'even the sight of the two poor men in irons on board her has affected me more than I can express'.[94] Nelson was later sympathetic to the application from Captain George Scott of the *Stately* for the court martial for John Burn, a royal marine, who had struck an officer, to be withdrawn on the grounds that the 'offence was occasioned by insanity'.[95]

It was customary for naval lunatics to be sent to public asylums, especially Bethlem Hospital, which would receive such men when 'if upon examination he appears to be a fit object of the charity' and for which since 1743 the Admiralty had paid a subsistence allowance of £4 12s a head.[96] The governors of Bethlem considered that the hospital, 'independently of the great advantage arising from them to the public at large, has always received and harboured great numbers of the soldiers and Sailors of his Majesty's army and navy, where by a very great saving hath annually, for a long period of time, accrued to his Majesty's government, which would have been otherwise under the necessity of maintaining those unfortunate objects at the private houses established for the reception of such as are afflicted with derangement.'[97] Nevertheless, the naval lunatics at Bethlem were not given the best of treatment, considered to be 'injudicious, and that uncalled severity is practised towards them'. Patients were left 'lying perfectly naked and covered up in straw'. An 'indiscriminate system of bleeding and purging in the spring months' and the 'mixing the mild and frantic patients together' tended to 'inspire maniacs with a dread of their keepers'.[98]

Bethlem, founded as the Hospital of St Mary of Bethlehem in 1247, had specialised in the treatment of the insane since at least the fourteenth century. It occupied once palatial buildings in Moorfield designed by Robert Hooke in 1675. Its cells, lit by small unglazed windows high in the wall, were strung along communication galleries which were used for exercise in bad weather and from which visitors could peep into the cells to watch the madmen. Most of the inmates rarely left their cells and were often chained to their beds. By the early nineteenth century these buildings were in a poor state of repair and new buildings, designed by the hospital's surveyor James Lewis, were erected in Lambeth, now occupied by the Imperial War Museum. It opened in 1815 but was immediately condemned for having been too expensive because of 'the unnecessary thickness of the walls'. As in the old premises, the central administration block was flanked by accommodation for the inmates with a gallery on one side and cells on the other. The new hospital was criticised for being gloomy because many of its rooms were overshadowed by the 'immense portico that is in front of the building'. The government had proposed that a semaphore should be erected on the 'pumpkin-shaped cupola' to warn of a French invasion. However, the building was not fireproof and the privies were badly positioned. After 1818, most naval lunatics were treated in special wards opened at Haslar Hospital.[99]

Meanwhile, officers and some other seamen were also sent to the Retreat at York, famed for its humane treatment and 'moral management' of its more genteel class of patient, and to other private asylums where treatment was not always so good. Conditions for those placed in many private asylums were not generally any better than in Bethlem and the public asylums. Hoxton House Asylum in East London was contracted by the Navy to house lunatic officers and seaman from 1792 onwards. The asylum had first been opened in 1695 and had been owned by the Miles family since 1715. The essayist Charles Lamb and his sister Mary were both patients there, as was James Hadfield who had attempted to assassinate George III, together with a number of criminal lunatics from Newgate prison. Sir Jonathan Miles, paid an annual retainer of £100 to the apothecary at Bethlem to refer incurable patients to Hoxton House. The asylum was overcrowded both with naval and poor law patients resulting in an over-reliance on the use of leg manacles, handcuffs and straitjackets which enabled a small number of staff to control the inmates.[100]

By 1812 the 'abominable conditions in the asylum' and 'the harsh treatment of the seamen, some of whom had served under Lord Nelson' were a public scandal at 'the house of Messrs Miles and Co. at Hoxton for the cure of mental derangement'. There, twenty patients were kept in a small room under the care of 'one keeper, who was supposed to see their clothes taken off and put on, their skin washed and kept clean, their hair combed, and to shave them' with many of the men 'unnecessarily handcuffed and chained to their beds or benches'. Violent and quiet patients were not separated and 'since there was no sick room, the sick remained with the healthy.' Very little was done to deal with the psychiatric condition of the patients, the doctors being brought in to see the patients confining themselves to their physical condition. The medical attendant of the naval lunatics was criticised for his excessive use of drugs, for which 'he had prescribed the mercury for mental derangement with good results, but he agreed that the mouths of the patients suffered badly. Purging, bleeding, cupping, or blistering was carried out, but never to excess'. The exercise grounds were cramped, with no shelter, and a high wall and it was impossible to offer much recreation or work to keep the patients occupied because of the lack of space. The asylum was judged 'unhealthy and improper'.[101]

It was expected that even in an asylum distinctions between officers and men would be observed. At Hoxton naval officers suffered the indignity of sharing a small sitting room 'indiscriminately with other maniacs, some of whom have been common maniacs and were now only rendered qualified for admission by payment having been insured to the proprietors of the concern for their accommodation.' While some of the patients were quiet and placid in manner, others were 'raging with inconceivable fury.' Some of the inmates were chained to their seats and others were handcuffed, such men 'frequently answering the calls of nature in the very room they are sitting in.' A number of the officers had been in the establishment for two years without receiving any medication and their diet of tea, beef, mutton, veal, cheese and small beer was deemed far too stimulating for their mental condition. Perhaps one of the greatest faults of the establishment was the 'impropriety of mixing officers indiscriminately with others' such as civilians, ordinary seamen and marines since 'in all our naval hospitals, officers are not put in the same ward or cabin together unless they have been accustomed to mess or associate with each other on board ship, or unless they enjoy similar rank'.[102]

It was through the maintenance of morale that an efficient ship and effective fleet could be maintained. Nelson and his fellow naval officers were aware of this, though the incidence of mental illness remained high during the years of monotony at sea, blockades and stressful battles of the French wars. Control of the men, ship and emotions was essential. For Admiral Collingwood, 'it has always been a maxim with me to engage and occupy my men, and to take such care for them that they should have nothing to do for themselves beyond the current business of the day.'[103] A well-organised and highly disciplined ship with a motivated crew was the key to success at sea.

# 7
# Keeping the Seamen Healthy

It was Nelson's firm belief that 'the great thing in all military service is health and it is easier for an officer to keep men healthy than for a physician to cure them'.[1] John Snipe, Physician to the Mediterranean Fleet, urged the vital importance of paying close attention to shipboard hygiene, ensuring that seamen were adequately clothed, that the ships were well-ventilated, clean and dry, that sick berths were fit for purpose and that there should be 'as nourishing a diet as situation and local circumstances will permit, composed of fresh meat and succulent vegetables'. This was possible only if naval officers at all levels collaborated with the ships' surgeons since 'nearly the whole of this is hinged on the improved mode of discipline which at this moment enables the British fleet to ride triumphant on the seas, and bid defiance to the hostile bands of our combined foes'.[2] Nelson was adamant that in order to wage a successful naval war 'the health of our seamen is invaluable, and to purchase that no expense ought to be spared'.[3]

If the crew were to be kept healthy, it was essential that the vessel on which they sailed should be a clean ship. Yet warships were designed to be formidable in battle or in maintaining a blockade rather than for the health of the men on board. Disease was perhaps a greater danger than death in battle and it was not easy to prevent infection from getting hold and spreading. The battleships were overcrowded. A third rate ship of 1800 tons would have about 600 men. A 100-gun, three-decker such as *Victory* carried some 900 men. Much healthier were the single-decked fifth or sixth rate frigates where the air could circulate more freely. Yet, the close proximity of the men to each other where 14 inches was officially allowed for each man to sling a hammock, meant that infection could spread quickly.[4]

Ventilation was a particular problem that was exacerbated in stormy weather and high seas when the ports and hatches had to be closed. In the totally unventilated well of the ship with its ballast it was necessary, as in contemporary coalmines, to lower a lighted candle into the well to test for noxious gases and firedamp before a carpenter would descend to inspect the pumps. If a candle was unavailable, the quality of the air in the hold would be tested by seeing how long it took for a silver spoon to tarnish. Gilbert Blane commented that 'it will appear hardly credible to succeeding generations that the air of the well of a ship could become so contaminated as in innumerable instances to produce instantaneous and irremediable suffocation'.[5]

At that time it was believed that infection was caused by miasma or foul-smelling bad air emanating from decomposed organic matter. It was held that good ventilation and circulation of air was essential to prevent miasmatic disease, but actually proved beneficial in an unintended way by reducing the risk of airborne bacterial infection. Various mechanical contrivances were devised to overcome the ventilation problem. Windsails on deck had long been used to conduct air through the hatchways. An improvement on this was the invention of a windmill operated ventilator by Dr Stephen Hales, originally devised for use on the roof of Newgate prison but enthusiastically taken up by the Sick and Hurt Board of the Royal Navy. This proved awkward to use on ships and Hales produced an improved machine for naval use in the form of a bellows in a large box with hinged sides that could be opened and closed by hand-worked rods. This 'Ship's Lungs' was installed on the *Prince* in 1753 and the *Namur* in 1758 before becoming compulsory on all naval vesssels.[6]

A rival method of ventilation was the brewer Samuel Sutton's Air Pump, which Sutton claimed to have an advantage over Hales's cumbersome machines since 'his ventilators, he tells us, will keep a prison sweet, but my pipes will sweeten even a boghouse'.[7] A series of pipes throughout the ship connected to fires in the hold helped the air to circulate. It was a method recommended by the court and society physician Richard Mead and by Admiral Sir Charles Wager in 1739,[8] but did not prove as popular with the Royal Navy as Hale's ventilator, though it had its admirers including Thomas Trotter. James Lind related how the good health of *Sheerness* on a long voyage to the Cape was attributed to the use of Sutton's Air Pump until it was noticed that the cocks of the 'fire pipes' had never been opened.[9]

A 'flue for conducting from the lower part of the deck the air vitiated by respiration' was devised by Captain Cuthbert Collingwood on *Barfleur*, to which Collingwood attributed the health of his seamen. Thomas Trotter believed that such ventilators should be fitted to most vessels considering 'the great advantages of pure air to life and health'. He also argued that parts of the ship which could not be easily ventilated should have their own windsails, especially the bread room of the ship which 'from its present pent-up condition, the number of lights so frequently burning in it, and the noxious effluvia issuing from cheese etc., is a species of volcano that is constantly throwing out pestiferous fumes to shorten and weaken life'.[10] Other inventions of a similar type were also devised by men on board the ships keen to improve their living and working conditions. Scuttles cut above the gun-ports were proposed by William Thompson, surgeon of the *Royal Oak*, and fitted throughout the fleet by order of Lord Mulgrave, Lord of the Admiralty, in 1777.[11] Another naval surgeon, W. Fullerton of the *Prince* invented an air pump to ventilate the more inaccessible parts of the ship in 1804.[12]

However, little realistically could be done to overcome the problems of damp and foul air. There was little option but to batten down the gun ports and hatchways in rough weather. Nothing could be done to prevent stocks of cheese and butter going rancid or the bilge water from stinking. Foetid conditions were the result of condensation from wet clothes, the sweating of unseasoned timbers used when in wartime ships needed to be constructed quickly and corners cut, and from the constant washing of the decks. Indeed concern with hygiene could make worse the problems of ventilation. Whilst the washing of clothes, hammocks and the decks was vital for the combatting of infectious disease, the water used could make worse the problems of rheumatism, tuberculosis and other respiratory diseases caused by the dampness of the ship. It was also believed that the bad odours resulting from the accumulation of water contaminated by decaying matter in the bilges was responsible for disease-causing miasmas. The problem was one of how to achieve both a clean and dry ship. The surgeons argued against anything that would encourage damp but the captains and commanders generally preferred a clean, white deck.

Cleaning the decks was a constant necessity in a situation where 'cleanliness, dryness and good air are essentially necessary to health' but dirt was inescapable. The upper decks were supposed to be washed every morning and the lower decks when the weather allowed them to be properly dried. At the very least the decks were to be swept daily and the collected dirt thrown overboard. Some admirals preferred the decks of their fleets to be washed down with water, others favoured vinegar and others ordered the use of sand. Almost universal was the use of holystones, blocks of pumice shaped like Bibles, for cleaning, by means of which 'the utmost cleanliness is preserved in the ship'.[13] Holystoning may have avoided problems of damp, but was harsh labour for the men carrying it out who 'suffer from being obliged to kneel down on the wetted deck, and a gravelly sort of sand strewed over it. To perform this work they kneel with their bare knees, rubbing the deck with a stone and the sand, the grit of which is often very injurious'.[14] The sand used could be hot and 'if you go between decks while the process is in operation, you will find yourself in a constant dust, which the men employed must inhale. If a black handkerchief be tied over their mouths, a crust of dust will be formed, where the breath moistens it; and which without this precaution would be inhaled'.[15] Admiral Lord Keith considered the custom of daily washing the decks to result in 'the destruction of the health and lives of valuable men' and in 1801 ordered that in the Mediterranean fleet the Lower Deck was only to be washed once a fortnight, swabs were not to be used on the Orlop and the Cockpit was to be dry-cleaned. It remained the duty of the messes to clean the decks daily with 'wood or stone rubbers'.[16]

Gilbert Blane, following the earlier advice of James Lind, recommended that the decks should be cleansed by scouring with hot sand or dry rubbing rather than with water. Portable stoves were to be used to reduce the humidity and dry out the lower decks.[17] These proved a particular success on the *Spencer* in January 1804 in drying out the lower deck after squally weather.[18] Nelson approved the use of such stoves and of ventilation devices to overcome the problem of humidity and increase the air flow. Aware of the unhealthiness caused by dampness and an unwholesome atmosphere, he also restricted the use of water to wash the middle and lower decks in an attempt to tackle the problem of dampness.[19]

Fumigation was seen as a way of expelling foul odours and purifying the ship of its noxious airs, as well as disinfecting the filthy clothing of pressed men. John Snipe recommended that all wood brought on to a ship should be smoked to remove the noxious effluvia contained in green wood.[20] Lind recommended the use of brimstone burnt in pots, supplemented by the destruction of foul bedding and the baking of infected clothes in an oven. The Sick and Hurt Board adopted this method in 1756 and then in 1782 ordered that ships should be fumigated with a hot lime wash as well as the placing of pots of smoking sulphur or charcoal on the decks. In a badly infected ship, the hatches and ports were to be closed for five or six hours a day for three days while the pots of brimstone were burning. Gunpowder, tar and tobacco were also to be used as fumigants.[21] An alternative method was devised by Dr J. Carmichael Smythe by which vitriol was poured over powdered nitre and warmed over a lamp which had the advantage of not needing to light potentially dangerous fires below deck. The system was used on the hospital ship *Union* in November 1795 and then in 1796 on the typhus-infected ships of the Russian squadron operating with the North Sea fleet.[22] Thomas Trotter, however, believed that brimstone was useless and nitre dangerous, and was critical of Carmichael Smyth having been awarded £500 for his 'demonstrated quackery' at a time when 300 naval surgeons were discharged without pay on the signing of peace.[23] He condemned sick berths that were 'half enclosed with hammocks, being fixed near the galley, more with a view to stifle contagion with the smoke from the fire than to keep the patient comfortable' and complained that 'even if infection was roasted to a cinder, the poor man was in danger of losing his eyes from the wood smoke in undergoing this fiery ordeal'.[24]

Sanitary facilities were sparse and inadequate for the number of seamen. Located on the beakhead, on either side of the bowspit, the heads consisted of 'seats of ease' with a clear drop to the sea and were completely exposed. On *Victory* there were only six seats of ease for

820 men. The captain had his own 'quarter gallery' at the end of stern gallery, while in larger ships similar quarter galleries were provided for the officers on the lower decks. In smaller ships the officers used buckets or their own chamber pots which their servants emptied. Meanwhile there were also two roundhouses, semi-circular cubicles offering a degree of privacy and shelter, near the heads, one for the use of midshipmen and warrant officers and the other for patients in the sick bay. The quarter galleries on *Malta* impressed some elderly Spanish ladies from Cartagena in 1813, who commented to each other on 'what cleanliness! What convenience! ... Certainly the English are the neatest and cleverest people in the world'.[25] They would have been less impressed by the facilities for the seamen who complained on the *Nereid* in 1808 that 'we are more like a prison ship than a man of war. From gunfire in the morning until sunset the gangway is attended by the Master of Arms to prevent more than two at a time going to the privy, so that the pains we labour under is insupportable, some discommode their trousers thro' a griping'. The heads could be dangerous in rough seas. On one ship, 'the yeoman had drank too much grog and whisky that on his coming up from the cockpit to go to the head as was supposed, he crawled out of one of the main deck ports and fell overboard'.[26]

It was little wonder that many men preferred to relieve themselves where ever they could. Tubs were placed on the decks for the purpose and these pissdales were drained through lead, copper or wood drainage pipes over the side of the ship. On the *Prince Frederick* 'the people go into the galley to piss, where tubs are placed for them' with the result that 'the galley was wet'.[27] Many naval surgeons and captains attempted to maintain high standards of hygiene by trying to prevent men relieving themselves wherever they were. On the *Spencer* in 1803, able seaman William Willey was punished with twelve lashes for 'pissing in the cockpit'.[28]

In bad weather when the hatches were battened down, 'necessary buckets' were in use as toilets but could not be emptied until the rough seas had calmed down. Surgeon Robert Robertson on the *Rainbow* in the West Indies in 1777 described sanitary conditions in storms and their effects on the health of the seaman by which 'the foul air then being much more confined around the sick, and where the well people lie, is consequently drawn into the lungs again and by respiration, and soon becomes foul and noxious, which renders it unfit for the salutary purposes of both the sick and the healthy'. Robertson believed that 'this circumstance is perhaps a much more powerful agent in enfeebling the seamen, in depressing their spirits during bad weather, and in rendering the dysentery epidemic in the ship, than the inclemency of the weather to which they are exposed upon deck in their watches' and found that 'it is very pleasing to observe the immediate alteration which appears in the countenances of the men when the ship is well washed and aired, and when they have cleaned themselves after bad weather'.[29] Gilbert Blane also believed that a small ship could be healthier because environmental conditions could be more easily controlled as 'a small ship is more easily ventilated, and the mass of foul air issuing from the hold, from the victuals, water and other stores, as well as the effluvia exhaling from the men's bodies, is less than in a large ship'.[30]

Conditions on enemy ships were inferior to those on British ones. Gilbert Blane was scathing about the filthy state of the holds in French ships, especially when 'the blood, the mangled limbs, and even whole bodies of men were cast into the orlop or hold, and lay putrefying for some time ... When, therefore the ballast or other contents of the holds of these ships came to be stirred, and the putrid effluvia thereby let loose, there was then a visible increase of sickness.'[31] Similarly on Spanish ships, the seaman William Robinson observed 'the scene of carnage horrid to behold' in a vessel where the dead bodies 'in a wounded or a mutilated state' were piled up in the hold.[32] There was a prejudice against burial at sea in Roman Catholic countries which made it a duty for the dead to be taken ashore for a Christian burial. The results of such practices were more deaths. Not surprisingly, dysentery and typhus were rampant and went unchecked. After the battle of the Glorious First of June 1794, conditions on the captured French ships were filthy, overcrowded and typhus-ridden. Admiral Howe urged that it was 'requisite that the French prisoners (about 2300) should be taken out of His Majesty's ships the most speedily: for preventing the infection, which is to be apprehended from the unprovided condition, and confined situation wherein several of them unavoidably remain at this time: the seamen of the fleet being otherwise, for the most part, now in a very promising state of permanent good health.'³³ The British prize crews boarding *Northumberland* and *Sans Pareil* were infected with typhus and died, while French prisoners also took the disease with them to British ships. Despite attempts to contain the infection by isolating the sick, fumigating the holds, cleansing and drying the deck with smoke and fires, and washing and airing clothing and bedding, five hundred men were transferred to Haslar when the fleet returned there. The French prisoners also continued to suffer and the outbreak of typhus only abated at the end of September.³⁴

Fumigation may have dealt with the smells resulting from in-adequate sanitation thought to be the cause of infection, but was no answer to the problem of the large number of rats that infested the ships. They gnawed at provisions in casks and their faeces and fleas spread disease. Introduced on board in provisions and stores it was impossible 'for any vigilance to exclude them' despite them being 'a great nuisance, destroying not only stores and provisions, but, urged by the continual noise of the water, will sometimes eat their way through the timbers, thus causing leaks, which it is supposed have proved fatal to many vessels'.³⁵ On *Nisus*, the surgeon James Prior recorded that 'these animals had so much increased that they ran about the lower deck almost without dread'.³⁶ On *Culloden*, Robert Hay had witnessed 'them leave the marks of their teeth in the thick skin of men's toes when asleep and on occasion to draw blood'.³⁷ In extremity, rats could also be a source of food though not to the taste of many. When Marine Lieutenant Augustus Field caught four rats on *Brunswick* while in the West Indies, he baked them in a pie with some pork chops. After another lieutenant vomited at the sight of this, Field retired to finish his meal in his cabin, later commenting that 'one of the rats was not entirely to his taste as the flesh was black; but whether from a bruise or from disease he could not say, but he should be more particular in future in the post mortem examination'. Lieutenant James Gardner to whom he addressed these remarks simply recorded 'I never was more sick in my life'.³⁸

Monotonous though it may have been, naval diet was not usually dependent upon vermin. Rather it was 'composed of hard sea biscuit, fresh beef while in port, but salt pork and salt beef at sea, pea soup and burgoo'. Sometimes also known as 'skillagallee', burgoo was 'oatmeal boiled in water to the consistency of hasty pudding'. Commonly served was lobscouse, a stew of salt meat, onions, potatoes, any available vegetables and crushed ship's biscuit. There were few variations on this basic diet other than the once a week treat of 'duff' pudding made from raisins and flour and occasionally cocoa instead of burgoo. There were not many complaints about the foodstuffs on offer, which compared favourably enough with the diet of labourers ashore, but the seamen were critical of the amounts they received. Each of them was allocated a pound of bread and a gallon of beer a day. Weekly rations were more meagre: four pounds of salt beef, two pounds of salt pork, a quarter of a pint of dried peas, one and a half pints of oatmeal, six ounces of sugar, six to eight ounces of butter and twelve ounces of cheese. The purser was often accused of issuing short measures as he often only gave a pound when fourteen ounces were stipulated in the regulations.[39]

Even full rations were not adequate for hard labour on the ship and men complained of being hungry. George Watson, a marine serving in the Mediterranean at the age of eighteen, complained that 'the greatest inconvenience I suffered from was hunger, whether that was owing to my youth, or to not having supplies equal to the labour we had to endure'. He recognised that the rations might have appeared generous enough to a landsman, but 'it should be recollected, such allowance has to serve a man, both for night and day, instead of day only; as a sailor, especially a boatman, who has to work as much by night as by day, and consequently as much inclined to eat'.[40] Morale was higher and hunger pains less after a provisioning trip. The North Sea station was known by seamen as 'a full belly station' as it was easy to collect supplies from the ports at home on a frequent basis. Marine Daniel Goodall on *Flora* with the North Sea fleet watching the Dutch coast in 1805 welcomed provisioning trips to Great Yarmouth, when the *Flora* would take bags of vegetables and 30 or 40 live bullocks to sea with it, but 'good rations could not reconcile us to dull and disagreeable work'.[41]

Supplies of rum, beer, water, butter and salt meat were stored in wooden caskets in the hold and had to be hauled up when needed. Accidents were common. In 1805, Antonio Bernard, a Viennese Marine, had 'a fall from the fore ladder against the armourer's bench which produced a hernia on the left side' when he was helping with 'hoisting up water from the hold' on *Queen*.[42] The food stored in the hold was at the prey of vermin and weevils, occasioning other health hazards from its storage. Goods of inferior quality or contaminated were condemned. Rancid and maggoty cheese and butter had to be condemned on the *Victory* in August 1803. In January 1805, 372 pounds of rice had to be destroyed as a result of rats 'eating holes in the head of the cask', and in February 2,542 pounds of bread were found to be 'maggotty, weevilly and unfit for men to eat' on the *Victory* despite Nelson's insistence on the highest quality for his men.[43]

The men were divided into messes and each member of a mess would take his daily or weekly turn as 'mess cook'. Supplies had to be collected from the steward and the food prepared before being taken to be cooked in the galley with its coppers and cast iron stove on a brick or flagstone stand, often located under the forecastle on the upper deck or on the middle deck. Once cooked, the food was shared among the messmates and the cook then had the chore of cleaning the mess utensils and equipment. The cooking was actually done by the ship's cook, often 'men that have lost a precious limb, or otherwise maimed in the defence of their King and Country'.[44] Many of them were 'elderly men who have seen much of seafaring life, and when their work is finished for the day they'll take their pipes, seat themselves in the Copper Alley and spin you a long yard'.[45] Jack Robertson, the cook on *Amelia* and 'a first-rate specimen of the British seaman of the day, a frank, pen-hearted and open-handed fellow', had lost his left hand on the *Temeraire* at Trafalgar, and was popular with officers and men for his readiness to entertain with a song.[46] It was the cook's duty to ensure that 'every article into which the provisions are put is perfectly clean, 'and that all supplies were accounted for so that 'the serving out of the provisions out of the boilers or coppers is managed entirely by the cook himself, for if there is any deficiency, he is answerable for it'. When dinner was being served 'the ship's cook, with his one arm (for he has seldom more; or if he have two arms, he has certainly only one leg) empties the coppers by means of a monstrous fork' and 'allows the pease-soup to run off by a cock from another boiler into a huge tub'.[47]

The men were piped to their meals which they ate in their mess groups seated on benches, chests or casks around tables set between the cannons. These tables were wooden boards suspended by ropes from the deck above and were stowed against the side of the ship when not in use. Wooden plates and wooden tankards or beakers of animal horn were commonly used. The wooden plates were square for easy storage and offered the men the chance of enjoying a 'square meal'. Breakfast of burgoo and Scotch coffee, made by boiling burnt bread in water sweetened with sugar, was usually at eight o'clock. Dinner at midday was a mixture of ship's biscuit or bread, meat and pease pudding, though Mondays, Wednesdays and Fridays were meatless 'banyan' days. A cold meal of biscuit, bread and cheese or leftovers from dinner was offered at four o'clock for supper.[48] Mealtimes were noisy with 'the merry notes' of the pipes 'nearly drowned next instant in the rattle of tubs and kettles, the voice of the ship's cook and his mates bawling out the numbers of the messes, as well as by the sound of feet tramping along the decks and down the ladders with the steaming ample store of provisions'.[49]

For the new sailor, the first impression he gained of his food was unappetising. Salt meat might be so hard that it could be carved into keepsakes. When boiled it produced a thick salty, fatty scum known as 'slush', half of which was used to waterproof the rigging and the other half could be kept by the cook for sale to tallow merchants to build up a 'slush fund' to supplement his wages. For Archibald Sinclair who joined the navy in 1814, his first taste of salt beef evoked 'dismay and astonishment at the first presentation of what was universally known as a piece of mahogany, to which it bore a striking resemblance in hardness, dryness and polish'. Pork was no better, 'a shrivelled piece of something bearing a resemblance to a cut from the hide of a rhinoceros'. Supplies of cheese and butter soon became rancid and would often be sold to the midshipmen before becoming unfit to eat, when they 'afford the most disagreeable exhalations'.[50] Jeffrey Raigersfield's mess bought a firkin of butter that was 'so full of small hairs that however often we washed it we could not separate the hairs from the butter, so we swallowed both butter and hairs'. The reason for this became plain when they reached the bottom of the firkin and found 'a mouse with all its hairs off' which they thought had fallen in after the butter had melted.[51] Ship's biscuit was little more inviting and just as contaminated by pests, being 'so light that when you tapped it upon the table, it fell almost to dust, and there out numerous insects called weevils crawled'. If large white maggots with black heads emerged from the biscuit, the biscuits were not considered to be as decayed. Whereas the weevils were 'bitter to the taste', the maggots were 'fat and cold to the taste, but not bitter'.[52]

For many men suffering from dental decay, biscuit had to be soaked before they could eat it. It was little wonder that, according to George Watson, 'the first thing sailors generally buy, when they come into port, are soft bread and butter, which are considered and they truly are, a great treat to teeth, long inured to the uniform resistance of flinty biscuit'.[53] Edward Mangin, chaplain on the *Gloucester*, went ashore 'for the avowed purpose of eating soft-tommy', as freshly baked bread and butter was called, which he preferred to 'purser's nuts' or ship's biscuit.[54] The surgeon James Prior considered that fresh fruit and vegetables 'are luxuries more grateful to the eye of a sailor than the bones of a favourite saint to the most orthodox Catholic'.[55]

Nelson took pains to ensure that all the provisions in his fleet were of the highest quality. The fleet's masters were ordered in October 1805 to board the supply ships arriving from Malta in order to 'take a most strict and careful survey on the pork, tongues, pease and wheat' to check that the casks and bushels were complete. Officers were also expected to randomly select pieces of meat from the casks and boil them to make sure that they did not shrink.[56] Nelson also scrutinised the returns of the fleet's pursers for any signs of irregularity that might indicate fraud or negligence.[57] He was particularly concerned about the pursers appropriating provisions for general consumption that had been purchased as medical comforts. Nelson believed that onions were of great benefit nutritionally and medically because of their anti-scorbutic qualities, so was especially concerned to find that some pursers were appropriating onions bought for medicinal use and instead were using them in the seamen's soup instead of purchasing vegetables themselves. In 1803 he ordered that 'the pursers are obliged to purchase vegetables for the ships' soup'.[58] In May 1804 he queried an 'extraordinary charge' of £100 from Captain George Ryves of the *Gibraltar* for onions, cabbages, pumpkins and leeks which should have been paid by the purser.[59]

Notwithstanding this close financial scrutiny of their work, Nelson was keen to encourage the pursers to use their initiative in purchasing provisions when the opportunity arose.[60] Where the Mediterranean fleet paid regular watering and wooding visits, it was possible for extensive private provision markets to develop. On one visit to Pula Bay in April 1805 'hundreds of natives flocked down bringing quantities of provisions, animals, fruit etc., which of course met with a most welcome reception'.[61] Richard Ford, Agent-Victualler to the Mediterranean Fleet, and his assistants were successful in obtaining fresh provisions from North Africa, Sardinia and Italy. Between February 1804 and April 1805, the 6,000–8,000 strong Mediterranean fleet consumed a million pounds of fresh beef and some £47,000 was spent on fresh fruit and vegetables. From October 1804 and January, 62,400 oranges, 35,700 lemons, 34,051 lbs of onions, 200,000 gallons of wine and 40,000 gallons of brandy were consumed.[62] In victualling matters, Nelson also took account of the tastes of his men, pointing out in 1804 that there would be complaints if cheese was replaced by rice in their diet.[63]

Whilst the seamen preferred familiarity in their diet, they ate less fish than might be expected. Thomas Trotter praised Sir Edward Pellew for encouraging his men to catch fish 'which has much retarded the appearance of scurvy in his own ship and others' and Lord Duncan who 'has always been remarkable for his indulgence in this duty'. However, Trotter considered it 'a pity that this excellent practice is not general in the fleet when there is nothing else for employment'.[64] Turtle soup was more popular when available, since 'every part of it was good to eat, but the eggs ... taste rather fishy'.[65] Ascension Island was considered the best place to catch turtles which were kept alive until required on board ship in water tanks or on deck where 'a wet swab was kept under their heads' and 'their eyes were washed every morning'.[66] However if the turtle soup, 'that distinguished dish on the table of the voluptuary' was not well-cooked and made 'a very sorry dish', the crew would say that 'God sends meat but the Devil sends cooks'.[67]

Fresh meat, however, was available to the officers who were allowed to bring livestock aboard. Although the Admiralty supplied bullocks for the men, the quality was not always good. The crew of the *Berwick* mutinied 'in consequence of some bullocks that were anything but fat' when 'John Bull, thinking only of his maw, broke out into open rebellion'.[68] The captain of the *Crescent* off Jamaica in 1800 allowed the men 'to supply themselves with pigs', which 'indulgence contributed essentially to keep off the scurvy'.[69] Thomas Trotter, nevertheless, considered that 'nothing has been more offensive on the decks of our ships as pigsties' and praised Lord St Vincent for moving them from the forecastle into the waist to make more room for the sick berth. It was his belief that 'officers ought cheerfully to give up a few messes of fresh pork to their stomachs, to let their lungs have the full benefit of pure air in their sleeping and waking hours'.[70] Trotter also criticised 'the filthy practice' of ships hanging fresh carcasses under the half-deck or under the booms in the waist, 'places exposed to the breath of the whole ship's company' where the crew brushed past them when they passed.[71]

The number of animals on board placed greater demands on the limited fresh water supplies carried by the ships. Drinking water was available on deck from a scuttle butt, a cask with a square hole or scuttle cut in it, but it was sometimes necessary for a marine to be stationed next to it to prevent wastage. These casks, containing water collected from rivers, would be hauled up from the hold if it was not possible to pump up fresh water from them to the decks. It was not always easy to find good sources of water. On the island of Diego Garcia in the Indian Ocean, William Richardson and his crewmates were sent in search of fresh water so 'as we could find no watering place here, we had recourse to digging holes in the ground for each empty cask and generally in the course of a night they would be filled by the morning'.[72] It was easier for Jeffrey Raigersfield on Dominica in the West Indies where 'the casks were landed from the boats and rolled to a deep part of the river, filled and bunged up' before being rolled down to the salt water where 'the men floated them, and fastening them one to the other they were towed on board'.[73] At Cagliari, where 'never was a place better adapted for watering a fleet', in 1805 the ships could approach the shore within a few hundred yards and the casks were taken on shore in boats to be filled from the river and then returned to the boats and rowed back to the ship. There a fleet of 15 ships was able to load water for 12,000 men for four months in about two days.[74] However smooth the process of watering may have been, it exposed men to the dangers of malaria in mosquito-infested areas and to ruptures in any area.

After a few weeks of storage the water became slimy and stagnant. When Leonard Gillespie joined his ship at Yarmouth in 1788, he found 'Thames water filled six months ago at Deptford in unseasoned casks, which are now filled with a dilute sort of ink – putrefaction has made it foetid and stinking'.[75] Edward Mangin believed that illness among the crew was caused 'by the foul water they are obliged to drink'.[76] On the *Phaeton* in 1803, Midshipman James Scott was recovering from seasickness in the English Channel when 'the liberal portion of salt junk and stinking water brought within hail of my olfactory nerves threw me on my back again'.[77] Even when water was in short supply, it could be difficult to drink it. On a voyage from Gibraltar to Great Britain, Thomas Marmaduke Wybourn complained that 'the greatest misfortune was the want of water: we were allowed only one pint a day for these last five weeks, and this was so bad sometimes as to oblige us to hold our noses while drinking'.[78] It was little wonder that spirits and beer were found more palatable to drink than water.

Action was taken to preserve drinking water at sea. Attempts were made to sweeten it with burnt biscuit, while Gilbert Blane suggested that it should be infused with quick lime and, if this failed, wine or spruce beer should be issued in place of the water since 'there is no cordial equal to good wine in recruiting men who are recovering'. Porter was considered too expensive to give to the crew.[79] John Snipe insisted that only the purest water should be taken from the head of springs and that water casks should be carefully maintained to avoid contamination.[80] Attempts were also made to distill sea water and filter it through sand or gravel. However, the use of calcined bones and silver nitrate recommended by the Durham apothecary Joshua Appleby or powdered chalk suggested by Stephen Hales made the water undrinkable. James Lind found a solution in 1762 with his invention of an apparatus for the distillation of sea water by fitting still heads or musket barrels to large coppers to draw off the steam evaporating from boiling sea water. In 1771 this method of distillation was presented to Lind as a new method by Irving, the junior surgeon on *Arrogant*, whose only difference in his apparatus was the substitution of a long tin tube wetted by mops for Lind's still head, which Lind accepted because he was 'desirous that in any form so important a discovery as the freshening of sea water by distillation might be introduced into general use'.[81] A charcoal filter was used on the *Favourite* in October 1805, 'by which method, the most putrid water becomes immediately sweet; but it was insufficient to supply the whole ship's company'.[82]

Solace was found from poor food and water in tobacco which was more often chewed than it was smoked because of the dangers of smoking below deck. It could be bought from the purser and the cost deducted from a man's wage, but after 1806 each sailor was given an allowance of two pounds of dried tobacco leaf a month, which would be soaked in rum and then rolled tightly in canvas to be stored until it matured sufficiently for chewing or smoking. Midshipman George Jackson was put off tobacco for life when he first tried to smoke a pipe, considering that 'from being considered a filthy indulgence, it has become a gentlemanly habit' though he had become 'so horribly ill' from trying it.[83] An officer such as Thomas Fremantle was more likely to take snuff, though 'I don't take more than I did, but full enough' when 'my snuff is just out and I shall be obliged to manufacture more from ships tobacco'.[84] Instead of snuff he had 'got perhaps a worse habit, which is smoking cigars – which does not agree with me, notwithstanding which I continue to do so like a child and deserve whipping'.[85]

The officers fared better with food and drink than the men under their command, often eating in some style from fine china and glassware with silver cutlery, and even had their own cooks, who were personal servants, unlike the ship's cook who was a warrant officer, and were often 'most haughty in their exalted stations'. An admiral like Cuthbert Collingwood who prided himself on serving salt meat and wine that cost no more than sixpence per gallon, was considered mean, Collingwood being nicknamed 'Salt Junk and Sixpenny'.[86] Nelson liked to live in some style as an admiral, breakfasting with his senior officers on tea, rolls, toast and cold tongue and dining leisurely on 'the best wines and most exquisite viands'.[87] The sick occasionally benefitted from the superior quality of food on the tables of the officers. Although they were supplied with medical comforts by the surgeon, these, in the opinion of Thomas Trotter, could have been better and that 'a little mutton broth is so nourishing under debility and so desirable in many cases after a long cruise that to grant it would be the *ne plus ultra* of our improvements'. However, mutton broth was only available due to the generosity of the officers who 'have kindly shared their stock with the sick; but look at their pay! Alas! They cannot afford it.'[88]

Diet had an important art to play in the prevention of scurvy, the scourge of the seaman on long voyages. Often referred to as the 'plague of the sea', scurvy, caused by a deficiency of vitamin C, had been a problem ever since men began to make long sea voyages from the fifteenth century onwards, yet it was only on lengthy voyages that it was a major problem. It has, nevertheless, even been suggested that a million British seamen died from it in the eighteenth-century, which is probably twice the number of sailors who served in the Royal Navy in that time.[89] It was characterised by 'large discoloured spots dispersed over the whole surface of the body; swelled legs; putrid gums; and, above all, an extraordinary lassitude of the whole body especially after any exercise, however inconsiderable; and this lassitude at last degenerates into a proneness to swoon on the least exertion of strength, or even the least motion.'[90] The skin would become dry and rough, the flesh became flaccid and, as the gums became purple and swollen, the teeth would be loosened. Wounds failed to heal.

Ideas about the causes and treatment of scurvy were dominated until late in the eighteenth-century by the account given in the seventeenth-century by John Woodall in his classic textbook for ships' surgeons *The Surgion's Mate* :

> Another cause of the disease to the ordinary sort of poor man is want of fresh apparel to shift them with ... partly also by the not keeping their apparel sweet and dry, and the not cleansing and keeping their cabins sweet, this also engendreth and increaseth the infection. Some charge biscuit as a cause of the scurvy, but I am not of their opinion. Some say inordinate watchings are cause thereof. Some say extreme labour wanting due nourishment. Some also affirm cares and grief to be some cause thereof, others affirm the very heat of the air, resolving the spirits and vapours, and engrossing the thick humours, causeth the scurvy; but what shall I amplify further, for it is also true that they which have all the helps that can be had for money, and take as much care as men can devise are even by the evil

disposition of the air, and the cause of nature, struck with the scurvy, yea and die thereof at sea and land both.[91]

A variety of approaches to the treatment of scurvy had been tried out on ships throughout the eighteenth century. Edmund Neeler invented a medicinal belt, which he claimed could cure scurvy, itch and infestation by vermin, which was tried out on various ships in 1746, though these rolls of canvas filled with a dried herbal mixture proved slow to cure the itch and were useless for scurvy or anything else.[92] Men unlucky enough to wear them got caught in the rigging and went down with colds when they took the belts off, despite a request from Captain Robert Harland for some, 'being glad to use every expedient to preserve the health of my people.'[93] William Cockburn, physician to the Royal Hospital at Greenwich, urged use of Elixir of Vitriol as a treatment for scurvy and had recommended its inclusion in surgeon's sea chests in 1732, although it was his sensible belief that it was more important to look for a method of preventing scurvy rather than one that would cure it.[94] Spinach was suggested as a preventative and Cockburn debated whether 'spinach would be useful in scorbutic cases', but the general opinion was against its adoption. Then 1757 a portable soup was introduced, made of beef and mutton leftovers from the salted naval rations formed into small cakes that could be mixed with boiling water, and acclaimed as something that 'every British seafaring man in His Majesty's Navy ought to be thankful for this great refreshing benefit.'[95] In 1771 the Society of Arts sent the Admiralty a recipe for a carrot marmalade as a cure for scurvy sent to them by Baron Stosch, one of their corresponding members from Berlin, which was tried out on Cook's *Resolution* and *Adventure*.[96]

James Cook was to be remarkably successful in avoiding scurvy during his three voyages to the Pacific and around the world made between 1768 and 1780. This was because he only had small crews and could put into land whenever he needed. He realised the curative potential of green vegetables and regularly foraged ashore when his ships were at anchor. He considered malt, from which was made sweet wort, to be 'without doubt, one of the best anti-scorbutic sea medicines then discovered, when used in time.'[97] When he reached Tahiti in April 1769 the ship's company had in general been very healthy owing in great measure to 'the sour krout, portable soup and malt' and to the 'care and vigilance of Mr Monkhouse the surgeon'; this sauerkraut and portable soup would be served to the men on alternate beef and banyan days, whilst the malt was given to any men showing the first signs of scurvy. The crew initially had been reluctant to eat sauerkraut until Cook had provided it as a luxury on the captain's table 'for such are the tempers and dispositions of seamen in general that whatever you give them out of the common way, although it be ever so much for their good, yet it will not go down well with them and you will hear nothing but murmurings against the men who first invented it; but the moment they see their superiors set a value upon it, it becomes the finest stuff in the world and the inventor a damn'd honest fellow.'[98] Joseph Banks, the botanist on the *Endeavour,* was less enamoured of sauerkraut or malt wort which had no effect on him when he began to show the symptoms of scurvy but when he made 'every kind of liquor which I used … sour with the lemon juice', he was surprised to find that 'in less than a week my gums became as firm as ever, and at this time I am troubled with nothing but a few pimples on my face.'[99]

Cook's success in keeping his crew free of scurvy was used as an argument against the issue of citrus fruits in the form of lime or lemon juice as an antiscorbutic, despite the numerous observations made since the sixteenth century that these fruits could be beneficial.[100] In May 1747 James Lind, the surgeon on *Salisbury,* conducted an investigation of various remedies for scurvy on 12 diseased seamen on his ship, which has been hailed as the first double-blind medical trial, but was ignored by his contemporaries and recognised as being of significance only in the twentieth-century when vitamins and vitamin deficiency were at last beginning to be understood. The twelve seamen were divided into six pairs, each of which was given a different possible cure: a quart of cider, a dose of elixir vitriol, vinegar, sea water, oranges and lemons, and electuary of garlic. After a fortnight, the pair fed on oranges and lemons had shown substantial signs of recovery, but the other couples had either progressed very little or not at all.[101] However, Lind, despite citing numerous references from earlier writers of the curative qualities of oranges, lemons and limes, failed to make clear any conclusions or any explicit recommendation that the Admiralty should supply citrus fruit to the fleet to help maintain its health.[102]

Lind continued to see scurvy as the result of faulty digestion and excretion, which require a reasonably varied diet to function efficiently. If a man's diet is monotonous 'these excrementitious humours naturally destined for this evacuation, when retained long in the body, are capable of acquiring the most poisonous and noxious qualities, and a very high degree of putrefaction'.[103] On long sea voyages in wet, humid weather, the healthy seaman was unable to properly digest his diet of ship's biscuit and salted meat resulting in his developing scurvy. The implication was that it was the conditions on board ship that were responsible for this rather than a monotonous, fruit- and vegetable free diet on its own, since Lind acknowledged that 'it appears, I think, very plainly, that such hard dry food as a ship's provisions, or the sea-diet, is extremely wholesome; and that no better nourishment could be well contrived for labouring people, or any person in perfect health, using proper exercise in a dry pure air; and that, in such circumstances, seamen will live upon it for several years without inconvenience.'[104] Lind placed more emphasis on the improvement of the general conditions in which the seaman lived and worked than on diet, for, with this, 'moderate exercise, cleanliness of body, ease and contentment of mind, procured by agreeable and entertaining amusements, will prove sufficient to prevent this disease from rising to any great height where it is not altogether constitutional.'[105]

When Lind's most prominent follower Gilbert Blane admitted that he had never been able to satisfy himself 'with any theory concerning the nature and cure of this disease, nor hardly indeed of any other',[106] it was little wonder that the treatment of scurvy continued to be hit or miss, with no real understanding of how it could be prevented or treated. Thomas Trotter, influenced by Joseph Priestley's work on oxygen, surmised that the presence of oxygen in citrus fruits purified the system but, 'whatever, therefore may be the theory of sea scurvy, we contend that vegetable matter imparts a something to the body, fortifies it against the disease: and that in proportion to the quantity of this something imparted, making allowance at the same time for external causes which counteract its effects on the constitution, the symptoms will sooner or later disappear.'[107]

There remained a prejudice against the use of fresh fruit as an antiscorbutic. Lemon juice was found to be ineffective as a means of preventing scurvy on the *Ajax* in 1800.[108] Thomas Trotter, while supporting the issue of lemon juice as a cure for scurvy, was against it being used as a preventative as he thought it 'cold and fat-consuming' and debilitated the system, and protested when it was issued generally that 'from the whole of my reports from the surgeons of the ships of the line, I do not find a single fact that can justify the general use of lemon juice as lately administered.'[109] This was no different to the attitudes of 1769 when a request that was made by the commander of the sloop *Ferret* for the repayment of money he had spent on the purchase of orange juice for members of the ship's company who had scurvy had been disallowed because orange juice was 'not included in the establishment of surgeon's necessaries and a precedent should not be set.'[110]

More dubious treatments continued to be employed. Buccaneers in the Caribbean were said to have buried men in the earth as a treatment for scurvy. Lind admitted that this could be efficacious when he recorded that men on a supply ship bringing seasonable green vegetables to the fleet off Belleisle in 1761 had suffered from scurvy through not enjoying the benefit of their cargo. They were then 'carried on shore and after being stripped of their clothes were buried in a pit dug in the earth (the head being left above the ground), their bodies were covered over with the earth and permitted to remain thus interred for several hours, until a large and profuse sweat ensued. After undergoing this operation, many who had been carried on men's shoulders to those pits were of themselves able to walk to their boats; and what was very extraordinary, two of them who had been quite disabled by this disease recovered so perfect a state of health that they soon after embarked for the West Indies recovered, and in good spirits, without once tasting any green vegetables'.[111] The surgeon on the *Albion* in 1799 attempted to use similar means to cure scurvy by burying a sufferer up to the neck in earth brought on the ship especially for the purpose, but to no effect. However 'the use of the lime juice had a good effect and which I allowed in considerable quantities'.[112] Similarly Peter Henry, surgeon on *Daedalus* noticed that there had been no incidence of scurvy during a voyage to Bombay in 1802 despite the crew having had only six weeks' supply of fresh meat in sixteen months, but unlimited supplies of fruit and vegetables.[113]

This was a vindication of the decision of the Sick and Hurt Board in 1795 to recommend the issue of lemon juice to the fleet 'as the best substitute for fresh fruit and vegetables, and the most powerful corrective of the scorbutic qualities of their common diet.' Lemon juice was much easier to store and ship than fresh vegetables and live oxen and so could be considered a dietary substitute as 'it is also well ascertained that a certain proportion of lemon juice taken daily, as an article of seamen's diet, will prevent the possibility of their being tainted with the scurvy, let the other articles of their diet consist of what they will.'[114] It was a response to the growing recognition of the value of lemon juice when it was used as an antiscorbutic and growing demand from naval commanders. Rear-Admiral Alan Gardner had asked in December 1793 'whether a few chests of lemons may not be productive of great benefit to the crews of the respective ships'[115] when requesting a supply of lemon juice for his expedition to take Mauritius and the two medical members of the Board, Robert Blair and James Johnston, had endorsed this proposal.[116] Commodore Peter Rainier's success in keeping scurvy at bay on the *Suffolk* on a four month journey to India was attributed to the daily distribution of lemon juice and sugar.[117] Vice-Admiral Elphinstone, Lord Howe and Admiral Duncan were all demanding supplies of lemon juice, which Blair and Johnston agreed would be a protection against scurvy. However demand exceeded supplies and in 1796 lemon juice as a preventative was restricted to ships going on foreign service though it continued to be available for curative purposes in home waters.[118] Only after 1800 when Lord St Vincent's demanded that the Channel fleet should receive lemon juice for prevention as well as cure did it become widely available again to fight the scourge of scurvy.[119]

Inevitably the acceptance and adoption of citric acid as a preventative against scurvy was to result in a shortage of citrus fruits. Thomas Trotter suggested that if lemon juice was unavailable, the strength of the small beer issued to the men should be doubled, but this was twice rejected by the Sick and Hurt Board.[120] However, the Board was more receptive to the idea of trying out alternatives. In the summer of 1800 trials of a crystallized form of lemon juice devised by a chemist Coxwell were carried out on *Superb, Ajax* and *Renown.*[121] Sir Roger Curtis at the Cape of Good Hope was also asked to conduct a trial but took no action.[122] The results of a trial ordered by Lord Hugh Seymour on the *Cambridge* in the West Indies were unfavourable.[123]

The Sick and Hurt Board was willing to carry out trials and investigate practical means of maintain the health of the navy.

Nelson himself accepted, following the advice of John Snipe, that 'it is necessary in order to remove an inveterate scurvy to give each man so afflicted six ounces of lemon juice, and two ounces of sugar.'[124] Prey to most of the diseases that afflicted the seaman, Nelson could not avoid 'the plague of the sea' when his crew were 'all knocked up with scurvy' on a two month's cruise on the *Albemarle* to Canada in 1782 before which there had been little time to re-provision and he and the officers had lived off salt beef. He commented that he was 'quite well; better than for a long time past' and put this down to the congenial climate of Canada after the Indies.[125] Nelson firmly believed that salt was the cause of scurvy and had given up using it on his food, but he was aware that citrus fruits could prevent it.[126]

Reacting to a temporary disruption to the provision of fresh supplies of citrus fruits and vegetables in the winter of 1804–5 caused by the Spanish entry into the war, he made sure that supplies of lemons and oranges from Sicily were available, remaining confident that 'we shall do very well' since 'I have always looked too far forward ever to be really distressed'.[127] Snipe and John Gray, surgeon of the hospital in Malta, were sent to Sicily to find new sources and collect 'on the spot every information relative to this valuable antiscorbutic', finding that 'if the person employed to see it squeezed, strictly does his duty, it will be of a superior quality to any I ever saw issued to His Majesty's fleets.'[128] The lemons were supplied by a Messina merchant John Broadbent, who already had a significant export business sending Sicilian lemons to Hamburg and St Petersburg. The fruit was then squeezed in Malta under the supervision of George Saunders, the dispenser of the Malta Naval Hospital, and then mixed with one tenth-part of brandy to preserve it before being stored in chestnut pipes. Nelson considered that 'immense sums might be saved … in their future purchase of this article, which I understand from the physician of the fleet, may be had in any quantity' and was eight times less expensive than inferior juice supplied by the Victualling Department.[129] Snipe judged this lemon juice from Sicily to be 'of the first quality.'[130] It was to have a good effect on the health of the fleet. Gillespie noted that 'several of the ship's companies appear to be slightly affected with scurvy indicating the want of fresh meat and vegetables, it is probable that this disposition would have been much more manifest had it not been for the supply of lemons and oranges lately furnished, the use of which has been attended with the most salutary effects.'[131]

Edward Jenner's vaccine against smallpox was quickly adopted by the Navy even though smallpox was not so grave a problem at sea as it was on land. However, the sailor was more vulnerable than the landsman when exposed to the smallpox virus as he had had little opportunity to develop any natural immunity. It was for this reason that Thomas Trotter, Physician to the Channel Fleet, became one of the earliest supporters of Jenner's cowpox vaccination and urged the Admiralty to issue an order for voluntary vaccination as 'there is scarcely a village that has not long shared its blessing', an exaggeration intended to warn the Admiralty against being backwards in adopting the latest in medicine. Trotter even proposed that the Navy should have its own source of cowpox for producing a vaccine when he suggested that 'some of the Gloucestershire cows should be transferred to the navy farm that surrounds the walls of Haslar Hospital for the purpose of inoculating the whole seamen of Spithead and thus prevent any return to that infection in our ships of war that we are now employed to defeat.'[132] Despite Trotter's lobbying it was not until September 1800, two years after the publication of Jenner's paper on vaccination that an order for voluntary vaccination was issued; a remarkably rapid response for any government department. Vaccination was now tried out in the Channel fleet after Veitch, the surgeon on the *Magnificent* had proposed it, having 'of late heard many respectable testimonies in its favour.'[133] Subsequently all marines joining up at Chatham were vaccinated.[134]

Vaccination was an improvement on the dangerous and uncertain method of variolation as a preventative method against smallpox popularised earlier in the eighteenth century by Lady Mary Wortley Montagu, who had observed its use in the Ottoman empire. Pustular matter from someone suffering from smallpox would be rubbed into the scarified skin of the person being inoculated against the infection. Before his enthusiastic adoption of Jenner's vaccination, Trotter had been keen to introduce inoculation into naval medical practice and boasted about having been the first to inoculate seaman volunteers in 1795.[135]

Earlier in the summer of 1800 Joseph Marshall and John Walker were sent out to join the Mediterranean fleet with a supply of Jenner's cowpox vaccine. The vaccine could only be kept alive by a chain of human carriers through arm to arm transfer. A black sailor on board their ship *Endymion* was vaccinated as the first link in the chain and from his arm several other members of the crew were vaccinated. One of them, a marine, almost died although not from the medical trial but when he fell overboard after getting drunk on spirits and had to be rescued by a young officer.[136] At Gibraltar, they vaccinated eleven men on *Endymion*, effectively starting the first naval vaccination programme, followed by mass vaccination of the Rock's garrison. Then on 19 October 1800 Vice-Admiral Lord Keith issued the order that 'any soldiers, seamen or marines in the Fleet, who may not have had the smallpox and wish to avoid that dreadful malady' should apply to Dr Marshall on board the flagship so that they could be inoculated with the cowpox which 'without pain or illness, or requiring particular diet or state of body, or leaving any marks, effectually excludes any possibility of the patient's ever being affected with the smallpox'.[137] However, almost as soon as the order had been issued, the fleet set sail and was dispersed making it impossible to proceed with mass vaccination.

Marshall proceeded to Menorca to continue with the programme of vaccination only to find an epidemic in progress with 'patients daily falling victims to its horrid ravages'. He also found that the local people in Port Mahon were receptive to the idea of some means of checking the disease, which could easily have spread from them to the seamen in port. He began a programme of vaccinating the local children and was so confident of the efficacy of his procedure that on the fourth day after vaccinating one of the children, he deliberately exposed him to the disease by inoculating him with smallpox at the bedside of a patient suffering from the disease without the boy falling ill in a public display for the benefit of the leading doctors and inhabitants of Mahon, who themselves 'became anxious to participate in this happy discovery, calling down blessings upon the head of its promulger to the world.'[138] On Malta, Marshall and Walker again found an outbreak of smallpox affecting the fleet and also took on the task of inoculating the civilian population to prevent them from infecting the army and navy stationed among them. The governor of Malta, Sir Alexander Ball commented that Marshall 'has performed this service, without receiving any pecuniary reward from me, as I conceive that the British Government know best how to appreciate and remunerate his services', a commendation which Marshall was keen to publicise.[139] Meanwhile, Walker and Marshall moved on to Sicily, and Naples, continuing to vaccinate the armed forces in their wake, Marshall not returning home until January 1802 and Walker continuing with his work in Egypt.[140]

The early adoption of Jenner's vaccine was rightly seen as a triumph for the Admiralty in safeguarding the health and efficiency of the naval forces. In February 1801, Trotter and some of his fellow naval surgeons presented a medal to Jenner depicting Apollo, god of medicine, presenting a young vaccinated seaman in full health to Britannia, who in turn holds out a civic crown to Jenner in homage to the importance of vaccination against smallpox and commemorating its introduction into the naval branch of public service. Trotter commented that 'although secluded by their office from the earliest communication with the progress of medical science', naval surgeons had taken a keen interest in Jenner's ideas and that 'the whole of your opinions and practice have excited uncommon attention amongst us.'[141]

Nelson was also to take a keen interest in vaccination. He was impressed by 'a full trial with the cow-pox' when he heard from an acquaintance that 'his child was inoculated with the cow-pox and afterwards reined in a house where a child had the smallpox the natural way, and did not catch it.' Convinced of its value, he nonetheless had problems in convincing Emma Hamilton that their daughter Horatia should be vaccinated even though he had stressed that 'the child is only feverish for two days; and only a slight inflammation of the arm takes place, instead of being all over scabs.'[142] His charge to Lady Hamilton to 'do you what you please' left her free to leave Horatia unvaccinated for a while, though when it was later undertaken Nelson could only 'wish I had all the smallpox for her, but I know the fever is the natural consequence'.[143]

Understanding the causes and consequences of a problem was believed in the age of Enlightenment to lead to improvement. Thomas Trotter praised the beneficial changes being introduced into naval medicine and believed that 'the complete mode of discipline carried out in His Majesty's ships at this time throughout the navy is, on the whole, so happily conducted for answering the purpose and securing the health of the ship's company'. The advantages of improving the conditions that caused ill-health were also seen as having wider advantages:

> It is not just health that is the fortunate result of these judicial forms of discipline: the morality of seamen is undergoing a revolution for the better. Nastiness, drunkenness and theft are almost banished from a man of war; the rough sailor is daily losing his ferocity of manners while the true courage which distinguishes the British tar is increased and blends itself with more polished notions of principle and honour.[144]

It was an optimistic assessment, but reflected the improving image of the seaman as wartime naval victories made him a more popular figure.

The success of preventative medicine in safeguarding the health of the Royal Navy is indicated by the low rate of sickness in the Mediterranean fleet on the eve of Trafalgar. Despite having pursued Villeneuve's combined fleet to the West Indies and back to the Mediterranean from May to July 1805, with little opportunity to resupply when the ships 'received not the smallest refreshment, or even a cup of water',[145] Nelson was able to report that 'the squadron is in the most perfect health, except some symptoms of scurvy'[146] and that 'we have lost neither officer nor man by sickness since we left the Mediterranean'.[147] Despite there being 276 seamen and marines on four ships showing signs of scurvy and who 'stand in need of the salutary aid of vegetables and fresh meat in order to re-establish a vigorous state of health', only seven of them were confined to the sick berths, and, after Nelson had arranged for fresh fruit, beef and water to be waiting for the fleet when it reached Tetuan, by mid-August 1805 'the number of scorbutics in the fleet is considerably diminished'.[148] In the two years before August 1805, only 110 seamen and marines had died and 141 been hospitalized in the entire Mediterranean fleet at a time when most of the ships had been continuously at sea. The sick list had averaged 190 in that period.[149] This was an impressive achievement in a fleet of ten or twelve ships of the line and two or three frigates carrying between 6,000 and 8,000 men. On the *Victory*, there had been only five deaths from fever, consumption and spinal injury and two hospital cases suffering from consumption in the period from 29 December 1804 to 20 October 1805.[150] The effect of preventative medicine in the navy during Nelson's career was just as impressive. Whereas the average sick rate during the American War of Independence had been 29.7 percent of official strength, during the French Revolutionary and Napoleonic Wars it was only 11.8 per cent.[151] It was an achievement to take pride in.

# 8

# Hospitals and Convalescence

As well as being concerned about preventative medicine, Nelson also showed a great interest in the naval hospitals to which his sick and wounded men were sent, offering his advice and opinions on hospital management down to the level of commenting on hygiene and nutrition. Nelson's interventions undoubtedly demonstrated his humane concern for the men under his command, although his influence was limited to the hospitals in the Mediterranean and his command did not extend to the great naval hospitals at home.

Nelson paid particular attention to the staffing of the hospitals, exercising patronage in ensuring that his favoured surgeons were rewarded with hospital posts and unsuitable members of hospital staff were dismissed. The purser at Malta proved unsatisfactory and was dismissed, as was a dishonest dispenser at Gibraltar whom Nelson considered to be 'a character so dangerous, not only to the individual, but also to the public service' as he was someone who had tried to advance his own interests by 'sacrificing the upright and honest man.'[1] Leonard Gillespie was to have been the first physician to be appointed to the hospital in Malta, but, instead of taking up the appointment, was selected to be Physician to the Mediterranean Fleet under Nelson. Michael Jefferson – who was surgeon on Nelson's first ship of the line *Agamemnon*, gave pain relief following the amputation of Nelson's right arm and treated his wound at the battle of the Nile – was rewarded for his loyalty with a shore posting to run the Malta hospital. However, he was soon relieved of his post as a result of his excessive drinking 'and by his own misconduct, he got out of a good employ, and he has seen another person, at Malta Hospital, put over his head'.[2]

Jefferson's replacement was another of Nelson's favoured surgeons, George Magrath, surgeon on the *Victory*, a man 'whom I admire for his great abilities every day I live', and Nelson recommended him as 'by far the most able medical man I have ever seen'.[3] When Emma Hamilton tried to persuade Nelson to get Jefferson a place on the *Victory*, he told her that 'with respect to Mr Jefferson, I can say nor do anything', especially as Magrath, 'the surgeon of the *Victory* is a very able, excellent man, and the ship is kept in the most perfect state of health; and I would not, if I could – but I cannot – do such an unjust act, as to remove him'.[4] In 1804, Nelson promoted Magrath to be surgeon of the hospital at Gibraltar.

Naval hospitals were essential in the Mediterranean and the West Indies where a lethal combination of scurvy, tropical disease and fever could decimate crews. Unable to make easy provision for its men on foreign shores, the navy had no choice but to establish its own hospitals. Hospitals were established in major ports such as Gibraltar, Port Mahon in Menorca, Halifax in Canada, the Cape of Good Hope, Madras, Antigua, Barbados and Bermuda. They were located wherever the navy was active. While hospitals may have been necessary, they were often overcrowded and, according to Gilbert Blane, 'crowding, filth and the mixture of diseases are the great causes of mortality in hospitals'.[5] Without them, though, the health of the navy overseas could not have been maintained.

The first purpose-built British naval hospital was opened on Isla del Rey in the middle of the harbour of Port Mahon in Menorca in 1711. Plans had been drawn up in 1709 for a hospital costing £9000 but it was never built and in 1710 Admiral Sir John Jennings ordered new plans. Here the sick were isolated unable to desert and away from the temptations of the bodegas of Port Mahon. The original hospital was single-storey with a chapel in the centre of the range flanked on each side by vaulted wards. The fourteen wards each housed twenty-four patients, offering beds for 336 wounded and sick seamen. New buildings in a more baroque style were erected during the second British occupation of Menorca. The new hospital constructed between 1771 and 1776 had two floors arranged around three sides of a courtyard in a u-shape and was surrounded by gardens. At the centre of the building was the square shaped tower that served as both a focal point for the hospital and a strategic viewing point over the harbour. There were 40 wards, a pharmacy, laundry, kitchen, rooms for the medical staff and bathrooms. Three natural wells supplied water. The hospital, with its 1,200 beds was abandoned when Spain regained Menorca in 1784, but in 1784 was reopened by the Spanish with a new chapel dedicated to St Charles. The hospital was regained by the British navy during the third occupation of Menorca between 1798 and 1802 before eventually becoming a Spanish military hospital.[6] There were differing views on the healthiness of the island location, known to the British as 'bloody island'. Admiral Jennings had praised it as 'a spacious and well-ventilated island' in 1711,[7] but by 1806 it was criticised for being 'very damp and intemperate', and 'uncomfortable for patients and staff, and quite unhealthy'.[8] Its main attraction as a British naval hospital was its comparative isolation in a busy harbour.

A second purpose-built naval hospital was built in 1741 at Gibraltar on a plateau a short way inland from Rosia Bay to confine the patients behind a shoulder of rock and remove them from the temptations of the town. Most of the building materials came from England, and craftsmen from Plymouth were contracted to work on the simple two-storey buildings ranged around a courtyard, accommodating 1000 men.[9] The hospital was regarded even by the Spanish as 'a magnificent work, spacious and designed in the form of an amphitheatre upon the living rock'.[10] As in the London hospitals of the time, there were long, interconnecting wards, but covered open-air verandas were an adaptation of the design suited to the local climate. The hospital had come under pressure during the great siege of Gibraltar from 1779 until 1783, but the buildings seem to have suffered from a lack of repair and maintenance and by 1788 were unfit to accommodate patients without essential repairs. With the outbreak of war with France in 1793, demands on the hospital increased, mainly for the reception of patients suffering from fevers.[11] The surgeon Edward Vaughan, dismissed as a 'sharp Westminster apothecary', was blamed for a lack of adequate medical care in the hospital, but he defended himself with the complaint that 'by far the majority of patients sent to these hospitals has laboured under complaints of long standing which have resisted medical treatment on board, and from their nature were likely to be considered objects of invaliding, rather than capable of receiving further benefit'. Furthermore, 'the utmost vigilance is required to preserve order and good government in the Naval Hospital at Gibraltar owing to the low price of wine and spirits and the disposition of the soldiers of the Garrison to convey liquor into the hospital'.[12] Vaughan was dismissed in 1802, but his successor William Burd was soon involved in a quarrel with the dispenser Paul Poggioli who accused him of 'embezzlement of medicines', a dispute that was never resolved when Burd died in the 1804 yellow fever epidemic.[13] Burd was also accused of converting the hospital into a bawdy house by hiring prostitutes as nurses and allowing the premises to become so filthy that if the dirt 'was up to his knees ... he would not see it'.[14] It was little wonder that Nelson wanted to dismiss Poggioli, replacing him with a competent surgeon he could trust like George Magrath. Ironically, this promotion was to deprive Magrath of the fame that would have come from having taken part in the battle of *Trafalgar* and the greater promotion awarded to Magrath's successor as the surgeon on *Victory* caring for the dying Nelson. By 1806 he had been transferred to the Mill Prison Hospital outside Plymouth and was dependent for promotion on a recommendation from his friend William Beatty at the peak of Beatty's fame as Nelson's surgeon at Trafalgar.[15]

In Malta, Nelson took great interest in the establishment of a permanent naval hospital. The island had been captured from the French in September 1800, two years after the French had taken it from the Order of the Knights of St John, and had a strategic importance at the crossroads of the Mediterranean, making it an ideal location for a British naval base. Nelson considered the temporary naval hospital set up at the Armeria in Vittoriosa to be totally unsuitable for a hospital and told John Snipe, whom he sent to Malta in 1803 to investigate possible sites for a permanent hospital, that 'the situation of the former Hospital at Malta was particularly unhealthy, it is my directions that you do not suffer that house to be received as an Hospital, or any other which, from situation, you may judge improper; but endeavour to procure a convenient and well-appointed house, in an airy and healthy situation for a Naval Hospital *pro tempore*.'[16] The Armeria, with its long corridors close to the ships at anchor in the Grand Harbour, originally had been built as an armoury before serving as a civil hospital. George Watson was a patient in the hospital at the Armeria and had nothing but praise for the surgeon, John Allen, and for one of the nurses, who was 'a generous kind hearted creature, and very fit to be a nurse to sailors as she was not overburdened with delicacy, and, being of a pleasing disposition, she could accommodate herself to the healthy as well as the sick'.[17] However, he was not so impressed when an insane marine chased a black seaman around the ward with a surgeon's knife before the other patients were able to overpower him, nor when two one-armed patients fought each other and fell on to Watson, breaking his thigh.[18]

Snipe believed that he had found the perfect spot for Nelson's preferred option of a completely new hospital in 'the Palace of Bighay which is a most desirable situation for a naval hospital, in summer it is cooled by a refreshing sea breeze, and in winter perfectly dry.' There was a convenient landing place for patients to be brought over from their ships and the building enjoyed 'sufficient ground belonging to it, in a high state of cultivation, to produce abundance of vegetables for the use of the sick, and if lemon and orange trees were planted, the Fleet, on this station, might be amply supplied with those anti-scorbutic fruit.'[19] The villa of Bighi, built in 1675 as a country residence for Giovanni Bichi, Knight of St John and nephew of Pope Alexander VII, was located on an impressive promontory overlooking the Grand Harbour of Valetta. Napoleon was said to have boasted that the site was perfect for his palace once Europe, Asia and Africa had all been subjugated to his Empire.[20] While Snipe had 'carefully examined every spot in and about the Harbour of Malta, and there is no situation so well calculated for a naval hospital as Bighay, it being nearly insulated, and some distance from any other houses', the existing buildings were inadequate for housing 500 patients; and, it would be necessary to build two wings on either side of the main palace buildings as well as other buildings for a dispensary, kitchen, storehouses and wash houses. Snipe reminded Nelson that 'there is no part of the service that requires more to be regarded than the choice of a proper situation for a hospital, and the right management of it, on which the health and strength of a fleet so much depends, for in wet and unwholesome seasons, if any infectious diseases get in into the hospital, which probably might have been prevented by proper care, they often weaken a fleet more than the sword of the enemy.'[21] Nelson, needing no convincing, agreed that adjacent land was needed to extend the buildings and provide gardens in which convalescent sailors and marines could enjoy exercise and fresh air, 'for with the ground it is the most healthy and eligible situation in Valetta Harbour; without it, confined within four bare walls, it would be the worst place in the place, for the heat would be intolerable.'[22]

Although a strong advocate for a new naval hospital in Malta, Nelson accepted that 'if we give up Malta it will be unnecessary to make a naval hospital'. In the meantime, the former Slaves' Prison in Valletta was converted into a naval hospital.[23] The Armeria was again reoccupied in 1819 although no more suitable than it had been when Nelson had condemned it in 1803. However Nelson's plans for Bighi were not forgotten and in 1829 it was finally decided that the villa should be converted into a naval hospital. Snipe's recommendations for the construction of two pavilions on either side of the villa were carried out; two wings with commodious balconies were built in the Doric style and the original villa was modified to harmonise architecturally with the new edifice.[24] A wide and high passage ran under the whole building; this was first used during the construction works for transporting construction materials by mule and later provided convenient communication links for the staff.[25] Although not opened until 1832, the grandiose buildings of the Royal Naval Hospital at Bighi, with its commanding position overlooking the Grand Harbour, was very much Nelson's in inspiration and formed an appropriate physical monument to his interest in naval hospitals.

Standards for the hospitals established overseas had been laid down by the Sick and Hurt Board in 1785. They should occupy open, elevated airy sites with an airing ground for convalescents. Each patient was to be allowed a minimum of 600 cubic feet of air. This was less than was allowed at the British naval hospitals of Haslar and Plymouth, which allowed a generous 864 cubic feet, but these were considered special cases as 'these are permanent hospitals built for long duration and at great expense'. It was not considered important whether the sides or heads of the beds were against the walls and cubicles were not to be built to shield a patient from the 'dying looks of his companion' as these might obstruct the air.[26] These standards were to be followed both overseas and in hospitals overseas built in response to the wars of the 1790s and 1800s.

Nelson's concern for the men in the naval hospitals extended to all aspects of the management of the hospitals themselves. The governor of the Gibraltar Hospital, Lieutenant William Pemberton was advised to give 'very strict and particular attention to the cleanliness and comfort of the patients.'[27] Nelson stressed to him the importance of attention to hygiene, a nutritious diet and a generous staffing ratio of one nurse to ten patients. Patients were allowed a pint of broth, a pound of mutton and a pound of fresh vegetables and fruit each day.[28] The surgeon of the Malta Hospital John Gray was given instructions to 'supply the necessary quantity of milk to the patients in their tea morning and afternoon' regardless of any additional costs that might imply.[29] Nelson's interest and concern extended to this minute level.

Regulations for the conduct of hospitals on foreign stations, published in 1809, formalised the management of the naval hospitals overseas. The surgeons were paid £500 annually with a free residence. They were expected to be constant in attendance, with both morning and evening visits to the sick, and were to act win conjunction with the the Agent for the purchase of stores and for the renting of sick quarters. Bedding was changed twice a week, and each new patient was to be examined and 'gently washed by a nurse', before being put to bed. If the ailment was infectious, the patient was to be given hospital clothing, old clothes being boiled or burned. Only those who could not be cured on board were to be accepted in the hospital, and no rupture cases were to be retained on shore once they had been issued with a truss. Every patient was to have first been issued a 'smart ticket' recommending him for treatment by the surgeon of his ship, and when discharged he was to be given a certificate or a recommendation to Greenwich Hospital. The dispenser, whose necessities for the sick included wine, porter, sugar, rice, sago, cocoa, arrow root, oranges, lemon juice, honey, barley, splints, trusses, sponges, lint and flannel, was to provide a prescription for each basket of medicines placed at the head of each bed. The wards were to be kept in a state of 'the most perfect cleanliness', officers and men, infectious and convalescent patients being carefully separated. Sponges and bandages were to be boiled or destroyed after use. The surgeon was given two complete sets of instruments, as well as the medicines he required. Finally, he was positively forbidden to practice privately, or to accept gratuities.[30]

Nelson, although he took a strong interest in the naval hospitals serving his fleet in the Mediterranean, had little contact with the great naval hospitals at home. It was only after 1746 that permanent naval hospitals were established in Britain. Up to then the navy had relied on the contracting system, placing the burden of finding board, lodging and medical care for sick and wounded sailors on the ports at which they were landed. St Bartholomew's and St Thomas's Hospitals were force to set aside beds for naval patients sent to London for care and treatment. The foundation of naval hospitals – at Haslar near Gosport and Plymouth – in the mid-eighteenth century recognized the need for a new solution to the problem of how to provide hospital care for the seaman.

Haslar was 'a strong, durable plain building consisting of three stories; the same to form a quadrangle with a spacious piazza within, the out fronts to be decent but not expensive' with attention given to 'the disposition, situation and dimensions of the wards for sick men, the convenience of light and air; to avoid narrowness as also crowding the beds too close together.'[31] Theodore Jacobsen, architect of the new Foundling Hospital in London, was appointed as architect and construction work began in 1746 though it was not to be completed until 1761, by which time only three sides of the proposed quadrangle had been built as a result of government pressure to economise. The only ornamentation was a pediment of Portland stone, displaying the arms of George II and personifications of Commerce and Navigation. Within the high walls of the hospital were houses for the officers of the institution, storehouses, workshops, a chapel dedicated to St Luke and a burial ground.[32] Haslar was built to house 1,500 patients in 114 wards, but by 1755 there were as many as 1,800 and by 1790 2,100 crowded together in cramped conditions.[33] It may have been one of the largest hospitals in Europe but Haslar, for all its solid and sober magnificence, was not always able to meet easily the demands placed upon it. Nevertheless, it still impressed visitors. When the physician George Pinckard was shown around Haslar in 1806, he 'felt it an honour to England that so noble an institution should offer, to our brave tars, the comforts required in sickness' and that 'the hospital like so many others of this island, from the grandeur of the edifice, might be mistaken for a palace.'[34] He was impressed that it had been built 'in an open, airy situation near the sea'.[35]

Work on the Royal Naval Hospital at Plymouth was not begun until 1758 (during the Seven Years War), but was relatively quickly completed in 1762 with accommodation for 1200 patients in sixty wards in detached blocks arranged around a courtyard and connected by a single-storey Tuscan colonnade, on the roof of which convalescents could take exercise and enjoy the fresh air. John Howard, the prison and hospital reformer, praised the Plymouth hospital for having detached ward blocks 'for the purpose of admitting freer circulation of air, as also of classing the several disorders in such manner as may best prevent the spread of contagion.'[36] This was also considered an admirable feature by Jacques Tenon and Charles-Augustin Coulomb when they visited Plymouth in July 1787 on behalf of a French Royal Commission to investigate foreign hospitals and declared that 'in not one of the hospitals of France and England, we would say in the whole of Europe, except the Plymouth Hospital are the individual buildings destined to receive patients as well ventilated and as completely isolated.'[37]

Haslar and Plymouth could be controlled more easily than the overseas hospitals because they were under the direct authority of the Navy rather than contracted out to an agent. The naval hospitals were isolated and had features in common with prisons to prevent the recovered seaman from deserting. Haslar, isolated from Gosport by marshes, was only accessible by an often impassable cart-track or by ferry. In 1755 it was necessary for the Admiralty to issue 'Protections' to the ferrymen to safeguard them against the Press Gangs active in the area just as it had earlier had to protect from impressment the carpenters, bricklayers and labourers employed to actually build the hospital.[38] The patients themselves were conveyed over from their ships anchored off Spithead to a specially constructed jetty and then transferred to the hospital in 'cradles on wheels'. Tall walls, twelve feet in height, surrounded the hospital to keep the sick seamen in rather than intruders out. There were iron grilles on the lower windows and the wards were locked at night. Lamps were 'placed on the outside wall of the Hospital, and sentinels fixed around the same by which means if the latter do their duty, the patients may be as effectually secured as on board an hospital ship and their cure sooner completed.'[39]

The patients were also made more conspicuous if they did manage to escape from the hospital by the issue of a 'Hospital Dress which would greatly tend to the people's recovery.' A hospital uniform would have been much cleaner than the men's own clothing, but would also enable the staff to control their movements. On arrival patients were bathed in hot soapy water, issued with clean hospital clothing and had their own clothes fumigated before they were admitted. Since these hospital uniforms were 'to be taken into the nurses' cabins when the men are in bed and delivered to them in the morning, they could not then escape but in their shirts.'[40] Nothing, however, could deter determined men from trying to escape down the latrines and through the sewers, which were also used for smuggling in liquor by the nurses just as keen on the solace of alcohol as their patients.[41] In 1794, 226 of the 8949 men at Haslar that year deserted. Men would immobilise the locks on the ward doors with sand, lower themselves from the upper windows with bed sheets and elude the guards to scale the perimeter wall. Such ingenuity and agility could be deemed the result of success-ful treatment at Haslar.[42]

The men sent to the hospitals were cases which the surgeons on their own ships could not deal with and 'lacked any prospect of being cured on board'. Among those men discharged by Robert Young from the *Ardent* in June and July 1797 were: Alexander Mitchell, a seaman diagnosed as insane; Charles Cain, a seaman with a maimed hand; John Halloran, a marine with venereal disease; and surgeon's mate John Todd who had scurvy.[43] After the battle of Camperdown, Young discharged to hospital 'those who survived to undergo amputation or be dressed'.[44] It was a miscellaneous assortment of cases but repre-sentative of the men being sent to the hospitals. Archaeological excavations in the cemetery area of Haslar have revealed that a significant number of men died as a result of amputation operations that went wrong, probably as a result of excessive blood loss or infection, and from scurvy.[45] There was also a danger that malin-gerers would fake their own illnesses 'to be an object for invaliding'. 'In his determination to watch for every opportunity for affecting his escape', such a man 'employs caustics to produce ulcers; inflates the urethra to give the scrotum the appearance of hernia; and drinks a decoction of tobacco to bring on emaciation, sickness at stomach and quick pulse.'[46]

The naval hospitals, unlike contemporary civil ones which often refused to admit chronic illnesses or fever cases, had no option but to admit all types of medical case, both sailors and marines, who were 'to be received and taken care of upon the same footing with seamen' just as at sea 'marines, sick or wounded are to be taken the same care of, by the surgeon of the ship, that the seamen are.'[47] In accordance with James Lind's belief that 'certain types of contagion automatically dissipate when patients are well separated' and that when this was done 'their range of infection is limited', patients at Haslar were separated according to how they had been diagnosed. Patients recovering from measles, scabies, syphilis, gonorrhoea and smallpox had their own galleries for walking in and had the name of the relevant disease they were suffering from written on the back of their hospital dress in case they tried to escape. Scurvy cases were also segregated, not because they were considered contagious, but because they were under a special therapeutic regime of vegetables, citrus fruit, wine, malt and 'land air' at a time when sea rations and sea air were considered responsible for their illness. Men suffering particularly malignant fevers and fluxes were isolated in fever wards at the far ends of the wings so as 'to cut off communications with other patients'.[48] The most contagious patients were assigned to wards on the top floors of the buildings, the less infectious to the middle wards and the convalescents to the ground floor convenient for their promenades.[49] At Plymouth too, particular cases were assigned to particular ward blocks with the most infectious again on the upper floors. The insane were also segregated at both hospitals before being quickly despatched to Bethlem Hospital in London.[50]

Daily routine in hospital was just as important as at sea. Patients were woken and washed at dawn. Beds were made, chamber pots emptied and the wards scrubbed and cleaned. The patients were washed daily, had their shirts and body linen changed twice a week and were regularly shaved. At 8 o'clock every morning in the summer and an hour later in winter, the assistant dispensers would inspect the wards, before the ward rounds of the physician or surgeon, accompanied by the dispenser and apothecary.[51] Thomas Trotter, second physician at Haslar in 1793–94, thought that the washing of men in bath tubs in the wards was demeaning and proposed that separate bath houses be built so the men could 'bathe like gentlemen' in facilities that might become 'as famous as those of Baiae in the days of ancient Rome.' He also wanted to improve diet with fresh milk, eggs and fruit, for 'how grateful is a dish of salad after a long cruise' and 'how delicious an apple, a pear or a plum after long sickness on board?' In order to do this and make Haslar self-sufficient, he recommended opening a farm in the grounds.[52] Trotter expected the nurses to be kind to their patients despite the strict discipline, as 'it is the lot of the sailor and soldier to languish under affliction and disease far from the cheering support and watchful attendance of his friends and relations; and hence a charge of another kind devolves on their physician, that nurses and others may be tender and assiduous in their respective duties.'[53]

In a hospital of the size of Haslar or Plymouth, it was not always easy to maintain the expected standards. Members of the medical staff were given permission to conduct their own private practices and were often neglectful absentees from their duties. At Plymouth, there was such neglect of the hospital by medical officers that at times a wounded man could not be admitted to the hospital because there was no one there to open the gate, admit him or treat him because the surgeon was away attending a 'gentleman of great fortune' in Cornwall, causing Thomas Trotter, Physician to the Fleet, to muse that 'by an irresistible impulse of imagination, the ghosts of so many thousands of brave men rise to my view, who have fallen into premature death by unprincipled neglect.'[54] This problem of absentee medical staff was solved in 1805 when hospital staff were forbidden to carry on civilian practices. Yet even when they were present in the hospital, the surgeons were not always competent at performing their duties. Stephen Love Hammick was accused of 'unskilfully performing several operations' at the Royal Hospital in Plymouth. Charges of having misdiagnosed 'a black man named Cook' were dismissed by Hammick, showing scant concern for the unfortunate patient's suffering, with the comment that 'whether the tumour was or was not subelavian aneurysm is merely a matter of conjecture'. In another case, that of Charles Marriner, whose leg he had amputated, he attributed Marriner's subsequent medical problems not to the operation but that 'in getting about he fell down, injured it and broke it up again.' He resented the slur on his competence brought against him by Mr Veitch, second surgeon to the Hospital, and asked 'what opinion must be formed of a man capable of entertaining the idea that any professional man could be so base and lost to feeling as to suppose I gave an opinion to mislead, is nothing more or less than the charge of wishing to commit murder on a fellow creature, the very insinuation makes me shudder.'[55]

An inspection of Haslar in 1794 concluded that 'the patients were in general well satisfied with the attendance given them, and also with respect to change of clean shirts, which they have twice a week'. However, they were less happy that their own clothes removed from them for fumigation were frequently lost and 'in many instances men, the whole of whose clothes have been lost, have been detained for weeks in the Hospital under the idea of looking for them'. Moreover, although the wards and bedding were clean, they were fumigated with inefficient fumigating lamps and the water closets 'smell offensively, and the floors seats and walls are constantly wet'. The dispensing of medicine was left to the nurses, many of whom were illiterate, with the result that 'the medicines prescribed for one man may be given to another or indeed not given at all.'[56]

The nursing staff was at first recruited from the wives and widows of sailors and marines. Despite it being stipulated that they should be 'the most sober, careful and diligent that can be had', at Haslar they had a reputation for stealing from their patients, forging wills and smuggling gin 'tied around their waists and under their stays in bladders'.[57] They were forbidden to undertake any duties which were considered the preserve of the surgeon. In 1805, Nurse Mary Bill was threatened with dismissal by one of the surgeons, Mr Delhuntry, who 'flew into a great passion at me' when he found her about to dress the ulcer of one of her patients who 'complained to me of being in great pain' at a time when neither of the surgeons were in the hospital.[58] Both she and Sarah Perrott, who had also been at the receiving end of Mr Delhuntry's temper when he forbade her to dress wounds, preferred the other surgeon Mr Tompson 'who treats the patients with great tenderness and attention.'[59] The patients themselves were not always so certain that the nurses would show kindness to them.

In 1780, Admiral Barrington was appointed to inspect the abuses at Haslar and recommended that control of the hospital be vested in a senior naval officer, 'used to command and well versed in the management of seamen', rather than in a physician because 'the patients at Haslar are too numerous and ungovernable, the character and authority of the present officers are without dignity or respect.'[60] After the pioneering James Lind's retirement as physician in 1783, a post he had held since 1758, the administrative control of the Hospital was transferred to a naval officer and the medical governance to Lind's son John, but it was not until 1795 that the real control of the hospitals at both Haslar and Plymouth passed out of medical control to a Governor with the rank of post captain. From 1795 naval discipline became paramount in the hospitals at home.[61]

At a time when status was as important in naval hospitals as on-board ship, the appointment of a serving naval officer as Governor of a naval hospital after 1795 resulted in friction between the executive and medical officers. William Yeo was appointed Governor of Haslar in 1795 and remained in post until 1808. Captain Richard Creyke was appointed Governor at Plymouth in 1795 to prevent 'in the most effective manner the inconveniences which have frequently been felt by the want of proper discipline and subordination.'[62] He immediately restricted private practice by the medical staff, more strictly enforced attendance at chapel, and ordered that a screen be erected in the chapel to separate the nurses from the men. When the medical assistants protested about Creyke's crude handling of the resignation of an assistant dispenser, he produced a letter from the Sick and Hurt Board threatening them with dismissal if they ever again questioned the authority of the Governor or showed him any signs of insolence or disrespect towards him. Creyke was angry when 'they showed no signs of sorrow for their improper conduct, made no apology for their contumacious behaviour' and continued to act like 'inconsiderate young men.'[63] He also banned Thomas Trotter in his role as Physician of the Channel Fleet from visiting the hospital without the permission of Dr Walker, physician to the Plymouth Hospital, after Trotter had challenged Walker's diagnosis of patients and had criticised the running of the hospital.[64] Trotter had claimed that men were being sent back to their ships with infected clothing and bedding after delays in treatment. The men were also given poor food and nauseous wine while in the hospital.[65] Creyke would accept no interference. In his opinion discipline in the hospital should be as stringent as on a ship where the captain's actions went unchallenged.

At Haslar, Captain Charles Craven felt that his authority as Governor, in succession to Yeo, was being challenged by the irregular arrivals and departures of a Lieutenant Gullifer, serving in the Channel fleet, disregarding Craven's rule that no one should enter or leave the hospital gates after ten in the evening. Gullifer was coming at all hours to visit his wife who kept house for her father Jacob Silver, who was in charge of the wing for lunatics. Eventually Gullifer was forbidden to live with his wife or even enter the hospital site, although on two separate occasions in July 1817 and September 1818 Craven allowed him entry to see his wife after she gave birth. The couple could only see each other away from Haslar. Craven unsympathetically considered that 'the conduct of Lieutenant Gullifer by no means merits the least indulgence from me and it is his own fault that his wife lives separately from him.'[66]

Although Haslar and Plymouth remained the principal naval hospitals at home, the strains of the naval warfare of the 1790s and 1800s and the demands of the sick of the Channel and North Sea fleets necessitated the establishment of smaller, temporary hospitals at Deal, Sheerness, Yarmouth and Dartmouth. Both the hospital built at Deal and the one at Great Yarmouth had 300 beds each. The hospital at Deal was first built in 1795 and then rebuilt in 1811.[67] The Royal Naval Hospital at Great Yarmouth lasted longer than most of these hospitals. Built by the Admiralty at a cost of £120,000 between 1809 and 1811, it remained in use until 1815, with both naval and military casualties from the battle of Waterloo being buried in the hospital square. It then became an army barracks until 1844 when it was used as a military lunatic asylum before the Admiralty claimed it back in 1854 for use as a naval hospital.[68]

Since the seventeenth century it had been the custom for each fleet to have a hospital ship to which the long term sick and wounded could be transferred. These were usually vessels that were about to be decommissioned, but generally were fit for their function. The mutineers at Sheerness in April 1797 were concerned about 'the state of the sick on board H.M. ships', but had no complaints about the *Spanker*, hospital ship for the Channel fleet, other than the quality of the food with its weak beer and coarse bread. Their main concern was the diseased state of the new recruits on the flagship *Sandwich*.[69] In 1802, the hospital ships, *Argonaut*, *Sussex* and *Matilda* were condemned for their ancient hulls, rotting timbers and low deck space.[70] Hospital ships also acted as the base of the Physician of the Fleet, as well as the surgeon, his three assistants and six landsmen nurses who dealt with the sick. It was the responsibility of the Physician of the Fleet to visit the other ships, inspect the surgeons' medical chests and journals, and prepare a weekly health report for the admiral. He lacked any direct responsibility over the surgeons, who were answerable to their captains, but was expected to encourage high medical standards.[71]

The hospital ship on which Thomas Trotter was based as Physician to the Channel Fleet in 1794 was perhaps typical of such ships. Built in 1778 with two decks and 44 guns, the 879–ton *Charon* was an old-fashioned cruising ship too small and too slow to be effective in naval warfare in the 1790s. It had been converted in to a hospital ship with one of the decks disarmed although the other deck still contained artillery and the crew of 120 included gunners. There were also marines on board not only to fight the enemy but to keep discipline among the crew and patients. The hospital was staffed by a surgeon, two mates, a matron, five nurses, three loblolly boys, six washerwomen and a baker.[72] Favoured fleet physicians such as Gilbert Blane and Leonard Gillespie were based on the flagship as part of the entourage of their admiral. Being on board the hospital ship, first the *Charon* and then the *Medusa* (until it was converted to a troop transport ship without the fleet physician being consulted) meant that for Trotter 'from my first appointment to the last hours in which I served in the fleet, my utmost exertions were employed to give the sick all the comforts which a sea life is capable of'. He prided himself that 'the hospital ship of the fleet was even stored with delicacies and a bill of fare such as no hospital in Europe at this moment can equal.'[73]

Despite the provision of hospital ships and naval hospitals, it sometimes remained necessary for local agents to be contracted to provide local care in the ports by the Commissioners of the Sick and Hurt Board, who were responsible for overseeing the health of seamen, administering navy pensions and looking after prisoners of war until their role was subsumed into the Transport Board in 1806. In 1799 when the Channel fleet anchored in Tor Bay, the sick had to be taken in open carts to the nearest sick quarters at Dartmouth where fever patients were crammed two in one bed. It proved necessary to set up a temporary hospital in the village of Torquay attended by local doctors as the accommodation in Dartmouth was inadequate to the demands made upon it.[74] Sick quarters and local doctors contracted to act as surgeon agents continued to be necessary to supplement the naval hospitals.

Officers were spared the indignities of treatment in the large naval hospitals until the beginning of the nineteenth-century but tended to be quartered in private houses and visited there by medical doctors. Nelson was assiduous in visiting his wounded officers, especially his protégés. In August 1801, his distress at the failure of an attack on Boulogne was increased by the wounds suffered by Captain Edward Parker and Lieutenant Frederick Parker; he wrote to Emma Hamilton that 'you will not believe how I am suffering and not well into the bargain'. Both young men were suffering from serious leg wounds and were lodged together in lodgings in Deal under the care of Dr Andrew Baird, sent to attend them by Lord St Vincent. Nelson visited the other wounded in the hospital at Deal, but went to see his two wounded officers as often as his duties would permit. At first Parker, whose thigh had been fractured, seemed to be recovering, but his leg had to be amputated close to the hip, and he died after four weeks in September 1801. In this time he became dependent on Nelson's visits for support and 'he got hold of my hand and said that he could not bear me to leave and cried like a child.'[75] He looked on Nelson as 'my friend, my nurse, my attendant, my patron, my protector, nay him whom the world cannot find words sufficient to praise.'[76]

Naval officers also flocked to the spas for their convalescence. Bath was the favoured resort, a fashionable town where the pleasures of society mingled with the pains of medical treatment. Patronised by all levels by royalty, aristocracy and gentry, its sulphurous thermal spring waters were said to relieve everything from gout to infertility, jaundice to deafness, and could be drunk in the Pump Room or bathed in up to the neck in one of the five pools. The town had a large population of doctors and apothecaries, both respectable physicians and quacks. Society gathered to gossip in the Pump Room and coffee houses. Intellectual stimulation was found in the circulating library, philosophical society and bookshops. Entertainment was sought in the Theatre Royal and Assembly Rooms. Although gambling was banned, it could easily be sought out, as could the prostitutes who roamed the streets. It was claimed that 'no place in a full season affords so brilliant a circle of polite company as Bath. The young, the old, the grave, the gay, the infirm, and the healthy, all resort to this vortex of amusement' in which 'ceremony, beyond the usual rules of politeness, is totally exploded'.[77]

Nelson was in no condition for such pleasures. He was there for the sake of his health only while convalescing from the San Juan expedition in 1781. He was 'so ill since I have been here that I was obliged to be carried to and from bed, with the most excruciating tortures, but, thank God, I am upon the mending hand.' His health regime was strict and he was 'physicked three times a day, drink the waters three times, and bathe every other night.'[78] He also abstained from wine. He was confident that he would soon be returned to good health as 'I most sincerely wish to be employed, and hope it will not be long.'[79] Bath was a favourite resort of Nelson's wife Fanny and father Edmund and he was to return to it in later years. Conscious of the benefits of spa treatment and following his eye injury at Calvi, Nelson went to take the medicinal waters at Pisa, accompanied in his convalescence by Josiah Nisbet and William Hoste.[80] Most convalescent naval officers, though, were more familiar with the spa resorts at home than abroad.

As an alternative to Bath, Tunbridge Wells was popular with similar opportunities to drink the spa waters and enjoy society at 'the general rendezvous of gaiety and politeness during the summer'.[81] However, there was an alternative to the spas in the new seaside watering places that had become fashionable during the reign of George III. Weymouth had become popular after George III recuperated there in 1789, taking regular dips in the sea from his bathing machine when 'he had no sooner popped his royal head under water than a band of music, concealed in a neighbouring machine, struck up 'God save Great George our King'.[82] His son the Prince of Wales patronised Brighton. In these newly fashionable resorts, sea bathing was promoted as having curative properties, having been popularised by the Sussex physician Richard Russell for whom 'the whole habit of body ought to be strengthened and rendered firm by cold bathing in the sea' and who believed the salt water of Brighton to be superior to the spa waters of Bath.[83]

In Jane Austen's novel *Persuasion*, the naval officer 'Captain Harville had never been in good health since a severe wound which he received two years before' and had gone to Lyme, 'which in the season is animated with bathing-machines and company', for the sake of his health. With him and his wife was a fellow officer the melancholy Captain Benwick, who was pining for the death of his fiancée, Harville's sister. Lyme had been chosen as suitable for the recuperation of both men, for 'Captain Harville had taken his present house for half a year: his taste, and his health, and his fortune all directing him to a residence unexpensive and by the sea; and the grandeur of the country, and the retirement of Lyme in winter, appeared exactly adapted to Captain Benwick's state of mind.[84]

Such gentility was not available to the ordinary seaman. Destitute sailors invalided out of service were a common sight in the streets. While the loss of a limb might not adversely affect the opportunities open to Nelson, a seaman who lost a leg or arm was unlikely to be able to continue in naval service and was compelled to resort to begging or the benevolence of a naval charity. The Royal Hospital at Greenwich had been established in 1694 for 'the relief and support of seamen serving on board the ships or vessels belonging to the Navy Royal' who 'by reason of age, wounds or disabilities shall be incapable of further service at sea, and be unable to maintain themselves',[85] and was the Royal Navy's equivalent of Chelsea Royal Hospital for army pensioners and Les Invalides in Paris. Robert Robertson found that 'some pensioners are extremely querulous, and run on, repeating the tedious history of their complaints again and again' and that 'some complain of having nothing to drink when several sorts of drink are beside them'. In his opinion the Greenwich pensioners 'retain little of the character of the sailor'.[86]

Although Nelson had declared that our grateful country is not unmindful of the sufferings of her gallant defenders' and described wounds as 'the marks of honour', he could not prevent wounded men from falling into poverty though he did what he could to help them.[87] He ordered the captains and surgeons in his fleet to issue the wounded with certificates that would enable them to claim pensions and promised to recommend casualties to the Patriotic Fund set up by Lloyd's of London to reward valour and assist injured officers, soldiers and seamen.[88] Lloyd's, handling marine insurance, had regularly established subscription lists for the relief of the widows and children of sailors killed in service, starting with a list for the dependents of those drowned when the *Royal George* capsized in 1782. Subscriptions had later been taken at Lloyd's for the United Society for the Relief of Widows and Children of Seamen, Soldiers, Marines and Militiamen, established in 1792, but subscription lists had continue to be opened following major naval battles that generated large 'butchers' bills'. After the Glorious First of June, £21,282 was raised. The Patriotic Fund, founded in 1803, was not specific to any particular battle or disaster and soon attracted support outside Lloyd's from the major City livery companies, the Bank of England, the East India Company and the Sun Fire Office.[89]

Yet for many of the disabled the only recourse was to the mercy of the parish under the poor law or to a state of beggary. Nelson was aware of the problems facing the poor on land and in 1792, near the end of five years spent on half-pay on land, took an interest in the plight of the Norfolk labourer. With his characteristic paternalism based on his Christian beliefs and his conception of the duties of a naval officer, he was concerned that the poor labourer was 'really in want of everything to make life comfortable'. They had 'not quite two-pence a day for each person, and to drink nothing but water, for beer our poor labourers never taste, unless they are tempted, which is too often the case, to go to the alehouse'.[90] The plight of the disabled seamen unable to work was even worse. They made not have made the ultimate sacrifice of their lives, but their service had reduced them to poverty and wasted lives.

# 9
# Trafalgar: Nemesis and Apotheosis

'Ah, Mr Beatty, you can do nothing for me. I have but a short time to live; my back is shot through.'[1] Nelson was well aware that there was nothing that his surgeon William Beatty could do for him when the injured vice-admiral was brought down to the cockpit of the *Victory* at the height of the battle of Trafalgar, as indeed was the surgeon. Nelson had been struck down on his quarter deck by a French musket ball at quarter past one on the afternoon of 21 October 1805. He died at half past four, two hours and forty-five minutes since he had been shot.[2] It was the manner of his death in the hour of victory that sealed Nelson's lasting fame.

Death and military glory went together, but there seemed something particularly tragic when it was the architect of victory who died at his moment of triumph. Death rather than survival attracts most attention. In his celebration of Lord Howe's victory on the Glorious First of June 1794, the painter Mather Brown depicted Lord Howe on the quarter-deck of the *Queen Charlotte*, dressed in full dress uniform rather than the old civilian coat and woollen knitted cap he actually wore during the battle, but the main focus of the painting is the dying Lieutenant Neville of the Queen's Regiment, fatally wounded when a cannon ball from the 'Jacobin' struck the sword he was holding and drove the hilt through his waistcoat into his blood-stained side. The blue-jacketed naval lieutenant Walter Lock holds Neville up by the shoulders, assisted by the kneeling Captain Tudor and Major Isaac. Sir Andrew Snape Douglas, flag-captain of the *Queen Charlotte* holds a hand over his own wounded forehead while he is supported by another lieutenant. A shortage of marines was compensated for by a military contingent aboard the ship. The whole painting shows the cost of victory while still showing Howe as a heroic figure.[3] Nelson, by contrast, was fated to be both the hero and victim in 1805.

The fatal shot came as Nelson paced up and down the quarterdeck between the steering wheel beneath the poop and the hatchway to the lower decks. A French marksman from the mizzen of the *Redoubtable* fired a shot at the close range of forty to seventy feet and hit him in the left shoulder, striking his epaulette and penetrating his chest. He was not the only casualty from the heavy fire of musketry from the tops of the French ship 'with destructive effect to the *Victory's* crew'.[4] In addition to the musketry fire, about 200 grenades were lobbed by the French sailors onto the forecastle, quarterdeck and poop. Within fifteen minutes of Nelson having been wounded, nineteen of the crew of the *Victory* had been killed, including the captain of marines William Adair, and twenty-two wounded.[5] Nelson collapsed on the very spot at which he had witnessed his secretary John Scott being cut in two by enemy shot an hour earlier and his body thrown overboard. Scott's blood still stained the sleeve and tails of Nelson's coat.[6]

According to a long established myth, Nelson's vanity made him a ready target as he was thought to be wearing his gold-encrusted full dress uniform and his many decorations, He was actually wearing a rather threadbare dark blue undress uniform with very little gold braid and only small wire-and-sequin facsimiles of his stars sewn on to the left breast of his coat.[7] Nelson wore embroidered versions of the Order of the Bath, the Ottoman Order of the Crescent, the Neapolitan Order of St Ferdinand and Merit, and the German Order of St Joachim on all his uniforms. These imitation stars made him an obvious target for enemy snipers, but also made his presence visible to his own men. Nelson, like many other naval commanders, was careful about his dress for battle, balancing show with convenience. Cuthbert Collingwood also 'dressed himself that morning with particular care' and advised one of his officers, Lieutenant Clavell, to pull off his boots and 'put on silk stockings as I have done, for if one should get a shot in the leg, they would be so much more manageable for the surgeon'.[8] Nelson wore cotton stockings that day and shoes, as he disliked wearing boots.

Thomas Hardy was also wearing shoes at Trafalgar and 'a shot struck the fore-brace bits on the quarter-deck, and passed between Lord Nelson and Captain Hardy; a splinter from the bits bruising Captain Hardy's foot and tearing the buckle from his shoe'.[9] After that incident, Nelson dismissed any suggestions that he change into a less conspicuous coat on the grounds that it was too late. What was noticed about Nelson was that he was not carrying his sword as he usually did in battle.

The missing sword and the flamboyance of the uniform have been interpreted as signs that Nelson had a death wish and was courting a glorious death in battle. It has even been suggested that his actions on his last day amounted to suicide in order that Emma Hamilton and Horatia would be provided for financially.[10] There is, however, nothing to suggest that Nelson was preoccupied with his financial position before he was struck down nor with his own death. He was optimistic enough to have written to tell Emma that 'we will look forward to many, many happy years and be surrounded by our children's children'.[11] Although he had requested to be relieved from his command in August 1804 after not having been ashore since June 1803 since this was 'absolutely necessary' to preserve his health, he hoped to return to action once his health was restored.[12] His own officers were concerned that 'his Lordship would be made the object of the enemy's marksmen' and hoped that 'he might be entreated by somebody to cover the stars on his coat with a handkerchief', although it was well known that 'he would be highly displeased with whoever should take the liberty of recommending any change in his dress on this account'.[13] Nelson himself accepted that 'I commit my life to Him who made me'[14] and that 'if it is his Providence to cut short my days upon earth I bow with the greatest submission'[15] but this was all part of the Anglican piety of a parson's son and in keeping with his general fatalism. He told Hardy that 'I shall probably lose a leg, but that will be purchasing a victory cheaply'.[16] Nelson was not acting out of character by placing himself at the forefront of action. His wounds before Trafalgar bore witness to that and he was consistent in the boldness of his attack. Wounds were the price he expected to pay for victory, and 'he was always prepared to lay down his life in the service of his country' and 'it was the ambitious wish of his soul to die in the fight, and in the very hour of a great and signal victory'.[17]

His head covered with a handkerchief so that his men would not see who was wounded and thus be demoralised,[18] he was carried by two sailors down to the cockpit, a very confined, poorly ventilated, damp and dimly-lit space described by Alexander Scott as resembling 'a butcher's shambles.'[19] In normal circumstances the living space of the midshipmen, master's mates and assistant surgeons, it was convenient for the dispensary and the hatchway down which the casualties were brought to be treated on mess tables or chests lashed together. On those makeshift operating tables, Beatty and his two assistant surgeons were to perform eleven amputations during the battle, all without benefit of anaesthetics other than brandy. As they operated the hull was shaken by the impact of enemy shot and the concussion of the ship's own gunfire. Close to hand were his surgical instruments in a portable wooden case, including long and short blade knives, a fine toothed bone saw, a screw tourniquet, two trephines, forceps, probes and scissors.[20] His medical stores additionally included fifteen tourniquets, splints of various lengths, 120 yards of linen and eight pounds of lint for dressing wounds and injuries. Laudanum was available to relieve pain, while olive or linseed oil mixed with ceruse was used to treat burns. Vinegar was used for disinfection and barrels stood around filled with water for rinsing the instruments, sponges and swabs. It was here that Nelson, lain on a bed of sails, stripped of his clothes and covered with a sheet and propped at an angle, supported by the purser Walter Burke, was examined by Beatty, who immediately realised that he could do little for him. Beatty had just pronounced death over the corpses of the captain's clerk Whipple and twenty-one year-old Lieutenant Alexander Ram, who had bled to death after tearing away the tourniquet the surgeon had applied when Nelson was brought down.[21] Nelson's coat was given to Midshipman George Augustus Westphal, who needed a pillow for his head wound.[22]

Beatty gently probed the wound with his right finger as Nelson informed him that 'he felt a gush of blood every minute within his breast: that he had no feeling in the lower part of his body: and that his breathing was difficult and attended with very severe pain about that part of the spine where he was confident that the ball had struck' and that 'I felt it break my back.'[23] He was later to say that 'all power of motion and feeling below my breast are gone'.[24] These symptoms reminded him of James Bush who had died on the *Victory* in July after thirteen days of suffering from a broken neck and were a sign that his own wounds would be fatal. In time 'his lower extremities soon became cold and insensible, and the effusion of blood from his lungs often threatened suffocation'.[25] Beatty soon abandoned trying to probe for the musket ball and, when Hardy came down with news of the battle, was ordered by Nelson to attend to the other wounded 'and give his assistance to such of them as he could be useful to; "for", said he "you can do nothing for me".'[26]

Leaving the Admiral to the care of the purser Burke and the chaplain Scott, Beatty went away to amputate the leg of a midshipman, William Rivers the seventeen year-old son of the *Victory's* gunner, who told his father that he had 'only lost my leg, and that in a good cause'. Not only was his foot injured, hanging on by a piece of skin above the ankle, but he had also lost three teeth, knocked out by shot. When Rivers saw the amputated limbs and dead bodies from the cockpit being thrown overboard, he asked about the fate of his own leg only to be told that 'I understand Old Putty Nose was to have them for fresh meat for the sick'.[27] Beatty performed nine leg and two arm amputations that day. Nine of these eleven amputation cases survived, including twenty-two year-old Daniel McPherson from Dumbarton, whose femur had been fractured by cannon shot that carried away 'several pieces of bone'. Less lucky was Richard Jewell, aged twenty-five, who perished from loss of blood after having had his leg amputated. Colin Turner, aged eighteen, died of gangrene after treatment for a stomach wound, while William Browne died of a haemorrhage in his chest caused by grape shot. These were only a few of the casualties treated that day.[28] The surgeon of the schooner *Pickle*, Simon Gage Britton, brought aboard after the battle to help with the casualties, was overwhelmed by the scene on the orlop deck.[29] Nelson was only one casualty demanding attention among many.

It is significant that both *Victory* and *Temeraire*, both at the centre of the battle, suffered higher casualties among their officers than other ships, possibly because their close engagement with French ships made it easier for the marksmen in the French rigs to target British officers. In general one third of the thirty British flag-officers and captains involved in the battle were killed or wounded, a high proportion for the time. *Colossus* was also heavily engaged throughout the fighting and, with 40 dead and 160 wounded, the casualties represented some thirty-five per cent of her complement of 571 when the other heavily damaged ships had casualty rates of between ten and twenty per cent. Other ships came off relatively unscathed in terms of casualties. Collingwood recorded 423 dead and 464 wounded from the British fleet in his casualty list on 28 October 1805, later revising this to 1663 casualties. Submissions to the Lloyds Patriotic Fund suggested 1734 casualties, but this was still considered a modest number especially in comparison with enemy losses.[30] It is estimated that 4400 French and Spanish sailors died in battle and 2500 were wounded at Trafalgar, but there were no official casualty lists in the wake of defeat.[31] The death, though, that was to eclipse all the other casualties was of the architect of the British victory.

Beatty returned in time to witness Nelson giving Hardy his last message to his mistress Lady Hamilton, stressing that 'I leave Lady Hamilton and my daughter Horatia as a legacy to my country',[32] and to hear his satisfaction at the outcome of the battle, 'Now I am satisfied. Thank God I have done my duty.'[33] He uttered the often quoted instruction to 'kiss me, Hardy' and expressed the desire that 'I could have wished to have lived to enjoy this, but God's will be done'.[34] Hardy left the cockpit and Nelson ordered his steward William Chevallier to turn him on to his right side to alleviate the pain. Lemonade, water and wine were given to assuage his thirst. In his last moments Nelson asked the chaplain Alexander Scott for water and air: 'Drink, drink, fan, fan, rub, rub.' He died at the moment of victory.[35]

It is through paintings that the classic image of the death of Nelson has been immortalised. Samuel Drummond's 1806 painting of the wounding of Nelson at Trafalgar owes its composition to paintings of the deposition from the Cross. In the foreground Nelson is held upright by two seaman and a marine who descend the companionway from the quarter-deck to the middle deck. A dead marine lies on the lower level with next to him an injured sailor, attended to by a kneeling soldier.[36] Similar religious connotations are evoked in the canvas of the death of Nelson painted by Arthur Devis and first exhibited in 1807.[37] Nelson, wrapped in a shroud-like sheet and the focus of the light in the painting is at the centre of the canvas surrounded by a sorrowing group of his men and surgeons. His wounded left shoulder is covered up and his blood-stained white shirt and uniform coat with its braid and decorations lie abandoned before him, symbolising the vanity of his worldly glory. His chaplain Alexander Scott rubs Nelson's chest trying to relieve the pain, his purser Walter Burke supports his pillow and his Neapolitan valet Gaetano Spedillo holds the glass from which Nelson sips water. Liberties have been taken with what actually happened and Captain Hardy, who was not present when Nelson died, is shown standing behind him, which would have been impossible for a man six feet tall even had he actually been there. Prominent in the painting is the kneeling figure of the surgeon William Beatty in the full dress uniform of a naval surgeon, taking Nelson's pulse and about to pronounce him dead while Nelson's steward William Chevailler looks intently at Beatty. Among the other figures are the dazed and wounded Lieutenant George Miller Bligh and the assistant surgeon Neil Smith. With its intentional echoes of the deposition of Christ from the Cross, it is a fitting depiction of the death of an iconic national hero.

Benjamin West, who painted a rival version of the death of Nelson, considered that Devis with his factual approach did not 'excite awe and admiration' and that it was unsuitable for the heroic Nelson to 'be represented dying in the gloomy hold of a ship, like a sick man in a prison hole.'[38] West himself also evoked the religious imagery of the pieta, with Nelson draped in a white sheet with his shirt ripped open and propped up on pillows supported by the purser Burke. William Beatty holds a handkerchief around the wound and the assistant surgeon leans forward to hear the admiral's dying words. Nelson's head is supported by his chaplain and Thomas Hardy holds his left hand. Chevailler holds Nelson's coat and breeches with the valet in attendance, Bunce the carpenter holds a hammer and has a bundle of plugs and oakum hanging from his shoulder and his mate steps over a coil of rope. In the background a wounded midshipman is brought down to the cockpit by two seamen. The pallor of the dying man, bathed in golden light, evokes the calm of a neo-classical statue.[39]

West, not considering the Cockpit a suitable location for the death of his hero, also painted an 'epic composition' of the death of Nelson in which he showed Nelson dying where he had fallen as 'all should be proportionate to the highest idea conceived of the hero', something for which 'a mere matter of fact will never produce this effect'.[40] This painting shows Nelson fully dressed, dying on deck surrounded by a reverent crowd of onlookers with the battle still raging in the background.[41] It was intended to inspire and uplift. Nelson had admired West's painting of the death in 1759 of his own idol General Wolfe at Quebec and had hoped that West might depict him at some time. Just as 'Wolfe must not die like a common soldier under a bush', Nelson too must be seen to die a heroic death.[42] West also painted an apotheosis of Nelson in which his corpse, draped in white and pale like a marble statue, is passed by the allegorical figures of Neptune and Victory to the arms of Britannia.[43] Devis and West both visited the *Victory* to see for themselves where their subject died, but what they depicted was what they thought suitable for an inspirational painting of the death of a national hero. What they saw was adjusted to fit in with their artistic vision.

The day following the battle Beatty began the task of preparing Nelson's body for its return home and 'measures were adopted to preserve them as effectively as the means then on board the *Victory* allowed'.[44] Hardy cut off Nelson's hair, with its pigtail, as a keepsake for Lady Hamilton.[45] Beatty then carefully positioned Nelson's body, stripped down to his shirt, into a large water cask now filled with brandy to preserve it for the voyage home so that the dead hero could be buried in England. On 24 October on the way to Gibraltar, there was a 'disengagement of air from the body to such a degree that the sentinel became alarmed on seeing the head of the cask raised'.[46] Beatty refilled the cask with brandy and noted that the body appeared to be absorbing the brandy. At Gibraltar, he obtained spirits of wine, which he considered a superior preservative, 'certainly by far the best when it can be procured.'[47] Twice more he had to refresh the spirits in the cask, in the proportion of two-thirds brandy to one-third spirits of wine, during the five weeks it took the *Victory* to sail home to Portsmouth from Gibraltar, by drawing off the liquor from the bottom of the leaguer and replacing it from above. This method managed to preserve Nelson's remains in a reasonable state, as Beatty found when he prepared the corpse for an autopsy, except for the bowels which were 'found to be much decayed and likely to communicate the process of putrefaction to the rest of the body; the parts already injured were therefore removed'.[48]

Nelson's body would have been sent home quicker had Collingwood carried out his original plan of transferring it from the badly damaged flagship to the faster frigate *Euryalus*. However, 'a very strong reluctance was manifested by the crew of the *Victory* to part with so precious a relic', to which they felt almost an exclusive claim. They had made representations for it remaining in their care on the grounds that 'the noble admiral had fought with them, and fell on their own deck', They were also concerned that 'if by being put on board a frigate, his body should fall into the hands of the enemy, it would make their loss doubly grievous to them; and, therefore they were one and all resolved to carry it safely to England'.[49] Such was the devotion of the ordinary seamen to the man who had had their welfare at heart.

Soon after arriving in Portsmouth, Beatty performed a post-mortem examination and removed the fatal musket ball. His emotionless, clinical report emphasised the horrifying nature of the wound and hints at the agony Nelson may have suffered in his last hours:

> The ball struck the forepart of his Lordship's epaulette and entered the left shoulder ... it then descended obliquely into the thorax, fracturing the second and third ribs, and after penetrating the left lobe of the lungs and dividing in its passage a large branch of the pulmonary artery, it entered the spine and lodged therein.[50]

On removing the ball, Beatty noticed that 'a portion of the gold-lace and pad of the epaulette, together with a small piece of his Lordship's coat, was found firmly attached to it'. This fatal musket ball was later mounted in a crystal case by Thomas Hardy and given to Beatty, who attached it to a fob on his watch chain.[51] The surgeon remarked of Nelson that 'there were no morbid indications to be seen; other than those attending the human body six weeks after death, even under circumstances more favourable to its preservation.' He found that 'all the vital arts were so perfectly healthy in their appearance, and so small, that they resembled more those of a youth, than of a man who had attained his forty-seventh year; which state of the body associated with habits of life favourable to health, gives every reason to believe that his Lordship might have lived to a great age'.[52] He concluded that 'the immediate cause of his Lordship's death was a wound of the left pulmonary artery, which poured its blood into the cavity of the chest'.[53]

Modern surgeons have challenged parts of Beatty's account of Nelson's injuries. Nelson was struck in the chest by a 20 gram lead ball, imparting 150–200 joules of energy, which having injured the ribs and lung, transected his spinal cord. If the bullet had severed the pulmonary artery and several intercostal vessels as Beatty stated, Nelson would have lost blood very rapidly and would not have survived for as long as he did. As Nelson had multiple rib fractures, the source of bleeding could have been a torn intercostal artery or vein, or else laceration of the lung. Nelson's description of 'a gush of blood every minute within his breast' was probably not bleeding from a pulmonary vessel but rather air or fluid shifting in his chest cavity. His eventual death would then have been due to severe hypotension from both blood loss and spinal shock, a conclusion supported by his pallor and ramblings. It was the damage to his spinal cord that killed Nelson. In such a case, in the unlikely event for the time of Nelson surviving the bleeding and the sepsis, he would have been left paraplegic, prone to bladder infections, pressure sores and eventual kidney failure. It is possible that modern surgery could have saved his life but he would have been paralysed.[54]

Significantly, there is no record of Nelson's death in the surgeon's journal for the *Victory* where it might have been expected to form a major part of the surgeon's report on Trafalgar. Compared with the journals of other Trafalgar surgeons, that of Beatty is poorly kept, but sloppy record keeping may not be the only explanation for the omission. It is highly likely that Beatty wanted to save the details so that he could publish them for his own benefit. His account of Nelson's death, published in 1807, was instrumental in forging the cult of Nelson; it also brought reflected glory on himself. Born in Londonderry in 1773, Beatty had joined the Navy in 1791 and had served on ten warships before being warranted to Nelson's flagship in December 1804. Earlier in his career he had been court-martialled for disrespectful conduct towards the captain of the *Pomona* but was exonerated in 1795. His principal role during Nelson's last hours was to bring him the fame and boost to his career that his own merits alone perhaps may not have achieved, including appointment as Physician of the Fleet in 1806 and Physician to Greenwich Hospital in 1822. He was knighted by William IV in 1831. His best quality as a naval surgeon was his ability to keep calm and cool under fire. In many ways a typical competent naval surgeon of his time, he owed his success to his association with the dying Nelson.[55]

Nelson himself was given a state funeral. After the post mortem had been carried out, Nelson's corpse was wrapped in cotton vestments and rolled in cotton bandages before being placed in a lead casket filled with 'brandy holding in solution camphor and myrrh'.[56] Such embalming methods were commonly used for the bodies of senior officers. Admiral Thomas Lewis was also embalmed when he died suddenly on board the *Canopus* off Alexandria in 1807. His surgeon Abraham Martin removed the stomach, intestines and spleen then washed the abdomen and 'other sound viscera' with spirits and sprinkled them with nitre and camphor. Then 'hemp soaked in spirits was also put in the cavity in place of the unsound viscera that were removed and the abdomen sewn up with the glover's suture'.[57]

Nelson's casket was made to be big enough to encase his own wooden coffin, constructed from a piece of the mainmast and spar of the French flagship *L'Orient* blown up at the battle of the Nile and given to him by Captain Benjamin Hallowell. The coffin was brought to the *Victory* by the London undertaker Peddison of Brewer Street and Nelson's body transferred to it. Beatty took on the task of helping to remove the linen wrappers from the embalmed body as there was a chance of 'the skin coming away from the body'.[58] The body was then dressed in uniform breeches, a shirt and silk stockings. A white cambric handkerchief was bound round the neck and forehead. The face was also gently rubbed with handkerchiefs in an attempt to restore the features in case it was exposed to public view while lying in state.[59] Although Beatty had referred to the uncorrupted state of the body and claimed that the facial features were 'somewhat tumid from absorption of the spirit but on using friction from a napkin they resumed in great degree their natural character',[60] it was thought that the face was beginning to decompose and it would not be appropriate to show it during the lying in state.[61] The wooden coffin in its lead cask within a wooden shell lay in state in the Painted Hall of Greenwich

Hospital for three days in January 1806 before being transported to the Admiralty in Whitehall from which the funeral procession wended its way to St Paul's Cathedral for a state funeral on 9 January 1806. The 'physicians of the deceased' were given an honoured place in the procession in a mourning coach behind representatives of the City commercial companies, a reminder of the importance doctors had enjoyed in Nelson's life.[62] After, the funeral ceremony, the catafalque was lowered through the floor of the crossing into the crypt and dropped into a marble sarcophagus designed for Cardinal Wolsey by the Florentine sculptor Benedetto da Rovezzano but never used until George III sent it from Windsor as an appropriate resting place for the great naval hero.[63] Such treatment in death sealed Nelson's status in the national pantheon.

A state funeral also awaited Cuthbert Collingwood in St Paul's in 1810 close to his friend Horatio Nelson. He had been wounded himself at Trafalgar through remaining in an exposed position in full uniform on the poop deck, stemming the flow of blood from a leg wound from a flying splinter with a pocket handkerchief applied as a tourniquet.[64] However, it was during his time as commander-in-chief of the Mediterranean fleet that his health began to fail. His greatest desire was to return home to Northumberland, though he acknowledged that 'the Admiralty have been exceedingly kind and attentive to me; they have sent me the best ship in the Navy and have reinforced my squadron; but what I most want is a pair of new legs and a pair of new eyes'.[65] He resorted to using spectacles to help his vision when working on his papers.[66] By 1809, he realised that 'tough as I am I cannot last much longer', though he and his dog Bounce seemed the most resilient when 'many about me are yielding to the fatigue and confinement of a life which is certainly not natural to man'.[67] The death of Bounce hit him hard, but by then he was complaining of severe stomach pains which his physician put down to 'entirely the consequence of the sedentary life I must have', directing the fleet from the desk in his cabin.[68] The diagnosis of 'a contraction of the pylorus', between the stomach and intestine, was believed to be caused by the months he had spent crouched over his desk, but was more likely to have been an ulcer or cancer. Finally relieved of his duties, he died at sea on the *Ville de Paris* on 7 March 1810. His surgeon could 'not believe it possible' that 'cruelly harassed by a most afflicting disease, obtaining no relief from the means employed, and perceiving his death to be inevitable, he suffered no sign of regret to escape'.[69] Despite his wish to be buried at sea or quietly in a private funeral, this neglected hero of Trafalgar, like Nelson, lay in state at Greenwich Hospital and was buried at St Paul's.[70]

Such grandiose funerals were not the norm. Instead burial at sea was the fate of most seamen, though officers were buried on land if that was at all possible. The Trafalgar Cemetery at Gibraltar contains such graves of naval officers, though very few actually from the battle of Trafalgar. For the humble sailor, his body was 'prepared for his deep-sea grave by his messmates, who, with the assistance of the sail-maker, and in the presence of the master-at-arms, sew him up in his hammock'.[71] Cannon shot, weighing some 32 pounds, would be placed at the feet to weigh down the body so that it would sink when committed to the deep. The body was placed on a grating and covered with the ship's ensign. After a short funeral service read by the chaplain, 'a seaman standing by took off the colours, and turning the grating launched' the dead man into the ocean. As the corpse 'splashed' into the water, the men and officers in attendance paid their respects, 'the multitude of stern looking men standing round; and preserving a profound silence'.[72]

In the heat of battle, there was not even time for such ceremonies or even for shrouds. William Dillon was shocked when he first witnessed this and 'the number of men thrown overboard that were killed, without ceremony, and the sad wrecks around us taught those who, like myself, had not witnessed similar scenes that war was the greatest scourge of mankind.' The seamen themselves were unsentimental and 'have a great objection to the body of anyone who has died remaining amongst them.' They were superstitious and 'an idea prevails amongst them, that sharks will follow a ship for a whole voyage which has a corpse on board; and the loss of a mast, or the long duration of a foul wind or any other inconvenience, is sure to be ascribed to the same influence.'[74]

For many men lost in a shipwreck there was not even the knowledge of the Christian commitment of their bodies to the sea to console their families, who remembered them with souvenirs from happier times now become *memento mori*. All that remains of Lieutenant James Wilcox, drowned when his ship the *Hero* was driven ashore on the Haak Sands off the Texel on the Dutch coast on Christmas Day 1811, is an oval miniature portrait of him as a dashing fashionable Regency officer in a locket containing a plait of his greying brown hair.[75] The *Hero* was wrecked in a storm, with Admiral Robert Carthew Reynold's flagship *St George* and the *Defence* from the Baltic fleet, while escorting a convoy of merchant ships from Gothenburg to London. Thirty of the merchant ships were also wrecked with great loss of life. Reynolds too lost his life. James Newman-Newman, captain of the *Hero* also went down with his ship, from which there were only eight survivors.[76]

Death was to be expected in battle or natural disaster, but in normal circumstances a high death rate represented a failure to maintain a healthy ship. Nelson was aware of this. Important to him and his compeers for the maintenance of a healthy fighting force was the control that came through self-discipline and ship's discipline. He may have occasionally exaggerated his achievements in the field of maintaining the health of his fleet just as he was prone to embellish most of his achievements, but such exaggerations clearly indicate the value he placed on the health of his fleet, and it was an area in which he indeed could pride himself on his achievements. Between 29 August 1803 and 21 August 1804, the wartime sick list fluctuated between 133 and 263, with an average of 17.3 men sick in each ship. Of these, the average number of men confined to the sick berth was even lower at 1.4 men.[77] Despite very few of the officers or men having 'had a foot on shore' in this period, the low number of sick was remarkable with most of the men on the sick list having sea ulcers. Nelson boasted that 'we are healthy beyond example, and in good humour with ourselves, and so sharp-set that I would not be a French admiral in the way of any of our ships'.[78] John Snipe believed that sobriety, ventilation, cleanliness, clothing and good food were 'absolutely required to keep up that muscular vigour, spirit of courage and adventure so necessary in the day of battle'. He considered that Nelson's 'attention on all occasions' to the health of the men under his command had 'made a deep impression on my heart, and the time I had the honour to serve under your lordship's commands I shall ever consider as the most fortunate period of my life'.[79]

It was this superiority in medicine and concern for the welfare of the seaman that gave the Royal Navy the advantage in the French Wars between 1793 and 1815. The advances made then had built on developments during the eighteenth century and contributed to the foundations of British naval supremacy during the *Pax Britannica* of the nineteenth-century. It was to keep those under his command in a condition fit to fight that Nelson took such an interest in their health and welfare. A risk taker and an ambitious naval officer thirsty for glory, he was focused on victory. His own personal health problems that reflected those of his men did make him sympathetic and encouraged him to take the advice of his surgeons. He summarised his own history of wounds as 'his eye in Corsica, his belly off Cape St. Vincent, his arm at Tenerife, his head in Egypt' and considered this 'tolerable for one war!'[80]

Those men serving under Nelson were absolutely convinced that his concern for their welfare was sincere and it was this that ensured the affection felt for him by the men who served under him. Seaman William Robinson on *Revenge* said that 'he was adored, and in fighting under him every man thought himself sure of success'.[81] An 'officer of rank' on *Britannia* called him 'the idol of his profession, the ornament and defence of his country, the greatest warrior of his age' and a man who 'died as he lived, a hero, and in the arms of victory'.[82] Such devotion came from a feeling that Nelson understood and had the welfare of his men at heart. John Snipe had no doubts that 'the triumphant state of health which this fleet has enjoyed for nearly twelve months ... points out in the clearest manner to the most superficial observer the good effects of the wise and salutatory measures pursued by our renowned commander-in-chief, under many untoward circumstances which formerly were not experienced in this country. When the thinking mind reflects on the ravages committed in our fleet by diseases in times past and contrasts it with the present we must be strongly impressed with sentiments of admiration and astonishment'.[83] It was an achievement and naval victory as great as that of Trafalgar.

# Notes

CHAPTER ONE

1. B. Crew, *Sea Poems* (2005), p. 19.
2. J. Sugden, Nelson: *A Dream of Glory* (2005), p. 36.
3. Ibid., p. 44.
4. J.S. Clarke and J. McArthur, *Life of Admiral Lord Nelson* (1810), vol. 1, pp. 2–3.
5. M. Duffy (ed.), *Naval Miscellany VI* (2003), p. 188.
6. Ibid., p. 197.
7. TNA, ADM 33/509, *Carcass*, paybook, 18 June 1773.
8. J. Charnock, *Biographical Memoirs of Lord Viscount Nelson* (1806), p. 161.
9. TNA, ADM 52/1639/7, log book of James Allen, *Carcass*, 4 August 1773.
10. H. Nelson, *Dispatches and Letters* (1844–6), vol. 5, p. 223.
11. H. Nelson, *Nelson's Letters to Lady Hamilton* (1815), vol. 1, p. 9.
12. Ibid., p.64.
13. Ibid., p. 85.
14. H. Nelson, *Dispatches and Letters* (1844–6), vol. 5, p. 261.
15. T. Pocock, *Horatio Nelson* (1994), p. 221.
16. H. Nelson, *Nelson's Letters to his Wife and Other Documents* (1958), p. 77.
17. Ibid., p. 82.
18. B.A.B. Ronald, *Young Nelsons* (2009), p. 86.
19. J. Raigersfield, *The Life of a Sea Officer* (1929) p. 8.
20. Ibid., pp. 7- 8.
21. TNA, ADM 101/102/3, L. Gillespie, surgeon's journal, *Vanguard*, 25 May 1787.
22. TNA, ADM 101/102/4, L. Gillespie, surgeon's journal, *Racehorse*, 19 January 1788.
23. Tunbridge Wells Museum, Nelson, *Victory*, to Camden, 11 October 1804; *Daily Mail*, 10 December 2012.
24. G.S. Parsons, *Nelsonian Reminiscences* (1843), p. 199.
25. W.H. Dillon, *A Narrative of my Professional Adventures 1790–1839* (1953), p. 13.
26. W. Hoste, *Memoirs and Letters* (1833), p. 10.
27. National Maritime Museum, MRF/88/1, letter from W. Hoste, 14 September 1795.
28. H. Nelson, *Dispatches and Letters* (1844–6), vol. 2, p. 304.
29. J. Raigersfield, *The Life of a Sea Officer* (1929) p. 9.
30. R. Woodman, *Of Daring Temper, 250 Years of the Marine Society* (2006), p. 24
31. Ibid, pp. 13–25.
32. J. Fielding, *An Account of the Receipts and Disbursements Relating to Sir John Fielding's Plan for the Preserving of Distressed Boys by Sending them to Sea* (1769), p. 5.
33. B.E. O'Meara, *Napoleon in Exile* (1822), vol. 2, p. 381.
34. *Middlesex Journal*, 5 January 1771.
35. *The Hampshire Courier, or Portsmouth, Portsea, Gosport and Chichester Advertiser*, 2 March 1812.
36. *Naval Chronicle*, 9 (March 1803), 243–4.
37. W. Hotham, *Pages and Portraits from the Past* (1919), vol. 1, pp. 94–5.
38. W. Robinson, *Jack Nastyface:*

*Memoirs of an English Seaman*
(2002), p. 26.

39. G. Price, *Pressganged* (1984), p. 7.

40. W. Robinson, *Jack Nastyface: Memoirs of an English Seaman* (2002), pp. 25–6.

41. Ibid., p. 27.

42. D. Goodall, *Salt Water Sketches* (1860), p, 5.

43. Ibid., pp. 2–4.

44. *The Times*, 8 October 1790.

45. J. Lind, *An Essay on the Most Effectual Means of Preserving the Health of Seamen in the Royal Navy (1774), p. 4.*

46. W. Turnbull, *The Naval Surgeon* (1806), p. 119.

47. R. Robertson, *Observations on the Jail, Hospital or Ship Fever* (1807), p. 19.

48. T. Trotter, *Medicina Nautica* (1803), vol. 3, p. 274.

49. G. Blane, *Observations on the Diseases Incident to Seamen* (1785), p. 242.

50. J. Lind, *An Essay on the Most Effectual Means of Preserving the Health of Seamen in the Royal Navy (1774), p. 3.*

51. C. Lloyd and J.L.S. Coulter, *Medicine and the Navy* (1961), vol. 3, p. 77.

52. J. Lind, *An Essay on the Most Effectual Means of Preserving the Health of Seamen in the Royal Navy (1774), p. 6.*

53. Ibid.

54. Ibid., p. 5.

55. Ibid., p. 6.

56. Ibid., p. 7.

57. G. Blane, *Observations on the Diseases Incident to Seamen* (1785), p. 317.

58. T. Trotter, *Medicina Nautica* (1797), vol. 1, p. 48; *Observations on the Scurvy* (1786), p. 153.

59. H.W. Hodges and E.A. Hughes, *Select Naval Documents* (1936), p. 168

60. T. Trotter, *Medicina Nautica* (1797), vol. 1, p. 48

61. C. Lloyd, *The Health of Seamen* (1965), p. 166.

62. T. Trotter, *Medicina Nautica* (1803), vol. 3, p. 93.

63. J. Lind, *An Essay on the Most Effectual Means of Preserving the Health of Seamen in the Royal Navy* (1774), p. 321.

64. G. Blane, *Observations on the Diseases Incident to Seamen* (1785), p. 226.

65. C. Barham, *Letters and Papers of Charles, Lord Barham* (1907), vol. 1, p. 304.

66. C. Lloyd and J.L.S. Coulter, *Medicine and the Navy* (1961), vol. 3, pp. 79–80.

67. Wellcome Library, MS 3680, letter from John Snipe to Nelson, 9 September 1803.

68. Ibid., MS3677, letter from Thomas Hardy to Nelson, 11 August 1804.

69. Ibid.

70. H. Nelson, *Dispatches and Letters* (1844–6), vol. 6, p. 154.

71. Ibid., p. 276.

72. T. Trotter, *Medicina Nautica* (1797), vol. 1, p. 446.

73. W. Beatty, *Authentic Narrative of the Death of Lord Nelson* (1807), pp. 80–1.

74. Ibid., p. 81.

75. R. Hay, *Landsman Hay* (1953), p. 171.

76. T.M. Wybourne, *Sea Soldier* (2000), p. 117.

77. J. Bates, *Autobiography* (1868), p. 45.

78. *The Times*, 12 September 1806.

79. G. Blane, *Observations on the Diseases Incident to Seamen* (1785), p. 45.

80. TNA, ADM 1/407, letter from J. Snipe to Nelson, 7 December 1803.

81. T. Trotter, *Medicina Nautica* (1797), vol. 1, pp. 443–4.

82. Privy Council, *Regulations and Instructions Relating to His Majesty's Service at Sea*, (1808), p. 139.

83. A. Fremantle, *The Wynne Diaries* (1940), vol. 3, pp. 118–19.

84. R. and L. Adkins, *Jack Tar* (2008), p. 140.

85. J.A. Gardner, *Recollections* (1906), pp. 89–90.

86. G. Cockburn, *A Voyage to Cadiz and Gibraltar* (1815), p. 2.

87. Ibid., p. 8.

88. J. Lowry, *Fiddlers and Whores* (2006), p. 93.

CHAPTER TWO

1. Nelson, *Dispatches and Letters* (1844–6), vol. 1, p. 476.

2. Ibid., pp. 3–4; J.S. Clarke and J. McArthur, *Life of Admiral Lord Nelson* (1810), vol. 1, pp. 22–3.

3. H. Nelson, *Dispatches and Letters* (1844–6), vol. 1, pp. 3–4.

4. J.S. Clarke and J. McArthur, *Life of*

*Admiral Lord Nelson* (1810), vol. 1, p. 23.

5. Ibid., p. 25.

6. H. Nelson, *Dispatches and Letters* (1844–6), vol. 1, p. 32.

7. Ibid., p. 100.

8. C. Lloyd and J.L.S. Coulter, *Medicine and the Navy* (1961), vol. 3, pp. 141–2.

9. H. Nelson, *Nelson's Letters to his Wife and Other Documents* (1958), p. 58.

10. H. Nelson, *Dispatches and Letters* (1844–6), vol. 1, p. 462.

11. J.S. Clarke and J. McArthur, *Life of Admiral Lord Nelson* (1810), vol. 1, p. 275.

12. H. Nelson, *Dispatches and Letters* (1844–6), vol. 2, p. 126.

13. Ibid., p. 140.

14. Ibid., p. 180.

15. J.S. Clarke and J. McArthur, *Life of Admiral Lord Nelson* (1810), vol. 1, p. 54.

16. Ibid., p, 57.

17. T. Dancer, *A Brief History of the Late Expedition against Fort Juan* (1781), pp. 43, 44, 53.

18. Ibid., p. 53.

19. A.M.E. Hills, 'Nelson's Illnesses', *Journal of the Royal Naval Medical Service*, 86 (2000), 72–80; *Nelson, A Medical Casebook* (2006), pp. 23–9.

20. B. Moseley, *Treatise on Tropical Diseases* (1803), p. 165

21. T. Dancer, *A Brief History of the Late Expedition against Fort Juan* (1781), p. 10.

22. Ibid., p. 36.

23. J. Sugden, *Nelson, A Dream of Glory* (2004), pp. 810–11.

24. J.S. Clarke and J. McArthur, *Life of Admiral Lord Nelson* (1810), vol. 1, p.58.

25. Ibid., p. 59.

26. T. Coleman, *The Nelson Touch* (2002), p. 34.

27. TNA, ADM 1/242, report on Nelson, 1 September 1780.

28. H. Nelson, *Dispatches and Letters* (1844–6), vol. 1, p. 10.

29. Ibid., vol. 4, p. 487.

30. Ibid., p. 37.

31. Ibid., p. 38.

32. Ibid., p. 41.

33. Ibid., p. 42.

34. Wellcome Library, MS 3676, account with R. Winch, 1781.

35. Ibid., p. 48.

36. Ibid., p. 67.

37. Ibid., vol. 6, p. 41.

38. W. Beatty, *Authentic Narrative of the Death of Lord Nelson* (1807), p. 78.

39. Ibid.

40. P.D.G. Pugh, *Nelson and his Surgeons* (1968), p. 5.

41. J. Lind, *An Essay on Diseases Incidental to Europeans in Hot Climates* (1808), p. 209.

42. G. Cleghorn, *Observations on the Epidemical Diseases in Minorca from the Year 1744 to 1749* (1779), p. 152.

43. Ibid., p. 135.

44. J. Lind, *An Essay on Diseases Incidental to Europeans in Hot Climates* (1808), p. 211.

45. Ibid., p. 203.

46. J. Lind, *An Essay on Diseases Incidental to Europeans in Hot Climates* (1808), p. 8.

47. T. Trotter, *A View of the Nervous Temperament* (1807), pp. 143–4.

48. J. Hunter, *Observations on the Diseases of the Army in Jamaica and on the Best Means of Preserving the Health of Europeans in that Climate* (1788), p. 24.

49. J. Lind, *An Essay on Diseases Incidental to Europeans in Hot Climates* (1808), p. 136.

50. G. Blane, *Observations on the Diseases Incident to Seamen* (1785), pp. 222–3.

51. R. Robertson, *Observations on Fevers, and other Diseases, which Occur on Voyages to Africa and the West Indies* (1792), pp. 9–10.

52. L. Gillespie, *Observations on the Diseases which Prevailed in HM Squadron in the Leeward Islands* (1800), pp. 89–91, 181.

53. F. Marryatt, *The Naval Officer* (1834), p. 138.

54. J. Lind, *An Essay on Diseases Incidental to Europeans in Hot Climates* (1768), p. 321.

55. R. Robertson, *Observations on the Jail, Hospital or Ship Fever* (1807) p. 97.

56. J. Lind, *An Essay on the Most Effectual Means of Preserving the Health of Seamen in the Royal Navy* (1778), pp. 67–79.

57. Wellcome Library, MS 3680, letter from J. Snipe to Nelson, 7 November 1803.

58. Wellcome Library, MS 3677, account of wine and spirits supplied to surgeon of *Spencer*, October 1804.
59. J. Boyle, *A Practical Medico-Historical Account of the Western Coast of Africa* (1831), p. 196.
60. J. Lind, *Diseases Incidental to Europeans* (1768), pp. 307–08.
61. G. Blane, *Observations on the Diseases Incident to Seamen* (1785), p. 224.
62. F.B. Spilsbury, *Account of a Voyage to the Western Coast of Africa* (1807), p. 17
63. R. Robertson, Observations *on the Jail, Hospital or Ship Fever* (1807) p. 80.
64. R. Robertson, *Directions for Administering Peruvian Bark, in a Fermenting State, in Fever, and Other Diseases* (1799).
65. R. Robertson, *Synopsis Morborum: Observations on Diseases Incident to Seamen* (1817), pp. 352–71.
66. Wellcome Library, MS 3680, letter from J. Snipe to H. Nelson, 7 November 1803.
67. Wellcome Library, MS 3677, Account of Wine and Spirit supplied to *Spencer's* Surgeon, October 1804.
68. S.F. Dudley, 'Yellow Fever, as seen by the Medical Officers of the Royal Navy in the Nineteenth Century', *Proceedings of the Royal Society of Medicine*, 26/4 (1933), 443.
69. Ibid., 443–56.
70. L. Gillespie, *Observations on the Diseases which Prevailed in HM Squadron in the Leeward Islands* (1800), pp. 60–78, 129–360.
71. F. Hoffman, *A Sailor of King George* (1901), pp. 63–4.
72. Ibid., p. 79.
73. J. Prior, *Voyage in the Indian Seas in the Nisus Frigate* (1820), p. 49.
74. Ibid., p. 54.
75. J. Veitch, *A Letter to the Commissioners for Transports, and Sick and Wounded Seamen, on the Non-Contagious Nature of the Yellow Fever* (1818), pp. 109–10.
76. Ibid., p. 131.
77. W.N. Boog Watson, 'Two British Naval Surgeons in the French Wars, *Medical History*, 13 (1969), 223.
78. Ibid., 220–23.
79. L. Brockliss and C. Jones, *The Medical World of Early Modern France* (1997), pp. 438–9.
80. W.N. Boog Watson, 'Two British Naval Surgeons in the French Wars, *Medical History*, 13 (1969), 222.
81. R. Robertson, *Observations on the Jail, Hospital or Ship Fever* (1807), p. 432.
82. Ibid., p. 301.
83. Ibid., p. 435.
84. E.A. Carson, 'The Customs Quarantine Service', *Mariner's Mirror*, 64 (1978), 63–9.
85. G. Hampson (ed.), *Portsmouth Customs Letter Books 1748–1750* (1994), pp. xxviii-xxix.
86. Ibid., p. 65.
87. Ibid., p. 185.
88. L. Brockliss, M.J. Cardwell and M. Moss, *Nelson's Surgeon* (2005), p. 103.
89. S. Benady, *Civil Hospital and Epidemics in Gibraltar* (1994), p. 76.
90. E. Desbrière, *The Naval Campaign of 1805* (1933), vol. 2, p. 94.
91. Ibid., p. 118.
92. J. de Zulueta, 'Trafalgar: the Spanish View', *Mariner's Mirror*, 66 (1980), 293–319; 'Health in the Spanish Navy during the Age of Nelson, *Journal of the Royal Naval Medical Service*, 86 (2000), 89–92.
93. E. Desbrière, *The Naval Campaign of 1805* (1933), vol. 2, p. 100; L. Brockliss, M.J. Cardwell and M. Moss, *Nelson's Surgeon* (2005), p. 126.

CHAPTER THREE
1. L.P. Le Quesne, 'Nelson and his Surgeons', *Journal of the Royal Naval Medical Service*, 86 (2000), 85–8.
2. H. Nelson, *Nelson's Letters to his Wife* (1959) pp.163–5.
3. J. Sugden, *Nelson, A Dream of Glory* (2004), p. 511.
4. H. Nelson, *Dispatches and Letters* (1844–6), vol. 2, p. 6.
5. H. Nelson, *Nelson's Letters to his Wife* (1959), p, 119.
6. H. Nelson, *Dispatches and Letters* (1844–6), vol. 1, p. 435.
7. H. Nelson, *Nelson's Letters to his Wife* (1959), p. 172.
8. H. Nelson, *Dispatches and Letters* (1844–6), vol. 1, p. 439.
9. H. Nelson, *Nelson's Letters to his Wife* (1959), p. 195.

10. H. Nelson, *Dispatches and Letters* (1844–6), vol. 1, p. 492; H. Nelson, *Nelson's Letters to his Wife* (1959), p, 119.
11. A.M. E. Hills, *Nelson, A Medical Casebook* (2006), pp. 62–4.
12. H. Nelson, *Dispatches and Letters* (1844–6), vol. 1, pp. 487–8.
13. Ibid., pp 488–9.
14. Ibid., vol. 2, p. 57.
15. Ibid., vol. 2, p. 2.
16. R. Southey, *Life of Nelson* (1813), vol. 1, p. 207.
17. *The Times*, 4 October 1804.
18. H. Nelson, *Dispatches and Letters* (1844–6), vol. 4, p. 309.
19. Ibid., p. 327.
20. W. Beatty, *Authentic Narrative of the Death of Lord Nelson* (1807), p. 70.
21. NMM, AAA6040, toby jug of Nelson, 1952.
22. W. Beatty, *Authentic Narrative of the Death of Lord Nelson* (1807), p. 70.
23. T. Trotter, *Medicina Nautica* (1801), vol. 3, p. 107.
24. H. Nelson, *Nelson's Letters to Lady Hamilton* (1815), vol. 1, pp. 21–2.
25. H. Nelson, *Dispatches and Letters* (1844–6), vol. 4, pp. 130, 141, 142, 146.
26. Ibid., p. 124.
27. British Optical Association Museum, London, LDBOA1999.167, portrait of Peter Rainier by Arthur Devis, c. 1805. Another version of the portrait owned by the Duke of Wellington is at Stratfield Saye.
28. C. Collingwood, *The Private Correspondence of Admiral Lord Collingwood* (1957), p. 141.
29. *The Times*, 5 February 1805.
30. Ibid., 2 July 1805.
31. P. Dollond, *Some Account of the Discovery, which led to the Grand Improvement of Refracting Telescopes, made by the late Mr John Dollond FRS., in order to correct some Misrepresentations in Foreign Publications, of that Discovery* (1789), pp. 1–15.
32. R. Blair, 'Experiments and Observations on the Unequal Refrangibility of Light', *Transactions of the Royal Society of Edinburgh*, 3/2 (1794), 3–76; A. Blair, 'On the Permanency of Achromatic Telescopes constructed with Fluid Object Glasses', *Edinburgh Journal of Science*, 7 (1827), 336–42.
33. H. Nelson, *Dispatches and Letters* (1844–6), vol. 4, p. 156.
34. T Cavallo, *Essay on the Theory and Practice of Medical Electricity* (1780), pp. 44–5.
35. G. Aldini, *An Account of the Late Improvements in Galvanism* (1803); pp 191–194.
36. In her youth Emma Hamilton was said to have had experience of 'electric medicine' when employed by James Graham as one of the scantily-clad young women who had posed among the classical statues in James Graham's Temple of Health and Hymen in Pall Mall, London, where visitors could view Graham's medico-electrical apparatus, with which he delivered electrical shocks to his patients. Graham had practised as an eye specialist in Philadelphia, where, influenced by Benjamin Franklin's electrical experiments, he had become convinced that electricity could be a universal cure. The highlight of the Temple of Health was the 'Celestial Bed', in the headboard of which was an electric current filling the air with a magnet fluid 'calculated to give the necessary degree of strength and exertion to the nerves' and which guaranteed fertility to anyone who slept in it. When Graham went bankrupt, he renounced electro-therapy and instead promoted mud baths as an elixir of life. While it is now considered unlikely that Lady Hamilton actually posed as Hygeia, goddess of health, at Graham's Temple, Nelson's resort to electric therapy for his eye problem was a case of him looking to contemporary science for an answer.
37. M. la Beaume, *On Galvanism* (1826), pp. 150–1.
38. L., Davidson, 'Identities Ascertained': British Ophthalmology in the First Half of the Nineteenth Century', *Social History of Medicine* 9/3 (1996), 313–333.
39. TNA, ADM 67/13, July 1805.
40. D.D. Edwards, 'Microbiology of the Eye and Ophthalmia' in Daniel Albert and Diane D. Edwards (ed.)

*The History of Ophthalmology* (1996), pp. 154–57.

41. J. Wardrop, *Essays on the Morbid Anatomy of the Human Eye* (1808).

42. H. Nelson, *Dispatches and Letters* (1844–6), vol. 2, p. 335.

43. C. White, 'An Eyewitness Account of the Battle of Cape, St Vincent', *Trafalgar Chronicle*, 7 (1997), 54.

44. H. Nelson, *Dispatches and Letters* (1844–6), vol. 2, p. 350.

45. Ibid., p. 383.

46. Ibid., vol. 6, pp. 41, 256.

47. H. Nelson, *Nelson's Letters to Lady Hamilton* (1815), vol.2, p. 85.

48. T.J. Pettigrew, *Memoirs of the Life of Vice-Admiral Lord Viscount Nelson* (1849), vol. 2, pp. 221–2.

49. C F. Vandeburgh, *The Mariner's Medical Guide*, (1819), p. 217.

50. W. Beatty, *Authentic Narrative of the Death of Lord Nelson* (1807), p. 374.

51. H. Nelson, *Nelson's Letters to his Wife* (1959), p. 374.

52. G. Blane, Observations *on the Diseases Incident to Seamen* (1785), pp 498–9.

53. H. Nelson, *Nelson's Letters to his Wife* (1959), p. 332.

54. Ibid., p. 374.

55. TNA, ADM 101/123, surgeon's journal, *Theseus*, James Farquhar, 25 July 1797.

56. H. Nelson, *Dispatches and Letters* (1844–6), vol.2, p. 423.

57. TNA, ADM 101/123, surgeon's journal, *Theseus*, James Farquhar, 25 July 1797.

58. C. Lloyd and J.L.S. Coulter, *Medicine and the Navy* (1961), p. 144.

59. TNA, ADM 101/123, surgeon's journal, *Theseus*, James Farquhar, 25 July 1797.

60. H. Nelson, *Dispatches and Letters* (1844–6), vol. 2, p. 444.

61. Ibid., vol. 3, p. 475.

62. H. Nelson, *Nelson's Letters to his Wife* (1959), pp. 332–3.

63. W. Northcote, *The Marine Practice of Physic and Surgery* (1770), p. 445.

64. TNA, ADM 101/123, surgeon's journal, *Theseus*, James Farquhar, 25 July 1797.

65. TNA, ADM 101/23/2, Surgeons' Journal, *HMS Seahorse*, 1797.

66. H. Nelson, *Dispatches and Letters* (1844–6), vol. 2, p. 448.

67. J. Charnock, *Biographical Memoirs of Lord Viscount Nelson* (1806), p. 104.

68. L. Haire,'Remarks on Mr Lucas's Practical Observations on Amputation', London *Medical Journal*, 7/4 (1786), 377.

69. *Medico-Chirurgical Journal*, 3 (1817), 2.

70. H. Nelson, *Nelson's Letters to his Wife* (1959), p. 375.

71. J.S. Clarke and J. McArthur, *Life of Admiral Lord Nelson* (1810), vol. 2, p.67.

72. H. Nelson, *Dispatches and Letters* (1844–6), vol. 2, p. 280.

73. Ibid., p. 441.

74. Ibid., p. 436.

75. Ibid., p. 435.

76. W. Beatty, *Authentic Narrative of the Death of Lord Nelson* (1807), p, 82.

77. H. Nelson, *Dispatches and Letters* (1844–6), vol. 2, p. 455.

78. TNA, ADM 101/124/1, surgeon's journal, *Vanguard*, 1 September 1798.

79. H. Nelson, *Dispatches and Letters* (1844–6), vol. 3, p. 66.

80. TNA, ADM 101/124/1, surgeon's journal, *Vanguard*, 1 September 1798.

81. J. Sugden, *Nelson, The Sword of Albion* (2012), p. 108.

82. H. Nelson, *Dispatches and Letters* (1844–6), vol. 3, p. 100.

83. TNA, ADM 101/124/1, surgeon's journal, *Vanguard*, 1 September 1798.

84. NMM, BHC 2903, Portrait of Nelson wounded at the Nile, possibly by Guy Head, 1798.

85. H. Nelson, *Dispatches and Letters* (1844–6), vol. 3, pp. 66–7.

86. J. Charnock, *Biographical Memoirs of Lord Viscount Nelson* (1806), p.159.

87. H. Nelson, *Dispatches and Letters* (1844–6), vol. 3, p. 424

88. Ibid., p. 83.

89. Ibid., p. 248.

90. The original is in the Admiralty Board Room, Ministry of Defence Art Collection. The copy in the National Maritime Museum (NMM, BHC2895, Leonardo Guzzardi, portrait of Nelson, 1799), may have been made for Nelson himself.

91. H. Nelson, *Dispatches and Letters* (1844–6), vol. 1, p. 70.

92. G. Blane, *Observations on the Diseases Incident to Seamen* (1785), p. 211.

93. J. Austen, *Persuasion* (1992), p. 20, 22, 61.

94. NMM, PAD 5574, Charles Heath, Cockpit of HMS *Vanguard*, 1 August 1798.

95. TNA, ADM 101/85, surgeon's journal, *Ardent*, Robert Young, 11 October 1797.

96. W. Northcote, *The Marine Practice of Physic and Surgery* (1770), vol. 3, p. 445.

97. W. Robinson, *Jack Nastyface* (2002), p. 50.

98. TNA, ADM 101/118/1, surgeon's journal, *Russell*, George Magrath, 1797.

99. W.H. Dillon, *A Narrative of my Professional Adventures* (1953), p.97.

100. W. Robinson, *Jack Nastyface* (2002), pp. 115-6.

101. S. Leech, *Thirty Years from Home* (1844), p.142.

102. *Ibid.*, p. 144.

103. J.C. Goddard, 'The Navy Surgeon's Chest: Surgical Instruments of the Royal Navy during the Napoleonic War', *Journal of the Royal Society of Medicine*, 97/4 (2004), pp. 191-197.

104. TNA, ADM 101/112/6, Medical Journal, *HMS Lion*, J. Young surgeon, 2 January 1798 – 1 January 1800.

105. W. Turnbull, *The Naval Surgeon* (1806), p. 259.

106. G. Blane, *Observations on the Diseases Incident to Seamen* (1785), p. 575.

107. Ibid., p. 498.

108. TNA, ADM 101/106/1, surgeon's journal, *Leviathan*, William Shoveller, 1805.

109. TNA, ADM 101/125/1, surgeon's journal, *Victory*, William Beatty, 21 October 1805.

110. TNA, ADM 101/72, surgeon's journal, *Pickle*, Simon Gage Britton, 24 October 1805.

111. TNA, ADM 101 125/1, surgeon's journal, *Victory*, William Beatty, January 1806.

112. J. Sugden, *Nelson, A Dream of Glory* (2004), p. 703.

113. TNA, ADM 101/106/1, surgeon's journal, *Leviathan*, William Shoveller, 1805.

114. W. Robinson, *Jack Nastyface* (2002), pp.61, 78.

115. H. Nelson, *Dispatches and Letters* (1844-6), vol.7, p. 227.

116. TNA, ADM 101/85, surgeon's journal, *Ardent*, Robert Young, 11 October 1797.

CHAPTER FOUR

1. H. Nelson, *Dispatches and Letters* (1844-6), vol. 1, p. 476.

2. Ibid., p. 273.

3. P.D.G. Pugh, *Nelson and his Surgeons* (1968), p. 3; A.M. E. Hills, *Nelson, A Medical Casebook* (2006), pp. 49-50.

4. J. Bell, *Memoir on the Present State of Naval and Military Surgery* (1798), p. 6.

5. M.J. Cardwell, 'Royal Naval Surgeons, 1793-1815: A Collective Biography' in D.B. Haycock and S. Archer (ed.), *Health and Medicine at Sea* (2009), pp. 40-4.

6. S. Lambert (ed.), *House of Commons Sessional Papers of the Eighteenth Century* (1975), vol. 73, p. 85.

7. Ibid., p.110.

8. T. Trotter, *Medicina Nautica* (1797), vol. 1, pp. 9, 322.

9. R. D. Leach, 'Sir Gilbert Blane MD, FRS', *Annals of the Royal College of Surgeons of England*, 62 (1980), 232-9.

10. B. B. Cooper, *The Life of Sir Astley Cooper*, (1843), vol. 1, p. 306.

11. R. D. Leach, 'Sir Gilbert Blane MD, FRS', *Annals of the Royal College of Surgeons of England*, 62 (1980), 232-9.

12. A.B. Granville, *Autobiography* (1874), vol. 1, p. 303.

13. Ibid., p. 260.

14. H. Nelson, *Dispatches and Letters* (1844-6), vol. 5, p. 439.

15. Ibid., vol. 6, p. 41.

16. H.G. Thursfield, (ed.), *Five Naval Journals* (1951), p. 49.

17. TNA, ADM 106/2896, p. 55, register of officers appointed to ships, 10 March 1739/40.

18. T. Smollett, *Roderick Random* (1979), p. 86.

19. Ibid., p. 149.

20. Ibid., p. 157.

21. Ibid., p. 191.

22. Ibid. p. 183.

23. C. Dunne, *The Chirurgical Candidate* (1808), p. 20.

24. Ibid., p. 26.
25. L. Brockliss, M.J. Cardwell and M. Moss, *Nelson's Surgeon* (2005), p. 18.
26. T. Trotter, *Medicina Nautica* (1797), vol. 1, pp. 14–15.
27. J. Dobson, 'Pernicious Remedy of the Naval Surgeon', *Journal of the Royal Naval Medical Service*, 43 (1957), 23 –8.
28. W. Turnbull, *The Naval Surgeon* (1806), pp. 309–11, 392–3.
29. J. Dobson, 'Pernicious Remedy of the Naval Surgeon', *Journal of the Royal Naval Medical Service*, 43 (1957), 23 –8.
30. M. Crumplin, 'Surgery in the Royal Navy during the Republican and Napoleonic Wars', in D.B. Haycock and S. Archer (ed.), *Health and Medicine at Sea* (2009), pp. 63–89.
31. TNA, ADM 101/106/1, surgeon's journal, *Leviathan*, William Shoveller, 1805.
32. TNA, ADM 101/118/2, surgeon's journal, *Russell*, George Magrath, 1801.
33. TNA, ADM 101/102/4, private diary, Lionel Gillespie, 1787.
34. TNA, ADM 101/93/1, Medical Journal, HMS *Canopus*, Abraham Martin, surgeon, July 1806.
35. Ibid., October 1806.
36. J.C. Goddard, 'Genitourinary Medicine and Surgery in Nelson's Navy', *Postgraduate Medical Journal*, 81 (2005), 413–18.
37. TNA, ADM 101/123/4. Medical journal, *HMS Theseus*, R. Tainish surgeon, 19 August 1797 – 19 August 1798.
38. TNA, ADM 101/80/3 Medical journal, *HMS Aboukir*, J. McMillan surgeon, 16 March 1808 – 15 March 1809.
39. TNA, ADM 101/81/1, Medical Journal, *HMS Etna*, J. Campbell surgeon, 9 July 1807 – 8 July 1808,
40. TNA, ADM 101/123/4. Medical journal, *HMS Theseus*, R. Tainish surgeon, 19 August 1797 – 19 August 1798.
41. TNA, ADM 101/ 83/4, Medical journal, *HMS Alfred*, J. Gray surgeon, 31 August 1810 –31 August 1811.
42. TNA, ADM 101/83/3, Medical journal, *HMS Alfred*, W. Warner surgeon, 1 October 1797 – 31 March 1798.
43. W. Turnbull, *The Naval Surgeon* (1806), pp. 281–5.
44. TNA, ADM 101/106/1, surgeon's journal, *Leviathan*, William Shoveller, 1804.
45. H.G. Thursfield, (ed.), *Five Naval Journals* (1951), p. 29.
46. E.P. Brenton, *Life and Correspondence of John Earl of St Vincent* (1838), vol. 2, p. 256.
47. M.J. Cardwell, 'Royal Naval Surgeons, 1793–1815: A Collective Biography' in D.B. Haycock and S. Archer (ed.), *Health and Medicine at Sea* (2009), pp. 57–8.
48. TNA, ADM 101/85, surgeon's journal, *Ardent*, Robert Young, 11 October 1797; C. Lloyd and J.L.S. Coulter, *Medicine and the Navy* (1961), vol. 3 p. 60.
49. L. Brockliss, M.J. Cardwell and M. Moss, *Nelson's Surgeon* (2005), p. 98.
50. TNA, ADM 101/125/1, surgeon's journal, *Victory*, William Beatty, 21 April 1805.
51. T. Trotter, *Medicina Nautica* (1803), vol. 3, pp. 441–6.
52. Ibid., vol. 3, p. 441.
53. H.G. Thursfield, (ed.), *Five Naval Journals* (1951), pp. 28–9.
54. TNA, ADM 101/85, surgeon's journal, *Ardent*, Robert Young, 11 October 1797.
55. TNA, ADM 101/118/1, surgeon's journal, *Russell*, George Magrath, 1797.
56. TNA, ADM 101/81/1, surgeon's journal, *Aetna*, James Campbell, 8 July 1808.
57. TNA, ADM 101/125/1, surgeon's journal, *Victory*, William Beatty, January 1806.
58. W. Beatty, *Authentic Narrative of the Death of Lord Nelson* (1807), p. 20.
59. Wellcome Library, MS 3680, report of John Snipe, 19 September 1803.
60. D. Pope, *Life in Nelson's Navy* (1981), p. 131; N. A. M. Rodger, 'Medicine and Science in the British Navy of the Eighteenth Century', *L'Homme, la Santé et la Mer*, ed. C. Buchet (1997), pp. 333–44.
61. *The Times*, 8 June 1833.
62. J. J. Keevil, 'Leonard Gillespie, MD, 1758–1842', *Bulletin of the History of*

*Medicine*, 28/4 (1954), 301–332.

63. W.N. Boog Watson, 'Two British Naval Surgeons in the French Wars, *Medical History*, 13 (1969), 215.

64. T. Pocock (ed.), *Trafalgar, An Eyewitness History* (2005), p. 8.

65. L. Brockliss, M.J. Cardwell and M. Moss, *Nelson's Surgeon* (2005), p. 15.

66. Ibid., p. 24.

67. NMM, ADM/F/36, Sick and Hurt Board, 8 December 1804.

68. J. Austen, *Mansfield Park* (1953), p. 314.

69. T. Trotter, *Medicina Nautica* (1804) in C. Lloyd (ed.), *The Health of Seamen* (1965), pp. 257–8.

70. A. Miller, *Dressed to Kill* (2007), pp. 48–9.

71. T. Trotter, *Review of the Medical Department in the British Navy with a Method of Reform Proposed* (1790).

72. T. Trotter, *Medicina Nautica* (1797), vol. 1, p.54.

73. NMM, ADM, F/28, Sick and Hurt Board, 6 February 1798.

74. T. Trotter, *Medicina Nautica* (1803), vol. 3, p. 40.

75. NMM, ADM, F/36, Sick and Hurt Board, 8 December 1805.

76. H. Nelson, *Dispatches and Letters* (1844–6), vol. 6, p. 237.

77. Ibid., p. 41.

78. BL, Add MS 34929, fo. 132, letter from L. Gillespie to Nelson, 15 April 1805.

79. K. Brown, *Passage to the World* (2013), pp. 73–7.

80. I. A. Porter, 'Thomas Trotter, Naval Physician', *Medical History*, 7 (1963), 155–64; B. Vale and G. Edwards, *Physician to the Fleet: The Life and Times of Thomas Trotter* (2011), pp. 145–55.

81. M.J. Cardwell, 'Royal Naval Surgeons, 1793–1815: A Collective Biography' in D.B. Haycock and S. Archer (ed.), *Health and Medicine at Sea* (2009), p. 61.

82. *The Lancet* (9 July 1870), 66–7.

83. Ibid., 66.

84. A. A. Cormack, *Two Royal Physicians: Sir James Clark, Bart., 1788–1870, Sir John Forbes, 1787–1861* (1965), p. 26.

85. *The Lancet* (9 July 1870), 66–7.

86. T.M. Wybourn, *Sea Soldier* (2000), pp. 57–8.

87. W.H. Dillon, *A Narrative of my Professional Adventures 1790–1839* (1953), vol. 1. p.144.

CHAPTER FIVE

1. E. Codrington, *Memoir of the Life of Admiral Sir Edward Codrington* (1873), vol. 1, p. 126.

2. W. Robinson, *Jack Nastyface* (2002), p. 87.

3. H.G. Thursfield, *Five Naval Journals*, (1951), p. 8.

4. R.M. Pallet, *Views of England* (1818), p. 218.

5. E. Hawker, *Statement of Certain Immoral Practices prevailing in His Majesty's Navy* (1822), p. 3.

6. W. Robinson, *Jack Nastyface* (2002), p. 89.

7. Ibid., p. 92.

8. R.M. Pillet, *Views of England* (1818), p. 218.

9. D. Goodall, *Salt Water Sketches* (1860), p.p. 25–6.

10. Ibid., pp. 26–7.

11. E. Hawker, *Statement of Certain Immoral Practices prevailing in His Majesty's Navy* (1822), p.2.

12. G. Watson, *Narrative of the Adventures of a Greenwich Pensioner* (1827), pp. 22–3.

13. J. Harris, *Harris's List of Covent Garden Ladies for the Year 1788* (1788), p. 91.

14. T. Pocock, *Sailor King: The Life of King William IV* (1991), p. 71.

15. D. Goodall, *Salt Water Sketches* (1860), pp. 25–6.

16. G. Pinckard, *Notes on the West Indies* (1806), p. 38.

17. D. Goodall, *Salt Water Sketches* (1860), p. 26.

18. E. Hawker, *Statement of Certain Immoral Practices prevailing in His Majesty's Navy* (1822), p.4.

19. J. Lowry, *Fiddlers and Whores* (2006), p. 119.

20. Ibid., p. 107.

21. Ibid., p. 31.

22. Ibid. p. 23.

23. B. Lavery (ed.), *Shipboard Life and Organisation* (1998), p.382.

24. J.D. Byrn (ed.), *Naval Courts Martial (*2009), pp. 328–9.

25. TNA, ADM 1/5346, Court Martial of Francisco Falso and John Lambert, 1798.

26. *Morning Chronicle,* 6 October 1806.
27. TNA. ADM 1/5383, Court Martial of William Berry, 1806.
28. *The Times,* 22 October 1807.
29. J. E.P. Brenton, *Life and Correspondence of John, Earl St Vincent* (1838), vol. 1, p.364.
30. J. Nagle, *Journal,* p. 211.
31. TNA, ADM 1/5337, Court Martial of Charles Sawyer, 1796.
32. F. Grose, *Dictionary of the Vulgar Tongue* (1811), p. 31
33. J.D. Byrn (ed.), *Naval Courts Martial (*2009), pp. 337–43.
34. TNA, ADM 1/5428, Court Martial of William Bouch, 1812.
35. B. Ruspini, *Treatise on Teeth* (1797), p, 64.
36. TNA, ADM 101/118/1, surgeon's journal, *Leviathan,* 1804.
37. K. Brown, *The Pox* (2006), pp. 86–90.
38. TNA, ADM 101/118/1, surgeon's journal, *Russell,* George Magrath, 1798.
39. TNA, ADM 101/10/4, surgeon's journal, *Racehorse,* Lionel Gillespie, 1797.
40. H.G. Thursfield, *Five Naval Journals,* (1951), p. 226.
41. P. Ziegler, *King William IV* (171), p. 51.
42. *The Medico-chirurgical Journal,* 1 (1819), 2.
43. TNA, ADM 101/ 82/3, Medical Journal, HMS *Albion,* J.C. Watson surgeon, *13 April 1799 – 2 January 1801.*
44. TNA, ADM 101/120/6, Medical Journal, HMS *Seahorse,* T. Shelby surgeon, 20 August 1797 – 20 August 1798.
45. TNA, ADM 101/ 80/5 Medical Journal, HMS *Adventure,* D. Parry surgeon, 12 June 1799–20 April 1800.
46. W. Northcote, *The Marine Practice of Physic and Surgery ( 1770),* p. 321.
47. BL, C112, collection of 185 advertisements, fo. 9, 2.
48. Ibid., fo. 9, 93.
49. BL, 551, collection of 231 advertisements, a.32, 14.
50. *Woolmer's Exeter and Plymouth Gazette,* 18 May 1809.
51. TNA, ADM 101/82/3, Medical Journal HMS *Albion,* S. Allen surgeon, 4 April 1802 – 5 May 1802.
52. T. Trotter, *Medicina Nautica* (1804) in C. Lloyd (ed.), *The Health of Seamen* (1965), p. 229.
53. R. Robertson, Observations *on the Jail, Hospital or Ship Fever* (1807) vol. 1, p. 479.
54. TNA, ADM 1/903, Sick and Hurt Board, 19 June 1740.
55. T. Trotter, *Medicina Nautica* (1804) in C. Lloyd (ed.), *The Health of Seamen* (1965), p. 229.

CHAPTER SIX
1. W. Turnbull, *The Naval Surgeon* (1806), p. 48.
2. A. Fremantle, *The Wynne Diaries* (1940), p. 205.
3. H. Nelson, *Dispatches and Letters* (1844–6), vol. 5, p. 438.
4. TNA, ADM 1/411, report of L. Gillespie, 14 August 1805.
5. D. Goodall, *Salt Water Sketches* (1860), pp. 51–2.
6. R. Hay *Landsman Hay* (1953), p. 94.
7. S. Leech, *Thirty Years from Home* (1844), pp. 90–1.
8. J. Durand, *An Able Seaman of 1812* (1926), p. 59.
9. T. Pocock (ed.), *Trafalgar, An Eyewitness History* (2005), p. 8.
10. A. Crawford, *Reminiscences of a Naval Officer* (1851), vol. 1, p. 78.
11. S. Leech, *Thirty Years from Home* (1844), pp. 90–1.
12. G. Watson, *Narrative of the Adventures of a Greenwich Pensioner* (1827), p. 88.
13. D. Goodall, *Salt Water Sketches* (1860), pp. 72–3.
14. TNA, ADM 101/108/3, Notes, *Maidstone,* Sampson Hardy, 1800–02
15. D. Goodall, *Salt Water Sketches* (1860), pp. 51–2.
16. Ibid., pp. 116–18.
17. C. Collingwood, *Correspondence* (1829), pp. 269–70.
18. J. Scott, *Recollections of a Naval Life* (1834), vol. 1, p. 40.
19. H.G. Thursfield, *Five Naval Journals,* (1951), p. 257.
20. S. Leech, *Thirty Years from Home* (1844), pp. 124–5.
21. A. Sinclair, *Reminiscences* (1857), p. 84.
22. T. Pasley, *Private Sea Journals* (1931),

p. 128.

23. A. Fremantle, *The Wynne Diaries* (1940), p. 261.

24. Ibid., p. 251.

25. J.A. Gardner, *Recollections* (1906), p. 42.

26. J. Scott, *Recollections of a Naval Life* (1834), vol. 2, p. 233.

27. A. Crawford, *Reminiscences of a Naval Officer* (1851), vol. 2, p.340.

28. S. Leech, *Thirty Years from Home* (1844), p. 74.

29. H.G. Thursfield, (ed.), *Five Naval Journals* (1951), p. 88.

30. C. Lloyd and J.L.S. Coulter, *Medicine and the Navy* (1961), vol. 3, p. 163.

31. T. Trotter, *A Practicable Plan for Manning the Royal Navy* (1819), pp. 22–3.

32. Ibid., p. 27.

33. Ibid., pp. 26–7.

34. E. Ford, *Life and Work of William Redfern* (1953), pp. 24–33.

35. W. Hotham, *Pages and Portraits* (1919), vol. 1, p. 119.

36. T. Fernyhough, *Military Memoirs* (1829), p. 57.

37. T.M. Wybourn, *Sea Soldier* (2000), p, 109.

38. S. Leech, *Thirty Years from Home* (1844), p. 104.

39. Ibid., p. 105.

40. BL, MS 34953, letter from H. Nelson to G. Gaskin, Secretary, S.P.C.K., 9 September 1803.

41. J. Bates, *Autobiography* (1868), p. 41.

42. T.M. Wybourn, Sea *Soldier* (2000), p. 122.

43. B. Lavery, *Royal Tars* (2010), p. 268.

44. S. Leech, *Thirty Years from Home* (1844), p. 112.

45. W. Turnbull, *The Naval Surgeon* (1806), p. 113.

46. Royal Marines Museum, Eastney Barracks, Portsmouth, recruiting posters.

47. G. Blane, *On the Comparative Health of the Navy* (1789) in C. Lloyd (ed.), *The Health of Seamen* (1965), pp. 162–3.

48. Ibid., p. 164.

49. TNA, ADM 1/232, order from Admiral Vernon, 21 August 1740.

50. D. Goodall, *Salt Water Sketches* (1860), p. 23.

51. T. Trotter, *Medicina Nautica* (1804), vol. 3, p. 129.

52. TNA, ADM 1/116, letter from St Vincent to Admiralty, 8 July 1800.

53. TNA, ADM 1/117, letter from St Vincent to Admiralty, 10 February 1801, enclosing letter of T. Trotter, 9 February 1801.

54. Lord Keith, *The Letters and Papers of Admiral Viscount Keith* (1926–55), vol. 3, p. 320.

55. G. Blane, *On the Comparative Health of the Navy* (1789) in C. Lloyd (ed.), *The Health of Seamen* (1965), p. 191.

56. TNA, ADM 101/125/1, surgeon's journal, *Victory*, William Beatty, 29 December 1804 – January 1806.

57. H.G. Thursfield, (ed.), *Five Naval Journals* (1951), p. 256.

58. W. Robinson, *Jack Nastyface* (2002), p.34.

59. S. Leech, *Thirty Years from Home* (1844), pp. 49–51.

60. G.V. Jackson, *The Perilous Adventures and Vicissitudes of a Naval Officer* (1927), p. 11.

61. D. Goodall, *Salt Water Sketches* (1860), p. 22.

62. J. Sugden, *Nelson: A Dream of Glory* (2004), p. 356.

63. TNA, ADM 101/125/1, surgeon's journal, *Victory*, William Beatty, 29 December 1804 – January 1806.

64. H. Nelson, *Dispatches and Letters* (1844–6), vol. 6, p. 211.

65. R. Hay *Landsman Hay* (1953), pp. 76–7.

66. D. Orde, *In the Shadow of Nelson* (2008), p. 7.

67. C. Collingwood, *A Selection from the Private and Public Correspondence* (1829), p. 413.

68. Ibid., pp. 51–2.

69. J.S. Clarke and J. McArthur, *Life of Admiral Lord Nelson* (1810), vol. 1, p. 130.

70. J. Sugden, *Nelson: A Dream of Glory* (2004), p. 340.

71. J. Briggs, *The History of Don Francisco de Miranda's Attempt to Effect a Revolution in South America in a Series of Letters* (1809), pp. 190–1.

72. K. Racine, *Francisco de Miranda: A Transatlantic Life in the Age of Revolution* (2002), p. 254.

73. Ibid., p. 164.

74. T. Trotter, *Medicina Nautica* (1797), vo. 1, p. 37.

75. H. Nelson, *Dispatches and Letters* (1844–6), vol. 3, p. 96.
76. Ibid., vol. 2, p. 230.
77. J.S. Clarke and J. McArthur, *Life of Admiral Lord Nelson* (1810), vol. 1, p. 14.
78. H. Nelson, *Dispatches and Letters* (1844–6), vol. 1, p. 186.
79. Ibid., vol. 4, p. 190.
80. Ibid., vol. 4, p. 401.
81. Ibid., vol. 6, 357.
82. Ibid., p. 392.
83. H. Nelson, *Nelson's Letters to Lady Hamilton* (1815), vol. 2, p. 87.
84. Ibid., vol. 1, p. 74.
85. H. Nelson, *Dispatches and Letters* (1844–6), vol. 6, p. 400.
86. W. Beatty, *Authentic Narrative of the Death of Lord Nelson* (1807), p. 80.
87. H. Nelson, *Dispatches and Letters* (1844–6), vol. 4, p. 401.
88. G. Blane, 'Statements on the Comparative Health of the Navy', *Medico-Chirurgical Transactions,* 6 (1815), 490–573.
89. C. Lloyd and J.L.S. Coulter, *Medicine and the Navy* (1961), vol.3, p. 354.
90. TNA, ADM 101/118/2, surgeon's journal, *Russell, 1801.*
91. W. Robinson, *Jack Nastyface* (2002), p. 113.
92. *Morning Chronicle,* 18 December 1787.
93. H. Nelson, *Dispatches and Letters* (1844–6), vol. 2, p. 394.
94. H. Nelson, *Dispatches and Letters* (1844–6), vol. 7, p. 58.
95. *Mariner's Mirror,* 92 (2006), 191.
96. NMM, 98/1, Sick and Hurt Board, 20 July 1743; J. Andrews, A. Briggs, R.
97. Porter, P. Tucker and K. Waddington, *The History of the Bethlem* (1997), p. 349.
98. *House of Commons Debates* (8 May 1811), vol. 19 cc. 1015–6.
99. J.W. Rogers, *A Statement of the Cruelties, Abuses and Frauds Practised in Mad-Houses* (1815), p. 194.
100. 'Committee on Madhouses', PP 1814–15 (296) IV.801, 26, 193.
101. E. Murphy, 'The Mad-House Keepers of East London', *History Today,* 51/9 (2001), 29–35.
102. TNA, ADM 105/28, remarks on lunatic cases at Hoxton, 13

November 1812.
103. Ibid.
104. C. Collingwood, *A Selection from the Private and Public Correspondence* (1829), p, 66.

CHAPTER SEVEN
1. H. Nelson, *Dispatches and Letters* (1844–6), vol. 5, p. 43.
2. Wellcome Library, MS 3680, report of J. Snipe, 19 September 1803.
3. H. Nelson, *Dispatches and Letters* (1844–6), vol. 7, p. 215.
4. C. Lloyd and J.L.S. Coulter, *Medicine and the Navy* (1961), vol. 3, pp. 70–1.
5. G. Blane, 'Statements on the Comparative Health of the Navy', *Medico-Chirurgical Transactions,* 6 (1815) 510.
6. S. Hales, *Description of Ventilators* (1743).
7. S. Sutton, 'Historical Account of a New Method of Extracting the Foul Air out of Ships' (1757) in R. Mead, *The Medical Works of Dr Richard Mead* (1762), p. 414.
8. Ibid., p. 443.
9. J. Lind, *An Essay on the Most Effectual Means of Preserving the Health of Seamen* (1773), p. 29.
10. T. Trotter, *Medicina Medica* (1797–1803), vol. 3, p. 285.
11. G. Blane, 'Statements on the Comparative Health of the Navy', *Medico-Chirurgical Transactions,* 6 (1815), 511.
12. NMM, ADM F/36, Sick and Hurt Board, 24 October 1804.
13. S. Leech, *Thirty Years from Home* (1844), p. 84.
14. W. Robinson, *Jack Nastyface* (2002), p. 6.
15. A.J. Griffiths, Observations *on some Points of Seamanship* (1824), pp. 192–3.
16. Lord Keith, *The Letters and Papers of Admiral Viscount Keith* (1926–55), vol. 2, p. 412
17. G. Blane, 'On the Comparative Health of the Navy' (1789), in C. Lloyd (ed.) *The Health of Seamen* (1965), p.p. 182–3.
18. TNA, ADM 51/1454.
19. TNA, ADM 1/411, report of Leonard Gillespie, 14 August 1805.
20. Wellcome Library, MS 36080, letter from J. Snipe to Nelson, 7 November

1803.

21. TNA, ADM 98/14, Sick and Hurt Board, 26 April 1782.

22. NMM, E/45, Admiralty to Sick and Hurt Board, 19 November 1795, 16 February 1796.

23. T. Trotter, *Medicina Medica* (1797–1803), vol. 1, p. 120.

24. Ibid., vol. 3, p. 441.

25. A. Crawford, *Reminiscences of a Naval Officer* (1851), vol. 2, p. 220.

26. Cited by R. and |L. Adkins, *Jack Tar* (2008), p. 140.

27. TNA, ADM 1/5346.

28. TNA, ADM 51/1454.

29. R. Robertson, Observations *on the Jail, Hospital or Ship Fever* (1807) vol. 1, pp. 432–3.

30. G. Blane, *Observations on the Diseases Incident to Seamen* (1785), p. 53.

31. Ibid., pp. 109–10

32. W. Robinson, *Jack Nastyface* (2002), p. 61.

33. S. Willis, *In the Hour of Victory* (2013), p. 73.

34. T. Trotter, *Medicina Nautica* (1797), vol. 1, pp. 55–6.

35. J. Prior, *Voyage in the Indian Seas in the Nisus Frigate* (1820), p. 49.

36. Ibid, p. 49.

37. R. Hay, *Landsman Hay* (1953), p. 102.

38. J.A. Gardner, *Recollections of James Anthony Gardner* (1906), pp. 244–5.

39. Wellcome Library, MS 3677, stores on *HMS Victory*, 1803–05.

40. G. Watson, *Narrative of the Adventures of a Greenwich Pensioner* (1827), pp. 126–7.

41. D. Goodall, *Salt Water Sketches* (1860), p. 67.

42. R. and L. Adkins, *Jack Tar* (2008), p.79.

43. Wellcome Library, MS 3677, stores on *HMS Victory*, 1803–05.

44. H.G. Thursfield, *Five Naval Journals*, (1951), p. 246.

45. Ibid., p. 247.

46. D. Goodall, *Salt Water Sketches* (1860), pp. 132–3.

47. B. Hall, *Fragments of Voyages and Travels* (1846), series 1, p. 137.

48. W. Robinson, *Jack Nastyface* (2002), p. 7.

49. B. Hall, *Fragments of Voyages and Travels* (1846), series 1, p. 138.

50. A. Sinclair, *Reminiscences* (1857), pp. 37–9.

51. J. Raigersfield, *The Life of a Sea Officer* (1929), p. 18.

52. Ibid., p. 24.

53. G. Watson, *Narrative of the Adventures of a Greenwich Pensioner* (1827), p. 148.

54. H.G. Thursfield, *Five Naval Journals*, (1951), p. 31.

55. J. Prior, *Voyage in the Indian Seas in the Nisus Frigate* (1820), p. 76.

56. H. Nelson, *Dispatches and Letters* (1844–6), vol. 6, p. 251.

57. Ibid., vol. 7, pp. 102–5.

58. Ibid., vol. 7, p. ccxvii.

59. Ibid., vol. 6, p. 27.

60. J. Bowden-Dan, 'Diet, Dirt and Discipline: Medical Developments in Nelson's Navy, Dr John Snipe's Contribution', *Mariner's Mirror*, 90 (2004), 260–72.

61. T.M. Wybourn *Sea Soldier* (2000), p.71.

62. Wellcome Library, MS 3678, provisions in the Squadron.

63. H. Nelson, *Dispatches and Letters* (1844–6), vol. 6, p. 74.

64. T. Trotter, *Medicina Nautica* (1804), vol. 3, p.129.

65. R. and L. Adkins, *Jack Tar* (2008), p. 86.

66. R. Hay *Landsman Hay* (1953), p. 170.

67. Ibid., p. 171.

68. J.A. Gardner, *Recollections* (1906), p. 139.

69. W.H. Dillon, *Narrative of my Professional Adventures* (1953), vol. 1, p. 397.

70. T. Trotter, *Medicina Nautica* (1804), vol. 3, p. 279.

71. Ibid., p. 280.

72. R. and L. Adkins, *Jack Tar* (2008), p. 91.

73. J. Raigersfield, *The Life of a Sea Officer* (1929), p. 23.

74. T.M. Wybourn, Sea *Soldier* (2000), p. 73.

75. J. J. Keevil, 'Leonard Gillespie, MD, 1758–1842', *Bulletin of the History of Medicine*, 28/4 (1954), 301.

76. H.G. Thursfield, *Five Naval Journals*, (1951), p. 29.

77. J. Scott, *Recollections of a Naval Life* (1834), vol. 1, p. 21.

78. T.M. Wybourn, Sea *Soldier* (2000), p. 66.

79. G. Blane, *Observations on the Diseases Incident to Seamen* (1785), pp. 295, 301, 307.
80. Wellcome Library, MS 36080, letter from J. Snipe to Nelson, 7 November 1803.
81. J. Lind, *An Essay on the Most Effectual Means of Preserving the Health of Seamen* (1774), p. 105; *An Essay on Diseases Incidental to Europeans in Hot Climates* (1808), pp. 351, 366.
82. F.B. Spilsbury, *Account of a Voyage to the Western Coast of Africa* (1807), p. 6.
83. G.V. Jackson, *The Perilous Adventures and Vicissitudes of a Naval Officer* (1927), p. 5.
84. A. Fremantle, *The Wynne Diaries* (1940), p. 245.
85. Ibid., p. 128
86. C.R. Pemberton, *Life and Literary Remains* (1843), p. 161.
87. J. J. Keevil, 'Leonard Gillespie, MD, 1758–1842', *Bulletin of the History of Medicine*, 28/4 (1954), 301.
88. T. Trotter, *Medicina Nautica* (1804), in C. Lloyd (ed.), *The Health of the Seaman* 1965), pp. 270–1.
89. N.A.M. Rodger, *Command of the Navy* (204), p. 308. Rodger is understandably dismissive of such exaggerated figures.
90. C. Lloyd (ed.), *The Health of Seaman* (1965), p.9.
91. J. Woodall, *The Surgion's Mate* (1978), p. 180.
92. TNA, ADM 354/132/41, James Cleveland, 19 February 1746.
93. NMM, ADM/E/43, Admiralty to Sick and Hurt Board, 1781–1783, 15 August 1782, ADM/E/12, Admiralty to Sick and Hurt Board, 1746–1750, 15 October, 11 December, 1747, 24 May, 27 December, 1748.
94. TNA, ADM 354/113/143, letter from W. Cockburn, 1 November 1740.
95. NMM, ADM/F/17, letter from surgeon on HMS Intrepid to Sick and Hurt Board, 4 January 1758.
96. NMM, ADM/G/785, Abstracts of Admiralty orders to Victualling Board, 1770–1774, 25 November 1771; ADM/E/41, Admiralty to Sick and Hurt Board, January 1770-December 1774, 20 January 1772.
97. J. Cook, *The Voyages of Captain Cook* (1999), p. 227.
98. Ibid., p. 38.
99. J. Banks, *Journal* (1896), p. 71.
100. See K. Brown, *Poxed and Scurvied* (2011), pp. 63–7.
101. J. Lind, *A Treatise of the Scurvy* (1753), pp. 145–8.
102. K. Carpenter, *The History of Scurvy and Vitamin C*, (1966), p.53. See also D. I. Harvie, *Limeys* (2002).
103. J. Lind, A Treatise of the Scurvy (1753), p. 203.
104. Ibid., p. 137.
105. Ibid., pp. 137–8.
106. G. Blane, *Observations on the Diseases of Seamen* (1789) in C. Lloyd (ed.), *The Health of Seamen* (1965), p. 160.
107. T. Trotter, *Medicina Nautica* (1797), vol.1, p. 424.
108. TNA, ADM 101/81/5, surgeon's log, James Scott, Ajax, 27 July 1799–31 January 1800.
109. T. Trotter, *Medicina Nautica* (1803), vol. 3, 390.
110. TNA, ADM 354/182/198, petition of Captain Murray, 1 September 1769.
111. J. Lind, *Treatise on Scurvy* (3rd. Edition, 1772) in C. Lloyd (ed.), *The Health of Seamen* (1965), p. 24.
112. TNA, ADM 101/82/3, surgeon's journal, Albion, 1799–1800.
113. TNA, ADM 101/96/1, surgeon's journal, Peter Henry, Daedalus, 1 January – 4 December 1802.
114. TNA, ADM 98/17, letter from Sick and Hurt Board, 27 May 1795.
115. NMM, ADM FP/36, letter from A. Gardner, 4 December 1793.
116. TNA, ADM 98/118, Sick and Hurt Board to Admiralty, 13 December 1793.
117. NMM, RAI/4, letter of P. Rainier to Sick and Hurt Board, 29 September 1794.
118. NMM, ADM d/40, letter of Sick and Hurt Board to Admiralty, 8 November 1796.
119. TNA, ADM 1/116, letter from St Vincent to Admiralty, 10 June 1800; TNA, ADM 2/948, Admiralty to St Vincent, 21 June 1800.
120. NMM, ADM F/26; Sick and Hurt Board to Admiralty, 27 May 1795; ibid., ADM F/27, 5 January 1797.
121. NMM, ADM E/47, letters from T. Trotter to Admiralty, 19 July, 28 September 1800.

122. NMM, ADM F/31, Sick and Hurt Board to Admiralty, 14 July 1800.

123. NMM, ADM F/32, Sick and Hurt Board to Admiralty, 27 January 1802.

124. Wellcome Library, MS 3680, report of L. Gillespie, 24 February 1805.

125. H. Nelson, *Dispatches and Letters* (1844–6), vol. 1, p. 67.

126. W. Beatty, *Authentic Narrative of the Death of Lord Nelson* (1807), p. 78.

127. H. Nelson, *Dispatches and Letters* (1844–6), vol. 7, p. 74.

128. Wellcome Library, MS 3677, correspondence of Nelson, Snipe, Saunders and Broadbent, 1804–05.

129. H. Nelson, *Dispatches and Letters* (1844–6), vol. 6, pp. 141–2.

130. Wellcome Library, MS 3681, letter from Sick and Hurt Board to Nelson, 29 May 1805.

131. Wellcome Library, MS 3680, report of L. Gillespie, 24 February 1805.

132. T. Trotter, *Medicina Nautica* (1799), vol. 2, p. 127.

133. NMM, ADM/F/31, Sick and Hurt Board, 7 September 1800.

134. Ibid., 13 September 1800.

135. T. Trotter, *Medicina Nautica* (1797), vol. 1, p. 387.

136. J. Baron, *Life of Edward Jenner* (1827), p. 402.

137. Ibid., pp. 396–7.

138. Ibid., p. 397.

139. Ibid., p. 400.

140. I. and J. Glynn, *The Life and Death of Smallpox* (2004), p. 121.

141. J. Baron, *Life of Edward Jenner* (1827), p. 406.

142. H. Nelson, *Letters to Lady Hamilton (1814)*, vol.1, p. 41.

143. E. Vincent, *Nelson, Love and Fame* (2003), p. 524.

144. T. Trotter, *Observations on the Scurvy* (1786), pp. 180–1.

145. H. Nelson, *Dispatches and Letters* (1844–6), vol. 6, p. 480.

146. Ibid., p. 474.

147. Ibid., p. 479.

148. TNA, ADM 1/411, report of L. Gillespie, 14 August 1805.

149. Ibid., 4 August 1805.

150. TNA, ADM 101/125/1, medical journal of W. Beatty, *Victory*, 1804–6.

151. M. Harrison, *Disease and the Modern World, 1500 to the Present Day* (2004), p. 68.

CHAPTER EIGHT

1. Wellcome Library, MS 3681, letter from Nelson to Sick and Hurt Board, 7 August 1804.

2. H. Nelson, *Dispatches and Letters* (1844–6), vol. 5, p. 439.

3. Ibid., vol. 6, p.36.

4. Ibid., vol. 5, p. 439.

5. G. Blane, *Observations on the Diseases Incident to Seamen* (1785), p. 338.

6. A.M. Akehurst, 'The Hospital de la Isla del Rey, Minorca: Britain's Island Hospital', *Architectural History*, 53 (2010), 123–61.

7. K Harland, 'The Royal Naval Hospital at Minorca, 1711: An Example of an Admiral's Involvement in the Expansion of Naval Medical Care', *Mariner's Mirror 94/1 (2008)*, 36–47.

8. Amics de l'Illa de l'Hospital Fundacion de la Isla del Rey, *The Hospital on the Island del Rey* (2010), p. 107; A.H. Morejón, *Topografia del Hospital Militar de Mahón, 1806* (2010), p. 202.

9. The buildings, now a private residential complex, are built in a vernacular style. Observed during visit of author, December 2010.

10. I.L. de Ayala, *Historia de Gibraltar* (1782), vol. 3, p. 370.

11. C. Lawrence, *The History of the Old Naval Hospital Gibraltar* (1994), p. 25.

12. Ibid., p. 28.

13. Ibid., p. 32.

14. BL, Add MS 34919, 34920, reports on Gibraltar Hospital, 1803.

15. Wellcome Library, MS 6242, letter from W. Beatty to Lady Hamilton, 15 October 1806.

16. TNA, ADM 1/407, letter from Nelson to J. Snipe, 25 November 1803.

17. G. Watson, *Adventures of a Greenwich Pensioner* (1827), p.187.

18. Ibid., p. 189.

19. TNA, ADM 1/407, letter from J. Snipe to Nelson, 9 December 1803.

20. C. Lloyd and J.L.S. Coulter, *Medicine and the Navy* (1961), vol. 4, p. 247.

21. TNA, ADM 1/407, letter from J. Snipe to Nelson, 9 December 1803.

22. Ibid., letter from Nelson to Dr.

Baird, 30 May 1804.

23. H. Nelson, *Dispatches and Letters* (1844–6), vol. 6, p. 41.

24. C. Savona-Ventura, *Contemporary Medicine in Malta* (2005), pp. 216–21.

25. The style of this communication corridor is very reminiscent in style of the entrance lobby at Haslar, though externally the classical grandeur of Bighi is totally different from the austerity of the naval hospital at Gosport. Observation of the author from visits to Haslar in November 2009 and Bighi in January 2010.

26. TNA ADM 98/14, report on 'what manner the hospitals abroad may be best conducted', 1785.

27. TNA, ADM 1/407, letter from Nelson to W. Pemberton, 21 December 1803.

28. Wellcome Library, MS 3681, contracts for victualling naval hospitals at Gibraltar and Malta, 1803.

29. Ibid., letter from J. Gray to Nelson, 22 February 1804.

30. C. Lloyd and J.S.L. Coulter, *Medicine and the Navy*, vol. 3 (1961), p. 149.

31. TNA, ADM 98/2, letter from Admiralty to Sick and Hurt Board, 18 June 1745.

32. H. Richardson, *English Hospitals 1660–1948* (1998), p. 79.

33. A.L. Revell, *Haslar the Royal Hospital* (2000), p. 25.

34. G. Pinckard, *Notes on the West Indies* (1808), vol. 1, p. 42.

35. Ibid., pp. 43–4.

36. J. Howard, *The State of the Prisons in England and Wales* (1784), p. 389.

37. J. Tenon, *Journal d'observations sur les principaux hôpitaux d'Angleterre* (1992), p. 150.

38. A.L. Revell, *Haslar the Royal Hospital* (2000), p. 21.

39. TNA, ADM 98/7, pp. 374–5, Sick and Hurt Board, 7 February 1759.

40. TNA, ADM 98/6, p. 150, Sick and Hurt Board, 19 January 1757.

41. C. Lloyd and J.S.L. Coulter, *Medicine and the Navy*, vol. 3 (1961), p. 253.

42. B. Vale and G. Edwards, *Physician to the Fleet: The Life and Times of Thomas Trotter* (2011), p. 90.

43. TNA, ADM 101/85, surgeon's journal, *Ardent*, Robert Young, June–July 1797.

44. Ibid., 11 October 1797.

45. Oxford Archaeology, *The Paddock, Royal Naval Hospital Haslar, Gosport (A2005.35) Archaeological Evaluation Report*, November 2005, https://librarythehumanjourney.net /1141/1/A2005.35.pdfA.pdf accessed 28 January 2015.

46. T. Trotter, *Medicina Nautica* (1797), vol. 1, pp. 36–7.

47. TNA, ADM 1/3533, Marine instructions for taking care of sick and wounded seamen, 12 January 1782.

48. J. Tenon, *Journal d'observations sur les principaux hôpitaux d'Angleterre* (1992), pp. 183–4.

49. Regulations drawn up by James Lind, 1777, in C. Lloyd and J.S.L. Coulter, *Medicine and the Navy*, vol. 3 (1961), pp. 219–26.

50. J. Tenon, *Journal d'observations sur les principaux hôpitaux d'Angleterre* (1992), pp. 154–5.

51. T. Trotter, *Medicina Nautica* (1797), vol. 1, pp. 27–8.

52. Ibid., pp. 15–27.

53. Ibid., p. 27.

54. T. Trotter, *Medicina Nautica*, (1803), vol. 3, p. 18.

55. TNA, ADM 1/3534, letter from Stephen Love Hammick, 4 September 1805.

56. TNA, ADM 1/3533, Remarks made upon an examination of the Royal Hospital at Haslar, 28 March – 4 April 1792.

57. E. Birbeck, A. Ryder and P. Ward, *The Royal Haslar Hospital* (2009), p. 65.

58. TNA ADM 1/3534, statement of May Bill, 27 February 1805.

59. Ibid., statement of Sarah Perrott, 27 February 1805.

60. TNA, ADM 98/13, report of Admiral Barrington to Sick and Hurt Board, 25 July 1780.

61. NMM, ADM E/45, Sick and Hurt Board, 14 August 1795.

62. C. Lloyd and J.S.L. Coulter, *Medicine and the Navy*, vol. 3 (1961), p. 266.

63. Ibid., p. 276.

64. NMM. ADM E/30, letter from Walker to Creyke, 23 October 1799; ADM E/47, Admiralty to Sick and

Hurt Board, 1 November 1799.

65. NMM, ADM F/30, T. Trotter to Admiralty, 24 October 1799.

66. C. Lloyd and J.S.L. Coulter, *Medicine and the Navy*, vol. 4 (1963), pp. 218–19.

67. H. Richardson, *English Hospitals 1660–1948* (1998), p. 82.

68. C. Lloyd and J.S.L. Coulter, *Medicine and the Navy*, vol. 4 (1963), p. 244.

69. NMM, ADM F/28, Sick and Hurt Board, 15 May 1797.

70. Ibid., 20 November 1802.

71. *Naval Chronicle* (1805), 2.

72. TNA, ADM 36/11831, muster roll, *Charon*, 1794.

73. T. Trotter, *A Practicable Plan for Manning the Royal Navy* (1819), pp. 26–7.

74. T. Trotter, *Medicina Nautica*, (1803), vol. 3, pp. 62, 84.

75. T. Pettigrew, *Memoirs of the Life of Vice Admiral Lord Nelson* (1849), vol. 2, p. 162.

76. Ibid., p. 169

77. W. Gye, *The New Bath Directory, for the Year, 1792: Containing an Historical Account of the Ancient and Present State of that Elegant City* (1792), p. 5.

78. H. Nelson, *Dispatches and Letters* (1844–6), vol. 1, p. 37.

79. Ibid., p. 38.

80. J. Sugden, *Nelson, A Dream of Glory* (2004), p. 521.

81. J. Sprange, *The Tunbridge Wells Guide: An Account of the Ancient and Present State of that Place* (1786), p. 93.

82. F. Burney, *Diary and Letters of Madam D'Arblay* (2013), vol. 5, p. 28.

83. R. Russell, *A Dissertation Concerning the Use of Sea Water in Diseases of the Glands* (1753), p. 15.

84. J. Austen, *Persuasion*, (1992), pp. 94, 95, 97.

85. Royal Charter of Greenwich Hospital, William III and Mary II, 25 October 1694.

86. R. Robertson, *Synopsis Morborum: Observations on Diseases Incident to Seamen* (1817), p. 779.

87. H. Nelson, *Dispatches and Letters* (1844–6), vol. 6, p. 109.

88. Ibid., vol. 7, p. 106.

89. C. Wright and C.E. Fayle, *A History*

*of Lloyd's* (1928), p. 228.

90. J.S. Clarke and J. McArthur, *The Life of Admiral Lord Nelson* (1810), vol. 1, p.120.

CHAPTER NINE

1. W. Beatty, *Authentic Narrative of the Death of Lord Nelson* (1807), p. 38.

2. Ibid., p. 84.

3. NMM, BHC2740, Mather Brown, 'Lord Howe on the Deck of the *Queen Charlotte*, 1 June 1794', c. 1794.

4. W. Beatty, *Authentic Narrative of the Death of Lord Nelson* (1807), p. 31.

5. Ibid., p. 54.

6. Ibid., p. 34.

7. NMM, UNI0024 (Greenwich Hospital Collection), Nelson's undress coat worn at Trafalgar, 1805.

8. C. Collingwood, *A Selection from the Private and Public Correspondence of Vice-Admiral Lord Collingwood* (1829), p. 124.

9. W. Beatty, *Authentic Narrative of the Death of Lord Nelson* (1807), p. 28.

10. Letter from H. Durrant, *The Times*, 26 June 1969.

11. H. Nelson, *Nelson's Letters to Lady Hamilton* (1815), vol., 2, p. 97.

12. J. Sugden, *Nelson: The Sword of Albion* (2012), p. 628.

13. W. Beatty, *Authentic Narrative of the Death of Lord Nelson (1807)*, pp. 19–22.

14. Ibid., p. 10.

15. H. Nelson, *Dispatches and Letters* (1844–6), vol. 6, p. 35.

16. *The Times*, 7 November 1805.

17. W. Beatty, *Authentic Narrative of the Death of Lord Nelson* (1807), p. 74.

18. Ibid., p. 35.

19. L.Brockliss, M.J. Cardwell and M. Moss, *Nelson's Surgeon* (2005), p. 120.

20. Beatty's case and instruments used in 1805 at the Battle of Trafalgar are held by the Royal College of Physicians and Surgeons of Glasgow.

21. W. Beatty, *Authentic Narrative of the Death of Lord Nelson (1807)*, p. 37.

22. H. Nelson, *Dispatches and Letters* (1844–6), vol.7, p. 249.

23. W. Beatty, *Authentic Narrative of the Death of Lord Nelson (1807)*, p. 39.

24. Ibid., pp.42–4

25. *Gibraltar Chronicle*, 2 November 1805.

26. W. Beatty, *Authentic Narrative of the Death of Lord Nelson (1807)*, pp. 42–4.

27. L. Brockliss, M.J. Cardwell and M. Moss, *Nelson's Surgeon* (2005), pp, 118–9. 'Putty Nose' was James Cosgrove, the purser's steward.

28. TNA, ADM 101/125/1, surgeon's journal, *Victory*, William Beatty, 21 October 1805.

29. TNA, ADM 101/72, surgeon's journal, *Pickle*, Simon Gage Britton, 24 October 1805.

30. S. Willis, *In the Hour of Victory* (2013), pp. 276–8.

31. Ibid., p. 280.

32. W. Beatty, *Authentic Narrative of the Death of Lord Nelson (1807)*, pp. 49–50.

33. Ibid., p. 84.

34. *Naval Chronicle*, 14 (1805), 38–40.

35. W. Beatty, *Authentic Narrative of the Death of Lord Nelson (1807)*, p. 84.

36. NMM, BHC0547, Samuel Drummond, 'The Death of Nelson', 1806.

37. NMM, BHC2894 (Greenwich Hospital Collection), Arthur William Devis, 'The Death of Nelson', 1805–7.

38. M. Lincoln (ed.), *Nelson and Napoleon* (2005), p.226.

39. NMM, BHC0566, Benjamin West, 'The Death of Lord Nelson in the Cockpit of the Ship 'Victory'', 1808.

40. M. Lincoln (ed.), *Nelson and Napoleon* (2005), p.226.

41. Walker Art Gallery, Liverpool, Benjamin West, 'The Death of Nelson', 1806.

42. M. Lincoln (ed.), *Nelson and Napoleon* (2005), pp.225–6.

43. NMM, BHC2905, Benjamin West, 'The Immortality of Nelson', 1807.

44. W. Beatty, *Authentic Narrative of the Death of Lord Nelson (1807)*, p. 61.

45. NMM, REL0116, Nelson's hair and pigtail.

46. W. Beatty, *Authentic Narrative of the Death of Lord Nelson (1807)*, p. 63.

47. Ibid., p. 62.

48. Ibid., p. 67.

49. *Naval Chronicle*, 14 (1805), 505–7.

50. Wellcome Library, MS 5141, report on the wounding, death and post-mortem examination of Viscount Nelson, 15 December 1805.

51. W. Beatty, *Authentic Narrative of the Death of Lord Nelson (1807)*, p. 71. It was later presented to Queen Victoria and is now in the Royal Collections at Windsor Castle.

52. W. Beatty, *Authentic Narrative of the Death of Lord Nelson (1807)*, p. 84.

53. Ibid., p. 70.

54. M.K.H. Crumplin, and A. Harrison, 'Death of an Admiral: The Death of Viscount Horatio Nelson', *Association of Surgeons of Great Britain and Ireland Newsletter*, 10 (May 2005), 3–5; M.K.H. Crumplin, 'The Most Triumphant Death: the Passing of Vice-Admiral Lord Horatio Nelson, 21st October 1805', *Journal of the Royal Naval Medical Service*, 91/2 (2005), 92–5; M.K.H. Crumplin, 'The Death of an Admiral : Surgery and Medicine in Nelson's Navy', *Journal of the Royal Naval Medical Service*, 98/1 (2012), 53; D. Wang, W.S. El-Masry, M. Crumplin, S. Eisenstein, R.J. Pusey and T. Meagher, 'Admiral Lord Nelson's Death: Known and Unknown, A Historical Review of the Anatomy' *Spinal Cord*, 43 (2005), 573–6.

55. L. Brockliss, M.J. Cardwell and M. Moss, *Nelson's Surgeon* (2005), pp. 195–6.

56. W. Beatty, *Authentic Narrative of the Death of Lord Nelson (1807)*, p. 72.

57. TNA, ADM 101/93/1, Surgeon's Journal, *Canopus*, Abraham Martin, 1807.

58. BL, Add MS 34992, memo from A. Scott, 20 December 1805.

59. H. Nelson, *Dispatches and Letters* (1844–6), vol.7, p. 259.

60. W. Beatty, *Authentic Narrative of the Death of Lord Nelson (1807)*, p.73.

61. BL, Ad MS 34992, letter from A. Scott to Earl Nelson, 15 December 1805.

62. *The Times*, 10 January 1806.

63. H. Nelson, *Dispatches and Letters* (1844–6), vol.7, p. p. 399–417.

64. D. Orde, *In the Shadow of Nelson* (2008), p. 198.

65. C. Collingwood, *A Selection from the Private and Public Correspondence* (1829), p. 511.

66. C. Collingwood, *The Private Correspondence of Admiral Lord Collingwood* (1957), p. 141.

67. Ibid., p. 529.

68. C. Collingwood, *Private Correspondence* (1957), p, 310.
69. *Quarterly Review*, 37 (1828), 390.
70. C. Collingwood, *A Selection from the Private and Public Correspondence* (1829), p. 419.
71. B. Hall, *Fragments of Voyages and Travels* (1846), p. 148.
72. H.G., Thursfield, *Five Naval Journals 1789–1817* (1951), p. 356.
73. W.H. Dillon, *A Narrative of my Professional Adventures* (1953), vol. 1, p. 138.
74. B. Hall, *Fragments of Voyages and Travels* (1846), p. 147.
75. NMM, MNT0115, oval miniature in locket of Lieutenant James Wilcox, 1806–9.
76. *Naval Chronicle*, 27(1812), 38.
77. Wellcome Library, MS 3680, sick reports, 1804–5.
78. Cited in J. Sugden, *Nelson: The Sword of Albion* (2012), p. 699.
79. Ibid., p. 690.
80. BL, Add MS 34992, 'Wounds received by Lord Nelson', c. 1802.
81. W Robinson, *Jack Nastyface* (2002), p. 49.
82. *The Times*, 2 December 1805.
83. Wellcome Library, MS 3680, report of J. Snipe, 7 May 1804.

# Bibliography

ARCHIVE SOURCES

BRITISH LIBRARY, LONDON
BL, Add MS 34992, Viscount Nelson papers

NATIONAL ARCHIVES, KEW
TNA, ADM, Admiralty
TNA, FO, Foreign Office
TNA, WO, War Office

NATIONAL MARITIME MUSEUM, GREENWICH
NMM, ADM, Admiralty, Sick and Hurt Board

WELLCOME LIBRARY, LONDON
MS 3667–81, Viscount Nelson papers
MS 5141, report on the wounding, death and post-mortem
    examination of Viscount Nelson, 15 December 1805

PRIMARY PRINTED SOURCES
Aldini, Giovanni, *An Account of the Late Improvements in Galvanism*,
    *London*, Cuthell and Martin 1803
Austen, Jane, *Mansfield Park*, London, Collins, 1953
____, _____, *Persuasion*, London, Everyman's Library, 1992
Ayala, Ignazio López de, *Historia de Gibraltar*, Madrid, Antonio de
    Sancha, 1782
Banks, Joseph, *Journal of the Right Honourable Sir Joseph Banks*

*during Captain Cook's first Voyage in HMS Endeavour*, London, MacMillan, 1896

Barham, Charles, *The Letters and Papers of Charles, Lord Barham*, ed. J.K. Laughton, London, Naval Records Society, 1907–11

Bates, Joseph, *The Autobiography of Elder Joseph Bates*, Battle Creek, Michigan, Seventh Day Adventist Publishing, 1868

Beatty, William, *Authentic Narrative of the Death of Lord Nelson*, London, Cadell, 1807

Beaume, Michael la, On *Galvanism*, London, Highley, 1826

Bell John, *Memoir on the Present State of Naval and Military Surgery*, London, J. Lee, 1798

Blackham, Robert J., 'Sea-Sickness', *British Medical Journal*, 1 (1939), 163–7

Blair, Archibald, 'On the Permanency of Achromatic Telescopes constructed with Fluid Object Glasses', *Edinburgh Journal of Science*, 7 (1827), 336–42

Blair, Robert 'Experiments and Observations on the Unequal Refrangibility of Light', *Transactions of the Royal Society of Edinburgh*, 3/2 (1794), 3–76

Blane, Gilbert, *Observations on the Diseases Incident to Seamen*, London, Cooper, 1785

____, _____, 'Statements on the Comparative Health of the Navy', *Medico-Chirurgical Transactions*, 6 (1815), 490–573

Boyle, John, A *Practical Medico-Historical Account of the Western Coast of Africa*, London, Highley, 1831

Brenton, Edward Pelham, *Life and Correspondence of John Earl of St Vincent*, London, Henry Colburn, 1838

Briggs, James, *The History of Don Francisco de Miranda's Attempt to Effect a Revolution in South America in a Series of Letters*, Boston, Oliver and Munroe, 1809

Burney Fanny, *Diary and Letters of Madam D'Arblay*, Cambridge, Cambridge University Press, 2013

Byrn, John D. (ed.), *Naval Courts Martial 1793–1815*, London, Navy Records Society, 2009

Cavallo, Tiberius, *Essay on the Theory and Practice of Medical Electricity*, London, P. Elmsley, 1780

Charnock, John, *Biographical Memoirs of Lord Viscount Nelson*,

London, H.D. Symons, 1806

Clarke, James Stanier, and McArthur, John, *The Life of Admiral Lord Nelson, K.B. from His Lordship's Manuscripts*, London, T. Cadell and W. Davies, 1810

Cleghorn, George, *Observations on the Epidemical Diseases in Minorca from the Year 1744 to 1749*, London, T. Cadell and G. Robinson, 1779

Cockburn, G, *A Voyage to Cadiz and Gibraltar, up the Mediterranean to Sicily and Malta in 1810*, London, J. Harding, 1815

Codrington, Edward, *Memoir of the Life of Admiral Sir Edward Codrington*, London, Longmans Green, 1873

Collingwood, Cuthbert, *A Selection from the Private and Public Correspondence of Vice-Admiral Lord Collingwood*, ed. G.L. Newnham Collingwood, London, 1829

____, _____, *Private Correspondence of Admiral Lord Collingwood*, ed. Edward Hughes, London, Navy Records Society, 1957

Cook, James, *The Journals*, ed. Philip Edwards, London, Penguin, 1999

____, _____, *The Voyages of Captain Cook*, ed. Jonathan Barrow, Ware, Wordsworth Editions, 1999

Crawford, Abraham, *Reminiscences of a Naval Officer during the Late War*, London, Henry Colburn, *1851*

Crew, Bob, *Sea Poems: A Seafarer Anthology*, Rendlesham, Seafarer, 2005

Dancer, Thomas, *A Brief History of the Late Expedition against Fort Juan*, Kingston, Jamaica, Douglas and Aikman, 1781

Dillon, William Henry, *A Narrative of my Professional Adventures 1790–1839*, ed. Michael Lewis, London, Navy Records Society, 1953

Dollond, Peter, *Some Account of the Discovery, which led to the Grand Improvement of Refracting Telescopes, made by the late Mr John Dollond FRS., in order to correct some Misrepresentations in Foreign Publications, of that Discovery'*, London, J. Johnson, 1789

Duffy, Michael (ed.), *Naval Miscellany VI*, London, Navy Records Society, 2003

Dunne, Charles, *The Chirurgical Candidate*, London, L. Harrison, 1808

Durand, James, *James Durand: An Able Seaman of 1812, his Adventures on Old Ironsides and as an Impressed Sailor in the British Navy*, ed. G.S. Brooks, New Haven, Yale University Press, 1926

Fernyhough, T, *Military Memoirs of Four Brothers engaged in the Service of their Country*, London, 1829

Fielding, John, *An Account of the Receipts and Disbursements Relating to Sir John Fielding's Plan for the Preserving of Distressed Boys by Sending them to Sea*, London, W. Griffin, 1769

Fremantle, A, *The Wynne Diaries*, Oxford, Oxford University Press, 1940

Gardner, James Anthony, *Recollections of James Anthony Gardner*, ed. R.V. Hamilton and J.K. Laughton, London, Navy Records Society, 1906

Gillespie, Leonard, *Observations on the Diseases which Prevailed in HM Squadron in the Leeward Islands*, London, J. Cuthell, 1800

Goodall, Daniel, *Salt Water Sketches, being Incidents in the Life of Daniel Goodall*, Inverness, Advertiser, 1860

Granville, Augustus Bozzi, *Autobiography of A. B. Granville, M.D., F.R.S. : being eighty-eight Years of the Life of a Physician who Practised his Profession in Italy, Greece, Turkey, Spain, Portugal, the West Indies, Russia, Germany, France, and England*, London, H. S. King, 1874

Griffiths, Anselm John, *Observations on some points of Seamanship*, Cheltenham, J.J. Hadley, 1824

Grose Francis, *Dictionary of the Vulgar Tongue*, London, C. Chappel, 1811

Gye, W., *The New Bath Directory, for the Year, 1792: Containing an Historical Account of the Ancient and Present State of that Elegant City*, Bath, W. Gye, 1792

Haire, Lancelot, 'Remarks on Mr Lucas's Practical Observations on Amputation', London *Medical Journal*, 7/4 (1786), 377.

Hales, Stephen, *Description of Ventilators*, London, Innys, 1743

Hall, B., *Fragments of Voyages and Travels*, London, H. Ellis and T. Pringle, 1846

Hampshire, Edward (ed.), *Brinestain and Biscuit: Recipes and Rules for Royal Navy Cooks*, London, National Archives, 2007

Hampson, G., *Portsmouth Customs Letter Books 1748–1750*, Winchester, Hampshire County Council, 1994

Harris, John, *Harris's List of Covent Garden Ladies or the Man of Pleasure's Kalendar for the Year 1788* London, H. Ranger, 1788

Hawker, E., *Statement of Certain Immoral Practices prevailing in His Majesty's Navy*, London, J. Hatchard, 1822

Hawksmoor, Nicholas, *Remarks on the founding and carrying on the building of the Royal Hospital at Greenwich*, London, N. Blandford, 1728

Hay, Robert, *Landsman Hay: The Memoirs of Robert Hay 1789–1847*, ed. M.D. Hay, London, Hart-Davies, 1953

Hervey, Augustus, *Augustus Hervey's Journal: The Adventures Afloat and Ashore of a Naval Casanova*, ed. David Erskine, Rochester, Chatham Publishing, 2002

Hodges, H.W. and Hughes, E.A. (ed.), *Select Naval Documents*, Cambridge, Cambridge University Press, 1936

Hoffman, Frederick, *A Sailor of King George: the Journals of Frederick Hoffman*, London, John Murray, 1901

Hoste, William, *Memoirs and Letters of Captain Sir William Hoste*, ed. Harriet Hoste, London, Richard Bentley, 1833

Hotham, William, *Pages and Portraits from the Past, being the Private Papers of Sir William Hotham*, ed. A.M.W. Stirling, London, Herbert Jenkins, 1919

Howard, John, *The State of the Prisons in England and Wales with Preliminary Observations and An Account of Some Foreign Prisons and Hospitals*, Warrington, W. Eyres, 1784

Hunter, John, *Observations on the Diseases of the Army in Jamaica and on the Best Means of Preserving the Health of Europeans in that Climate*, London, G. Nicol, 1788

Jackson, George Vernon, *The Perilous Adventures and Vicissitudes of a Naval Officer*, ed. Harold Burrows, London, Blackwood, 1927

Keith, George Keith Elphinstone, *The Letters and Papers of Admiral Viscount Keith*, ed. C. Lloyd, London, Navy Records Society, 1926–55

Lambert, Sheila (ed.), *House of Commons Sessional Papers of the Eighteenth Century*, Wilmington, Delaware, Scholarly Resources, 1975

Lavery, Brian (ed.,), *Shipboard Life and Organisation 1731–1815*, London, Navy Records Society, 1998

Leech, Samuel, *Thirty Years from Home, or a Voice from the Main Deck*, Boston, Tappan, Whitemore and Mason, 1844

Lind, James, *A Treatise of the Scurvy*, Edinburgh, Kincaid and Donaldson, 1753

\_\_\_\_, _____, *An Essay on the Most Effectual Means of Preserving the Health of Seamen in the Royal Navy, and a Dissertation on Fevers and Infection, Together with Observations on the Jail Distemper*, London, D. Wilson and G. Nichol, 1774

\_\_\_\_, _____, *An Essay on Diseases Incidental to Europeans in Hot Climates with the Method of Preventing their Consequences*, London, J. and J. Richardson, 1808.

Lloyd, Christopher, *The Health of Seamen: Selections from the Works of Dr James Lind, Sir Gilbert Blane and Dr Thomas Trotter*, London, Navy Records Society, 1965

Lowry, James, *Fiddlers and Whores: The Candid Memoirs of a Surgeon in Nelson's Fleet*, ed. J. Millyard, Barnsley, Seaforth, 2006

Marryatt, Frederick, *The Naval Officer*, London, Baudry, 1834

Mead, Richard, *A Discourse on Scurvy*, London, Brindley, 1749

\_\_\_\_, _____, *The Medical Works of Dr Richard Mead*, London, C. Hitch, L. Hawes, 1762

Monson, William, *The Naval Tracts of Sir William Monson*, ed. M. Oppenheim, London, Navy Records Society, 1902–14

\_\_\_\_, _____, (ed.) J.K. Laughton *Naval Miscellany*, London, Navy Records Society, 1902

Morejón Antonio Hernández, *Topografia del Hospital Militar de Mahón, 1806*, Mahon, Reial Acadèmia de Medicina de les Illes Balears, 2010

Moseley, Benjamin, *Treatise on Tropical Diseases and on the Climate of the West Indies*, London, T. Cadell, 1803

Nagle, Jacob, *The Nagle Journal: A Diary of the Life of Jacob Nagle, Sailor*, ed. John C. Dann, New York, Weidenfeld and Nicolson, 1988

Nelson, Horatio, *Nelson's Letters to Lady Hamilton*, London, Thomas Lovewell, 1814

\_\_\_\_, _____, *The Dispatches and Letters of Lord Nelson*, ed. Nicholas

Harris Nicolas, London, Colburn, 1844–6

____, _____, *Nelson's Letters to his Wife*, ed. G.P.B. Naish, London, Navy Records Society, 1959

Northcote, William, *The Marine Practice of Physic and Surgery*, London, T. Becket and P.A. de Hondt, 1770

O'Meara, Barry E., *Napoleon in Exile, or A Voice from St Helena*, London, Simpkin and Marshall, 1822

Parsons, George Samuel, *Nelsonian Reminiscences; Leaves from Memory's Log*, London, C. Little and J. Brown, 1843

Pasley, Thomas, *Private Sea Journals 1778–1782*, London, J.M. Dent, *1931*

Pettigrew, Thomas Joseph, *Memoirs of the Life of Vice-Admiral Lord Viscount Nelson*, London, T. and W. Boone, 1849

Pillet, René-Martin, *Views of England during a Residency of Ten Years, Six of them as a Prisoner of War*, Boston, Parmenter and Norman, 1818

Pinckard, G., *Notes on the West Indies written during the Expedition under the Command of the late General Sir Ralph Abercromby*, London, Longman, Hurst, Rees, and Orme, 1808

Pemberton Charles Reece, *Life and Literary Remains of Charles Reece Pemberton*, London, C. Fox, 1843

Pocock, Tom, *Sailor King: The Life of King William IV*, London, Sinclair-Stevenson, 1991

____, _____, (ed.), *Trafalgar, An Eyewitness History*, London, Penguin, 2005

Price, George, *Pressganged, the Letters of George Price of Southwark alias George Green*, Royston, Ellison, 1984

Prior, James, *Voyage in the Indian Seas in the Nisus Frigate*, London, Richard Phillips, 1820

Privy Council, *Regulations and Instructions Relating to His Majesty's Service at Sea*, London, W. Winchester, 1808

Raigersfield, Jeffrey, *The Life of a Sea Officer 1783–1828*, ed. L.G. Carr-Laughton, London, Cassell, 1929

Robertson, Robert, *Observations on Fevers, and other Diseases, which Occur on Voyages to Africa and the West Indies*, London, John Murray, 1792

____, _____, *Directions for Administering Peruvian Bark, in a*

*Fermenting State, in Fever, and Other Diseases,* London, T. Cadell and W. Davies, 1799

———, ———, *Observations on the Jail, Hospital or Ship Fever,* London, John Murray, 1807

———, ———, *Synopsis Morborum: Observations on Diseases Incident to Seamen,* London, T. Cadell and W. Davies, 1817

Robinson, William, *Jack Nastyface: Memoirs of an English Seaman,* London, Chatham Publishing, 2002

Rodger, N.A.M. (ed.), *Naval Miscellany V,* London, Navy Records Society, 1984

Rogers, John Wilson, *A Statement of the Cruelties, Abuses and Frauds Practised in Mad-Houses,* London, J. McCreery, 1815

Russell, Richard, *A Dissertation Concerning the Use of Sea Water in Diseases of the Glands,* London, James Fletcher, 1753

Russell, William Clark, *The Life of Admiral Lord Collingwood,* London, Methuen, 1895

Ruspini, Bartholomew, *Treatise on Teeth,* London, Johnson, and Kearsley, *1797*

Scott, James, *Recollections of a Naval Life,* London, Richard Bentley, 1834

Sinclair, Archibald., *Reminiscences of the Discipline, Customs and Usages of the Royal Navy in the Good Old Times,* London, Simpkin and Marshall, 1857

Smollett, Tobias, *The Adventures of Roderick Random,* Oxford, Oxford University Press, 1979

Spilsbury, Francis B., *Account of a Voyage to the Western Coast of Africa Performed by His Majesty's Sloop Favourite in 1805,* London, Richard Phillips, 1807

Sprange Jasper, *The Tunbridge Wells Guide: An Account of the Ancient and Present State of that Place,* Tunbridge Wells, Jasper Sprange, 1786.

Sutton, Samuel, 'Historical Account of a New Method of Extracting the Foul Air out of Ships' (1757) in R. Mead, *The Medical Works of Dr Richard Mead* (1762), pp. 397–437

Tenon, Jacques, *Journal d'observations sur les principaux hôpitaux d'Angleterre,* ed. Jacques Carré, Clermont-Ferrand, Université Blaise-Pascal, 1992

Thursfield, H.G., *Five Naval Journals 1789–1817*, London, Navy
Records Society, 1951

Trotter, Thomas, *Observations on the Scurvy*, Edinburgh, Elliot, 1786

_____, _____, *Review of the Medical Department in the British Navy
with a Method of Reform Proposed*, London, Bew, 1790

\_\_\_, _____, *Medicina Nautica*, London, Cadell, 1797–1803

\_\_\_, _____, *A View of the Nervous Temperament*, London, Longman,
Hurst, Rees and Orme, 1807

\_\_\_, _____, *A Practicable Plan for Manning the Royal Navy and
Preserving our Maritime Ascendancy without Impressment*,
Newcastle and London, Longman, Hurst, Rees and Orme, 1819

Turnbull, William, *The Naval Surgeon*, London, Phillips, 1806

Tunstall, Brian (ed.), *The Byng Papers*, London, Naval Records
Society, 1930

Vandeburgh, C. F., *The Mariner's Medical Guide*, (London, Baldwin,
Cradock, and Joy, 1819

Veitch, James, *A Letter to the Commissioners for Transports, and Sick
and Wounded Seamen, on the Non-Contagious Nature of the Yellow
Fever*, London, Underwood, 1818

Wardrop, James, *Essays on the Morbid Anatomy of the Human Eye*,
Edinburgh, George, Ramsay, 1808

Watson, George, *A Narrative of the Adventures of a Greenwich
Pensioner*, Newcastle, R.T. Egar, 1827

Wilson, John, *Outline of Naval Surgery, Edinburgh*, Maclachlan and
Stewart, 1846

Wybourn, T. Marmaduke, *Sea Soldier: An Officer of the Marines with
Duncan, Nelson, Collingwood and Cockburn, The Letters and
Journals of Major T. Marmaduke Wybourn*, ed. A. Petrides and J.
Downs, Tunbridge Wells, Parapress, 2000

SECONDARY PRINTED WORKS

Adkins, Roy and Lesley, *Jack Tar: Life in Nelson's Navy*, London,
Little, Brown, 2008

Akehurst, Ann-Marie, 'The Hospital de la Isla del Rey, Minorca:
Britain's Island Hospital', *Architectural History*, 53 (2010),
123–61

Albert, Daniel and Edwards, Diane D. (ed.) *The History of*

*Ophthalmology*, Oxford, Blackwell Science, 1996

Allison, R.S., *Sea Diseases: The Story of a Great Natural Experiment in Preventative Medicine in the Royal Navy*, London, John Bale, 1943

Amics de l'Illa de l'Hospital Fundacion de la Isla del Rey, *The Hospital on the Island del Rey, The King's Island, Port of Mahon*, Mahon, Grup Editorial Menorca, 2010

Anderson, Roy M. and May, Robert M., *Infectious Diseases in Humans*, Oxford, Oxford University Press, 1991

Andrews, Jonathan; Briggs, Asa; Porter, Roy; Tucker, Penny and Waddington, Keir, *The History of the Bethlem*, London, Routledge, 1997

Baron, John, *Life of Edward Jenner*, London, Henry Colburn, 1827

Benady, Sam, *Civil Hospital and Epidemics in Gibraltar*, Grendon, Gibraltar Books, 1994

Birbeck, Eric, Ryder, Ann and Ward, Philip, *The Royal Hospital Haslar: A Pictorial History*, Chichester, Phillimore, 2009

Boog Watson, William N., 'Two British Naval Surgeons in the French Wars', *Medical History*, 13 (1969), 213–25

Bowden-Dan, Jane, 'Diet, Dirt and Discipline: Medical Developments in Nelson's Navy, Dr John Snipe's Contribution', *Mariner's Mirror*, 90 (2004), 260–72

Brockliss, Laurence and Jones, Colin, *The Medical World of Early Modern France*, Oxford, Oxford University Press, 1997

Brockliss, Laurence, Cardwell, M. John and Moss, Michael, *Nelson's Surgeon: William Beatty, Naval Medicine and the Battle of Trafalgar*, Oxford, Oxford University Press, 2005

Brown, Kevin, *The Pox: The Life and Death of a Very Social Disease*, Stroud, Sutton, 2006

____, _____, *Poxed and Scurvied: The Story of Sickness and Health at Sea*, Barnsley, Seaforth, 2011

____, _____, *Passage to the World: The Emigrant Experience 1807–1940*, Barnsley, Seaforth, 2013

Buchet, C. (ed.), *L'Homme, la Santé et la Mer*, Paris, Champion, 1997

Cardwell, M. John, 'Royal Naval Surgeons, 1793–1815: A Collective Biography' in David Boyd Haycock and Sally Archer (ed.), *Health and Medicine at Sea* (2009), pp 38–62.

Carpenter, Kenneth, *The History of Scurvy and Vitamin C*, Cambridge University Press, 1966

Carson, E.A., 'The Customs Quarantine Service', *Mariner's Mirror*, 64 (1978), 63–9

Coleman, Terry, *The Nelson Touch: The Life and Legend of Horatio Nelson*, Oxfords, Oxford University Press, 2002

Cooper, B.B., *The Life of Sir Astley Cooper*, London, John W. Parker, 1843

Cormack, A. A., *Two Royal Physicians: Sir James Clark, Bart., 1788–1870, Sir John Forbes, 1787–1861*, Banff, Banffshire Journal, 1965

Crumplin, Michael K.H., 'The Most Triumphant Death: the Passing of Vice-Admiral Lord Horatio Nelson, 21st October 1805', *Journal of the Royal Naval Medical Service*, 91/2 (2005), 92–5

____, _____, 'Surgery in the Royal Navy during the Republican and Napoleonic Wars', in D.B. Haycock and S. Archer (ed.), *Health and Medicine at Sea* (2009), pp. 63–89

____, _____, 'The Death of an Admiral: Surgery and Medicine in Nelson's Navy', *Journal of the Royal Naval Medical Service*, 98/1 (2012), 53

Crumplin, M.K.H., and Harrison, A., 'Death of an Admiral: The Death of Viscount Horatio Nelson', *Association of Surgeons of Great Britain and Ireland Newsletter*, 10 (May 2005), 3–5

Davidson, Luke, 'Identities Ascertained: British Ophthalmology in the First Half of the Nineteenth Century', *Social History of Medicine*, 9/3 (1996), 313–333

Desbrière, Eduord, *The Naval Campaign of 1805: Trafalgar*, Oxford, Oxford University Press, 1933

Dobson, J., 'Pernicious Remedy of the Naval Surgeon', *Journal of the Royal Naval Medical Service*, 43 (1957), 23 –8

Dudley, Sheldon F., 'Yellow Fever, as seen by the Medical Officers of the Royal Navy in the Nineteenth Century', *Proceedings of the Royal Society of Medicine*, 26/4 (1933), 443–56

Edwards, Diane D., 'Microbiology of the Eye and Ophthalmia' in Daniel Albert and Diane D. Edwards (ed.) *The History of Ophthalmology* (1996), pp. 147–163.

Ford, E., *The Life and Work of William Redfern*, Sydney, Australian

Medical Publishing Company, 1953

Glynn, Ian and Jenifer, *The Life and Death of Smallpox*, London, Profile Books, 2004

Goddard, Jonathan Charles, 'The Navy Surgeon's Chest: Surgical Instruments of the Royal Navy during the Napoleonic War', *Journal of the Royal Society of Medicine*, 97/4 (2004), pp. 191–197

____, _____, 'Genitourinary Medicine and Surgery in Nelson's Navy', *Postgrad Medical Journal*, 81 (2005), 413–18

Goodyear, James D., 'The Sugar Connection: A New Perspective on the History of Yellow Fever in West Africa', *Bulletin of the History of Medicine*, 52 (1978), 5–21

Harland, Kathleen, 'The Royal Naval Hospital at Minorca, 1711: An Example of an Admiral's Involvement in the Expansion of Naval Medical Care', *Mariner's Mirror 94/1 (2008), 36–47*

Harrison, Mark, *Disease and the Modern World, 1500 to the Present Day*, Cambridge, Polity Press, 2004

Harvie, David I., *Limeys: The Conquest of Scurvy*, Stroud, Sutton, 2002

Haycock, David Boyd and Archer, Sally (ed.), *Health and Medicine at Sea*, Woodbridge, Boydell Press, 2009

Hills, A.M.E., 'Nelson's Illnesses', *Journal of the Royal Naval Medical Service*, 86 (2000), 72–80

____, _____, *Nelson, A Medical Casebook*, Stroud, Spellmount, 2006

Keevil, J.J., Lloyd, C.C., and Coulter, J.L.S., *Medicine and the Navy 1200–1900*, Edinburgh and London, E and S. Livingstone, 4 volumes, 1957–63

Keevil, J.J., 'Leonard Gillespie, MD, 1758–1842', *Bulletin of the History of Medicine*, 28/4 (1954), 301–332

Kiple, Kenneth F., *The Cambridge Historical Dictionary of Disease*, Cambridge, Cambridge University Press, 2003

Langley, Harold D., *A History of Medicine in the Early US Navy*, Baltimore, Johns Hopkins University Press, 1995

Lavery, Brian, *Royal Tars: The Lower Deck of the Royal Navy 875–1850*, London, Conway, 2010.

Lawrence, Christine, *The History of the Old Naval Hospital, Gibraltar, 1741–1922*, Southsea, C. Lawrence, 1994

Leach, R. D., 'Sir Gilbert Blane MD, FRS', *Annals of the Royal College of Surgeons of England*, 62 (1980), 232–9

Le Quesne, L.P., 'Nelson and his Surgeons', *Journal of the Royal Naval Medical Service*, 86 (2000), 85–8.

Lincoln, Margarette (ed.), *Nelson and Napoleon*, London, National Maritime Museum, 2005

Miller, Amy, *Dressed to Kill: British Naval Uniform, Masculinity and Contemporary Fashions 1748–1857*, London, National Maritime Museum, 2007

Murphy, Elaine, 'The Mad-House Keepers of East London', *History Today*, 51/9 (2001), 29–35

Orde, Denis, *In the Shadow of Nelson: The Life of Lord Collingwood*, Barnsley, Pen and Sword, 2008

Pocock, Tom, *Horatio Nelson*, London, Pimlico, 1994

Pope, Dudley, Life *in Nelson's Navy, Ann Arbor*, University of Michigan Press, 1981

Porter, I. A., 'Thomas Trotter, Naval Physician', *Medical History*, 7 (1963), 155–64

Pugh, P.D. Gordon, *Nelson and his Surgeons*, Edinburgh and London, E. and S. Livingstone, 1968

Racine, Karen, *Francisco de Miranda: A Transatlantic Life in the Age of Revolution*, Wilmington, New York, Rowman and Littlefield, 2002

Revell, A.L., *Haslar the Royal Hospital*, Gosport, Gosport Historical Society, 2000

Richardson, Harriet (ed.), *English Hospitals 1660–1948: A Survey of their Architecture and Design*, Swindon, Royal Commission on the Historical Monuments of England, 1998

Rodger, N.A.M., *The Command of the Ocean: A Naval History of Britain 1649–1815*, London, Allen Lane, 2004

____, _____, 'Medicine and Science in the British Navy of the Eighteenth Century', *L'Homme, la Santé et la Mer*, ed. C. Buchet (1997), pp. 333–44

Roddis, Louis H., *A Short History of Nautical Medicine*, New York, Paul B. Hoeber, 1941

Ronald, D.A.B., *Young Nelsons, Boy Sailors during the Napoleonic Wars*, Oxford, Osprey, 2009

Savona-Ventura, Charles, *Contemporary Medicine in Malta*, San Gwann, Publishers Enterprises Group, 2005

Southey, Robert, *Life of Nelson*, London, John Murray, 1813

Stevenson, Christine, *Medicine and Magnificence: British Hospital and Asylum Architecture 1660–1815*, New Haven and London, Yale University Press, 2000

Stewart, L., 'The Edge of Utility: Slaves and Smallpox in the Early Eighteenth Century', *Medical History*, 29 (1985), 54–70

Sugden, John, *Nelson, A Dream of Glory*, London, Jonathan Cape, 2004

____, _____, *Nelson, The Sword of Albion*, London, Bodley Head, 2012

Vale, Brian and Edwards, Griffith, *Physician to the Fleet: The Life and Times of Thomas Trotter*, Woodbridge, Boydell Press, 2011

Vincent, Edgar, *Nelson, Love and Fame*, New Haven, Yale University Press, 2003

Wang, D., El-Masry, W.S., Crumplin, M., Eisenstein, S., Pusey, R.J. and Meagher, T., 'Admiral Lord Nelson's Death: Known and Unknown, A Historical Review of the Anatomy' *Spinal Cord*, 43 (2005), 573–6

White, Colin, 'An Eyewitness Account of the Battle of Cape, St Vincent', *Trafalgar Chronicle*, 7 (1997), 54S.

Willis, Sam, *In the Hour of Victory: The Royal Navy at War in the Age of Nelson*, London, Atlantic Books, 2013

Woodman, Richard, *Of Daring Temper, 250 Years of the Marine Society*, London, Marine Society, 2006

Wright, Charles and Fayle, C. Ernest, *A History of Lloyd's from Founding Lloyd's Coffee House to Present Day*, London, Macmillan, 1928

Ziegler, Philip, *King William IV*, London, Fontana, 1971

Zulueta, Julian de, 'Trafalgar: the Spanish View', *Mariner's Mirror*, 66 (1980), 293–319

____, _____, 'Health in the Spanish Navy during the Age of Nelson', *Journal of the Royal Naval Medical Service*, 86 (2000), 89–92

# Index